THE ART CLASSIC ROCK

Paul Grushkin
based on the Rob Roth Collection

GOODMAN

Paul Grushkin

Very special thanks to Rob Roth for the opportunity to give historical context to a most magnificent collection.

Thank you to Joel Selvin for putting us together. And thanks to my wife, Jane Eskilson, for the encouragement that led to a speedy completion.

Thanks to all the collectors in my life who've helped me create my library and archive.

Finally, a tip-of-the-hat to editor Rod Green and everyone at Carlton Books for creating a beautiful and lasting work.

Rob Roth

Thanks to all who have indulged and encouraged my rock graphics collecting frenzy!

Patrick Meade; Mom and Dad; Sir Elton John; David Furnish; Alice Cooper; Sheryl Cooper; Bernie Taupin; Sir Tim Rice; Steve Miller; Kim Miller; Bob Ezrin; Shep Gordon; Bob Halley; Clare Graham; Brian Nelson; D C Parmet; Bob Pfeifer; Scott Boorey; Derek McKillop; Richard Marot; Gerald Scarfe; Herbie Herbert; Howard Rose; Joel Selvin; John Reid; Jonathan Wells; Jonny Podell; Keith Bradley; Lynn Goldsmith; Marty Maidenberg; Matt Lee; Merck Mercuriadis; Michael Hewitson; Pat Morrow; Paul Grushkin; Toby Mamis; Josh at J. Fields Studios for the expert linen mounting; Jonathan Goodman and all at Carlton Books.

Photography: Richard Marot
Assisted by Ryan Zimmerman, Mike Williams, Ken Chan, Michael LaMorté, Caitie McCabe

Design by Grade Design Consultants

Printed and bound in China

FOREWORD

Rob Roth is obsessive to say the least. Being obsessive is not always a bad thing. Some people can make it work for themselves in a really positive way. Having worked professionally with Rob on many occasions, I can attest to his obsessiveness. I mean, how many times do you have to rehearse stabbing an Alice Cooper look-alike, throwing her down the stairs, getting put in a straight jacket, and subsequently hung on the gallows by a noose? Then, and only then, if it looks perfect can we rehearse the second song.

The witnessing of 'Be Our Guest' in Rob's production of *Beauty and the Beast* was beyond excessive. It was insanity on the grandest scale. Everything that Rob does he does with vision and passion. Owning a few posters is fine. But why not own all of them? That's our Rob!

When I first saw Rob's collection, I was absolutely stunned. He had to redesign his penthouse on the Upper West Side just to accommodate them. I mean, he had things of mine that I had never seen. And they were all in perfect condition.

Obsessive? Rob? WELL YEAH!

It takes a compulssive OBSessive to appreciate another compulsive OBsessive

Alice Cooper

A LIFE IN MUSIC

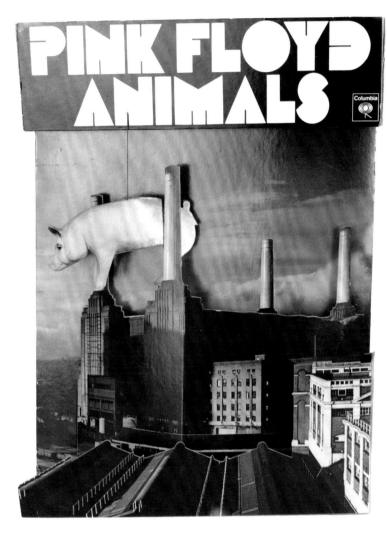

My passion for rock 'n' roll graphics began with the music of these great bands, which provided equal parts pleasure and refuge through my teen years. I spent many hours in headphones, poring over album covers, reading everything I could find about these bands that meant so much to me.

My introduction to promotional graphics came courtesy of a department store, E. J. Korvettes, which placed full-page ads in Sunday's *New York Times* announcing the week's new album releases (on sale for $3.99!). I was excited to get this first look at the album art, and began to collect these poster size ads and put them up on my bedroom walls.

Mondays after school I would race to the mall on my bike to check out the advertised albums as well as the amazing in-store promotional set-ups. These were elaborate combinations of posters, stand-up displays, mobiles and album flats surrounding stacks of albums, cassettes and 8-tracks. Sometimes, there were first-day give-away items: pins, keychains, t-shirts, stickers, book covers, etc.

The use of the album art in these various items was a source of great fascination for me, even as a kid. I would often ask the managers for the mobiles and displays. When I was lucky they would write my name on the back of the item to hold it for me.

One day someone had already claimed a Pink Floyd *Animals* stand-up display, which crushed me, so I decided to call Columbia Records and ask for one. A long shot, but it worked! A large box soon arrived with the coveted *Animals* stand-up display, along with posters, a mobile, bin dividers and album flats. Jackpot! I started calling the various promo and press departments to request materials, and to my surprise was rarely refused. (Led Zeppelin's Swan Song Records was a holdout, but they put me on their press list, sending releases on the tan Swan Song letterhead. Very cool!)

After high school, my collecting slowed for a time as I went to college, graduated and focused on my career as a theatre director. In 1994, I directed my first Broadway show, *Beauty and The Beast*, which subsequently was produced around the world. A life-altering experience to say the least, with the added benefit of allowing me to hunt record stores in many great cities.

During these years of travel, I discovered eBay, which had recently launched. I spent many nights in my hotel room hunting for promo items. I started by re-acquiring many pieces I had as a teen, along the way discovering tons of amazing artwork I had never seen. A nightly treasure hunt combined with shopping! I was quickly obsessed, and decided to collect every piece of graphic material from my eight favourite bands, along with selected items from many others. The collection now numbers over 3,000 pieces. And it is still growing…..

Assembling this collection and living life surrounded by such beautiful works of art has brought me much pleasure. The pieces showcased here represent the talents of many artists, musicians, managers and record execs. I thank them, one and all.

Rob Roth

INTRODUCTION

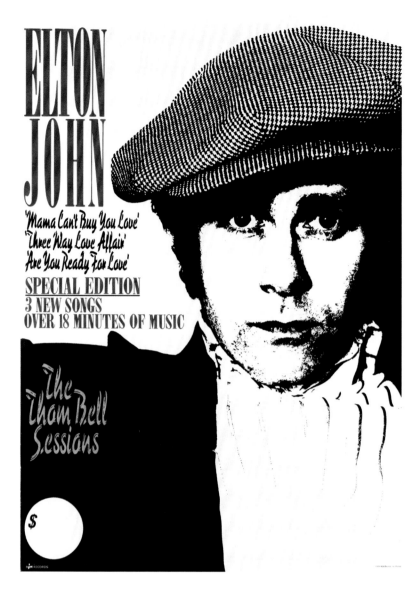

It was a time of fat cats and big bucks in rock music – those three decades, the 1970s, 1980s, and 1990s, which gave rock its most glorious artwork. There was a ton of money to be made producing both recordings and staged events, and just as quickly as it was amassed, more money was thrown at even greater promotion activities. This new and highly successful exploitation of rock music dramatically altered the course of the social movement that had been first built just years before, in the late 1960s. What we today call 'classic rock' was now 'mainstream' in popular culture, without the added element of social protest. Rock was everywhere on the radio dial. Rock was what you went to see, what you bought in the record store. Rock was both safe to listen to out in the open, and completely dominant, with the ability to drown out everything else. While, in due course, classic rock would become over-the-top with its own heady success, what you see in this long-anticipated book are all its finest promotions, from a time when promotion ruled.

At first, the financial clout of the now arena-sized, production-friendly music was a joyous achievement, certainly for the top bands and their managers, as well as the record execs and the merchandisers. It was also a portent of unimagined access for millions of new fans who eagerly joined in, post-Woodstock, in 1969, when large festivals – these were now rock concerts – began to flourish. But the advent of these most spectacular times would just as surely presage reactionary movements known as new wave, punk, heavy metal and hip-hop, as well as

new technologies beginning with the CD replacing the LP, which in turn would be supplanted by the MP3 digital file in the new millennium – developments which would see targeted, graphic-reliant campaigns supplanted by faceless, graphic-less viral marketing. So there would never be such a fun time of sheer indulgence and over-the-top marketing as were during these 30 years in rock history.

Whether it be a source of satisfaction – *We made it to the top!* – or a target for others' derision – *What happened to the revolution?* – rock's graphics and related ephemera from these three decades shows how the music had risen far beyond its modest 1950s inception and the counter-culture evolution which followed. By 1970, rock was simply the dominant popular music everywhere across the land, and its own success would be the cause of hugely popular aberrations like disco. You could see this in how rock was advertised and sold to the public: it was promoted as a reigning artform. Even glam and funky chic, and the beginnings of metal, were filtered through its by now across-the-board acceptance.

The focus of *Art of Classic Rock* is the graphic arts achievements that helped propel rock to centre stage worldwide. It's also the story of one of rock's foremost collectors, Rob Roth, a Tony-award nominated Broadway show director, who fell in love with great music and consequently all the products a true rock fan might ever desire – what Roth would call the 'great stuff of rock'. Like the rock that it mirrored, it nearly overwhelmed him.

Roth concentrated his collecting on eight bands and

musicians because for him (and for thousands of the most dedicated fans) these groups proved they had the 'greatest stuff':
- Rolling Stones
- Elton John
- Led Zeppelin
- Pink Floyd
- Alice Cooper
- Queen
- David Bowie
- The Who

The success of these particular musicians and bands, as seen by the sheer outpouring of outrageous and sophisticated graphics shown in this book, marked the peak of what could be accomplished by harnessing rock's musical power to the greatest-ever massing of youth. This was the first full realisation of rock's commercial potential and enormous marketability.

'Doing your own thing' was a hallmark of the psychedelic 1960s. That came to an end in the summer of 1971, when promoter Bill Graham closed his mid-sized Fillmore Auditoriums in both San Francisco and New York, opting to produce, as other promoters increasingly were, rock concerts in oversized indoor arenas and in outdoor amphitheatres and stadiums. Accordingly, rock entered a mainstream period in which the music took the broadest avenues to popular acclaim. The marketing, exemplified in large part by highly calculated album-advertising art, took on a commercial professionalism which in some circles

might be criticized as 'slick'. Not that this was all bad, mind you, because the graphics clearly beckoned to the rock fan, and the art was very capable of being thoroughly intoxicating. The point is: it was now intended to be successful in fulfilling its objective. Rob Roth was an example-target of all this marketing, and so that arrow found its bullseye in this most appreciative fan.

By the beginning of the 1970s, all the major touring rock bands were able to sell out arenas and stadiums coast to coast in the US and around the world. The rock promoter became firmly established as a fixture in the business, on an equal par with the record label executive. The transformation out of the idealistic late 1960s now also saw the most widespread use yet of rock – even beyond what Elvis and the Beatles had accomplished – to sell myriad products, from cars and chocolate to cosmetics and clothing. With all this exploitation came a lessening of the social commitment that many of the great rock bands of the 1960s had demonstrated as an integral part of their music. As the new decade proceeded, a rock band's impact was measured more and more by album and ticket sales, and less by their ability to effect change or 'make a difference'. Mass appeal was a numbers game. Radio and newspaper advertising supplanted the 1960s concert poster, which was relegated to an adjunct, support role. It was all about what a fan was likely to be impressed with in the record store, what the fan would slather over when seeing the full-page newspaper ad for an upcoming concert. And album cover art – remember, there was once 'album cover

art' –now, more than ever, ruled both the in-store and concert worlds.

And there was the rise of the merchandising companies. One of the first was Winterland Productions, a spin-off of Bill Graham's empire. It began, in 1971, as a t-shirt and poster store at Winterland dance arena in San Francisco but within its first ten years evolved to become a multi-million-dollar, rock-band-licensed merchandise organisation and licensing operation. Winterland and others developed the art and science of marketing rock merchandise to unprecedented levels, producing items that featured logo-like rock graphics commissioned by individual bands (a classic example being the Rolling Stones' tongue and lips, created by art director John Pasche).

This was a significant step in the evolution of rock itself, as graphics quickly became the basis of almost every band's 'line of product'. While the intentionally provocative new graphics had their origin in the freedom inherent in the rock concert posters of the late 1960s, the overall sales campaign would be worked in a far more sophisticated, focused manner.

Readers of *The Art of Classic Rock* will see some of the greatest campaign materials ever created for rock's biggest players. These graphics are reflected in a variety of formats: promotional posters, record store stand-up displays, counter-top displays, backstage passes and all manner of swag advanced by the record labels. Even the display ads in the Sunday entertainment sections of major newspapers benefited from all the new graphics activity. These ads

themselves swiftly developed into an almost distinctive genre of rock art, appealing enough to be collected by fanatics like Rob Roth because of their own sheer boldness (even if they did happen to appear in an instantly disposable medium).

All eras change the world, but these were perhaps more rapidly changing times than had ever been experienced. For those who came of age beginning in the 1970s, and as 1960s fringe lifestyle and culture mutated into staples of the middle-class status quo, the mainstream now belonged to the millions who forever would be rockin' out – those who came to the music by way of 'festival seating'. Today, we know that music, movies, fashion, and television programmes of the 1970s, 1980s, and 1990s are more popular than ever. The ascension of Led Zeppelin and the Rolling Stones to the notion of 'louder, harder, heavier' being best of all began then, and in no small measure that's due to the enormous proliferation of these bands' branding. They, and the other musicians depicted in *The Art of Classic Rock*, are the ones responsible for leading a mass population to rock, and for the emergence of collectors such as Rob Roth.

This book is not the first to say, 'Long live rock!' But its message is clearly, 'Hit me with your best shot!'

Paul Grushkin

1

THE ROLLING STONES

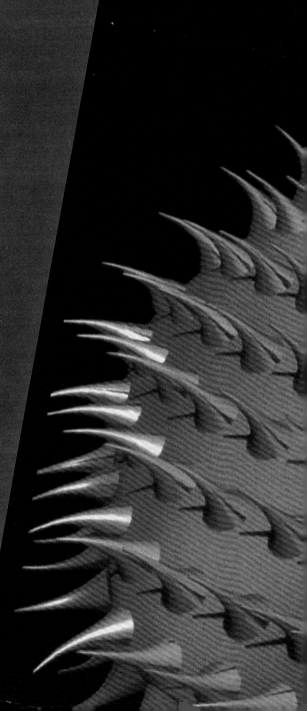

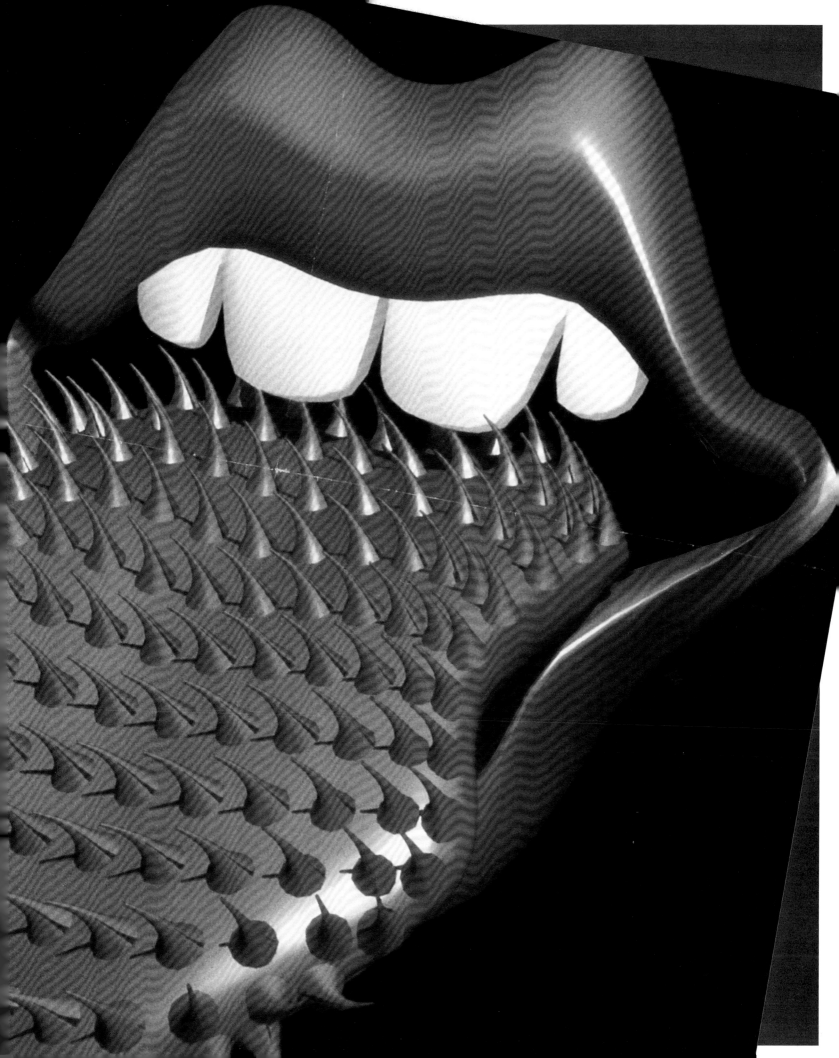

THE ROLLING STONES

During their 1969 tour of North America, the Rolling Stones were introduced every night on stage by their road manager, Sam Cutler, who proclaimed they were 'the greatest rock & roll band in the world'. Forty years on (plus seven prior, formative years when they were transitioning between a blue-eyed R&B band and the full-on rock band they became), they have punched out and smacked down every pretender to the throne.

The Stones came out on top because they were better organised over the long haul. Their albums consistently were among the most provocative in the stores, played the best at home, and on stage the band was the most impressive for the longest time. In pioneering the rock 'n' roll lifestyle, as well as in the aggressive way they promoted their product, they achieved a notoriety that was integral to the band's identity.

That identity was achieved in no small measure through savvily-managed graphics that attracted and held the attention of the public. Mick Jagger took a personal interest in every major product – starting with the albums and the tour sets the band would then approve.

It was Jagger who brought into the creative loop photographers David Bailey (*The Rolling Stones* and *Goats Head Soup*), Michael Cooper (*Their Satanic Majesties Request*) and Peter Frank (*Exile on Main Street*); pop-art god Andy Warhol (*Sticky Fingers* and *Love You Live*); surrealist Guy Peelaert (*It's Only Rock 'n' Roll*); sculptor Robert Brownjohn (*Let It Bleed*); and designers

John Pasche (the inestimable tongue-and-lips logo), Peter Corriston (*Some Girls*, *Emotional Rescue*, *Tattoo You*); John Van Hamersveld (*Exile on Main Street*); Kaz (*Still Life*); and Kosh (*Get Yer Ya-Ya's Out*) to name only a few of the many.

Corriston himself won a 1982 Grammy for 'Best Recording Package' for *Tattoo You*, the top industry award presented for the visual look of an album.

Many important commissions were contracted out as – certainly by the late 1970s – each graphic-arts package was intended to extend the band's identity and launch them anew. The last 20 years of Rolling Stones tours each took on a specific graphic-arts flavour that was imparted to the stage design, the advertising, and the merchandising campaign, sometimes – but not always – emanating from the album art itself.

Jagger's interest in branding the Rolling Stones with the tongue-and-lips logo is directly linked to their success. Seeing how American promoter Bill Graham used psychedelic concert poster art in the late 1960s to define

the public's image of his Fillmore Auditoriums on both coasts – effectively, to brand the experience – and observing how one American band in particular, the Grateful Dead, was so successful early on in the 1970s with their skeleton-and-roses logo helping form a bond between the band and audience, Jagger was determined to obtain a graphic identity that would serve the Rolling Stones forever.

John Pasche has stressed the importance of Jagger's involvement, telling *Business Week Magazine* in 2008: 'Mick Jagger was very interested and knowledgable about art history and graphic design. He's always taken a lot of interest in everything graphical and photographical related to the band and he understands the importance of image.

'Once Jagger was satisfied with a design, he would get the rest of the band to rubber-stamp it, but he was always the leader, and he took his role quite seriously.'

The bad boys of rock 'n' roll may have developed a reputation to live up to, but that reputation became part and parcel of the Rolling Stones' corporate image.

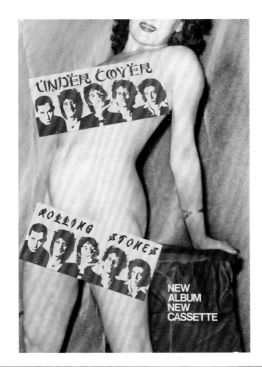

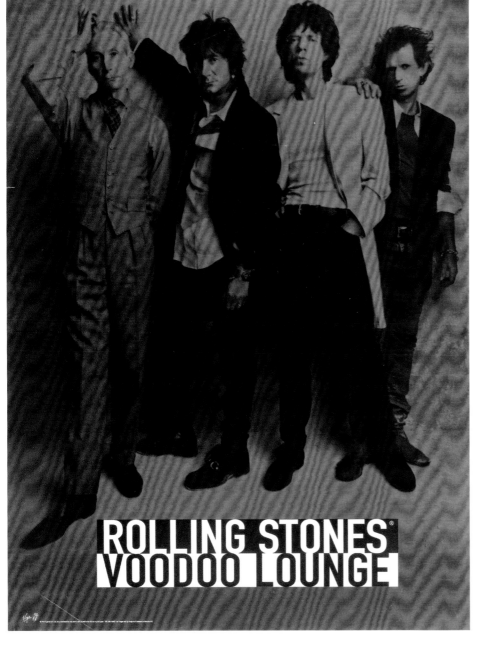

TOP, LEFT

Undercover, UK promo
poster, 1983

TOP, RIGHT

Some Girls, Japan
promo poster, 1978

BOTTOM, LEFT

Voodoo Lounge, US
promo poster, 1994

BOTTOM, RIGHT

Rolling Stones, US
promo poster, 1964

The Stones' first formal gig (under the name the Rollin' Stones) was on July 12, 1962 at London's Marquee Club. Their first UK tour began in September 1963 and their first US tour was in June 1964, on the heels of the release of their eponymously-named debut album (the cover art was a photo shot by acclaimed British photographer David Bailey). In the UK, the album hit No 1 and stayed at the top for 12 weeks.

By early 1965, the Stones were the talk of the UK and their second album, *The Rolling Stones No. 2*, spent 10 weeks at Number 1, beginning in January. That record and their third US album, *The Rolling Stones, Now!* would lead to their first tours of Scandinavia, France and Germany and back again to North America, during which time lightning would descend from the heavens bearing their all-time most memorable song (featured on their next American album, *Out of Our Heads*). '(I Can't Get No) Satisfaction', released in June in America, would establish them as a rock 'n' roll act now and forever, and was their first No 1 US single.

Between the Buttons (January 1967) saw the band moving further away from its R&B roots, now, not surprisingly, into artsy territory (in the manner of the Beatles, Bob Dylan, and the Beach Boys who also were

traversing similar paths). Then, following a brief late-spring European tour (their first forays to Poland, Greece, and Italy) and after enduring a number of court dates stemming from drug arrests, the band entered into the arduous process of recording a psychedelic opus, *Their Satanic Majesties Request* (December 1967), which was seen by some as deliberately intended to mix it up in the stores with the Beatles' *Sgt. Pepper's Lonely Hearts Club Band*. The singles that emerged were quite happily hippy-trippy: 'She's a Rainbow', and '2000 Light Years from Home'.

Esteemed photographer Michael Cooper (who also shot the iconic cover for *Sgt. Pepper's*) created the three-dimensional group picture for *Satanic Majesties*. The lenticular (shifting) image shows the band members (except Jagger) coyly glancing at each other. Then, looking more closely at the cover, the Stones' fans could see the Beatles pictured as well. But, due to excessive production costs, later editions of the album replaced the glued-on lenticular with a standard colour photo.

In total, four Stones albums feature a novelty cover (the others are the working zipper on *Sticky Fingers*; the cut-out faces on *Some Girls*; and the peel-back stickers on *Undercover*).

LEFT, BOTTOM
Tour programme, early 1960s

BELOW, MIDDLE
Tour programme, 1965

BELOW, TOP
Tour programme, 1964

BELOW, BOTTOM
Tour programme, 1966

OPPOSITE
UK and European tour programme, 1964

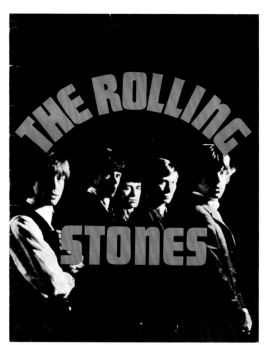

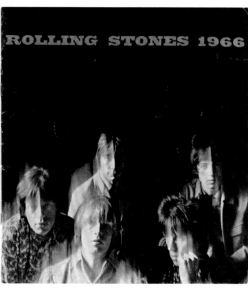

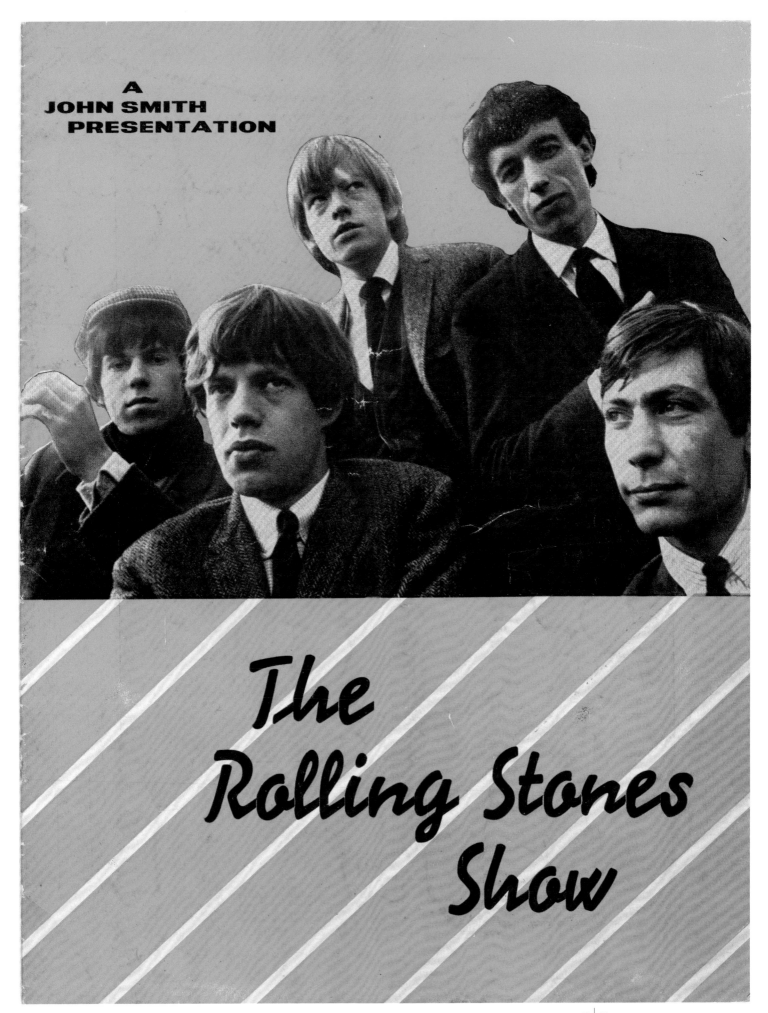

A
JOHN SMITH
PRESENTATION

The
Rolling Stones
Show

LEFT
US tour poster, 1972.
Art: David Byrd

TOP, LEFT

Get Yer Ya-Ya's Out,
UK press ad, 1970

TOP, RIGHT

'Jumpin' Jack Flash', UK
press ad, 1968

BOTTOM, LEFT

US tour programme,
1972. Art: David Byrd

BOTTOM, MIDDLE

Get Yer Ya-Ya's Out,
promo poster, 1970

BOTTOM, RIGHT

Get Yer Ya-Ya's Out,
US press ad, 1970

'Jumpin' Jack Flash', the single which heralded the arrival of *Beggars Banquet* (December 1968) famously never made it to the album itself; it was one of Brian Jones' last efforts with the Rolling Stones (he also contributed to 'No Expectations', 'Street Fighting Man' the king of all picture sleeves, and 'Stray Cat Blues'). The keynote track was, however, 'Sympathy for the Devil'.

The cover art originally proposed for *Beggars Banquet* – a bathroom wall showing smarmy graffiti – was rejected by both Decca Records in Britain and London Records in the US. But the Stones refused to budge, and the release date was put off for several months. In November the Stones relented, allowing the album's release in a plain, off-white jacket which represented a recreation of an RSVP card.

Sculptor Robert Brownjohn imagined the surreal cake which was the cover of *Let It Bleed* (November 1969). It was a Rube Goldberg-style absurdity of an antique turntable tone-arm joined to a record-changer-style spindle supporting (in lieu of LPs), a number of oddities stacked on a catering plate. The cake parts were prepared by a little-known cook who was to become a major celebrity food writer, Delia Smith.

Automatic Changer – the album's original title – inspired the food sculpture and the reverse of the LP sleeve shows the same sculpture ravaged, as if it had been the centerpiece of a gleeful (backstage?) rock & roll party.

The Stones' 1969 American tour was much publicised, written about, recorded, and filmed; it featured most of *Beggars*

Banquet and much from the not-quite-released-yet *Let It Bleed*. The poster and programme artwork was designed by David Byrd, who handled the promotional graphics for Bill Graham's Fillmore East in New York City.

The extraordinary 1970 live album *Get Yer Ya-Yas Out!* (it was unusual for a live album to reach No 1 in Britain) documented the tour, mostly based on the shows at New York's Madison Square Garden. The cover photography for *Ya Yas* featured Charlie Watts and a donkey, taken near London in early 1970. Apparently, the photo was inspired by the lyrics to Bob Dylan's 'Visions of Johanna'. The theme also echoes through the film *Gimme Shelter*, made of the American tour, with Jagger and Watts posing with the donkey on an Alabama road the month before.

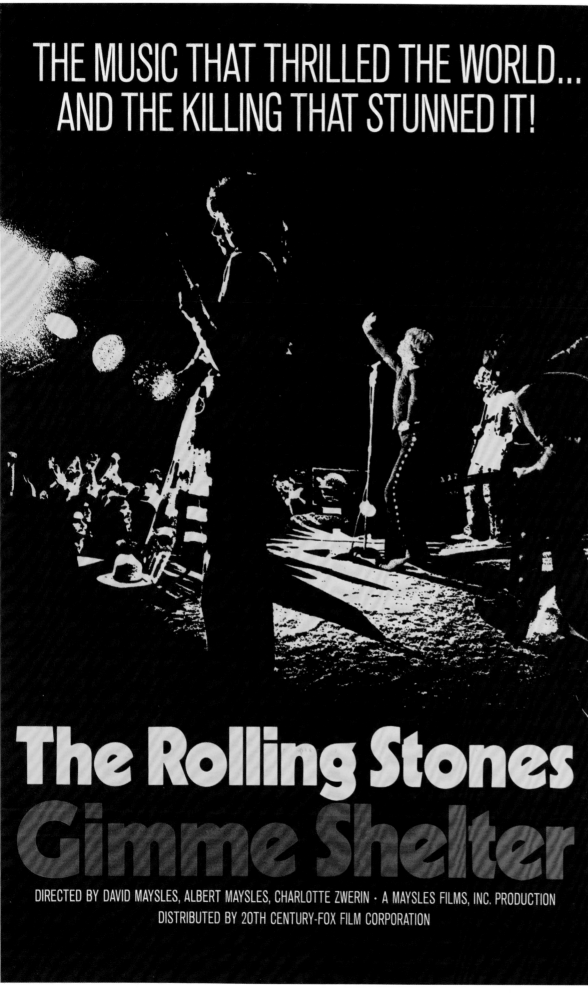

THE MUSIC THAT THRILLED THE WORLD...
AND THE KILLING THAT STUNNED IT!

The Rolling Stones
Gimme Shelter

DIRECTED BY DAVID MAYSLES, ALBERT MAYSLES, CHARLOTTE ZWERIN · A MAYSLES FILMS, INC. PRODUCTION
DISTRIBUTED BY 20TH CENTURY-FOX FILM CORPORATION

After the 1969 North American tour's planned denouement in West Palm Beach, Florida, the Stones were determined to give one last performance for the 1960s . . . which became the disastrous free show at Altamont Raceway in the far hills east of Oakland in northern California on 6 December. An horrific scene ensued with stabbings and beatings occurring throughout the day

Filmmakers Albert and David Maysles directed a documentary about the tour, *Gimme Shelter*. Much of the film depicted the quixotic dealmaking that was the making and unmaking of the event. Long afterwards, what's remembered from *Gimme Shelter* is the concert itself and the grim-faced, heavy-handed 'security' provided by the inebriated and unrepentant Hells Angels.

George Lucas, shortly to become known worldwide for his *Star Wars* film epics, was a cameraman for the Maysles at Altamont. Ironically, none of the footage he shot was incorporated into the final cut, as his camera jammed after he shot only 100 feet of film.

LEFT
Gimme Shelter, US movie
promo poster, 1970

OPPOSITE, TOP LEFT
Gimme Shelter, German
movie promo poster, 1970

OPPOSITE, BOTTOM LEFT
Gimme Shelter, UK movie
promo poster, 1970

OPPOSITE, FAR RIGHT
Gimme Shelter, Japanese
movie promo poster, 1970

THE ROLLING STONES

HEISS-HEISSER-AM HEISSESTEN

GIMME SHELTER

Regie: David Maysles, Albert Maysles · Charlotte Zwerin · Eine Maysles Films, Inc Produktion

The Rolling Stones Gimme Shelter

■カラー作品■超ステレオ音響

〈アイム・フリー！〉ミック・ジャガーが叫んだ
30万人の若者たちがみた衝撃の未来──
興奮と熱狂が支配した太陽のオルタモント！

"ローリング・ストーンズ" イン ギミー・シェルター

■出演ローリング・ストーンズ■監督デビッド・メイスルズ／アルバート・メイスルズ／シャーロット・ツワーリン

◆ジャンピング・ジャック・フラッシュ ◆サティスファクション ◆ユー・ゴッタ・ムーブ ◆ワイルド・ホース ◆ブラウン・シュガー ◆むなしき愛 ◆アイヴ・ビーン・ラビング・ユー・トゥ・ロング ◆ホンキー・トンク・ウィメン ◆ストリート・ファイティング・マン ◆シックス・デイズ・オン・ザ・ロード ◆ジ・アザー・サイド・オブ・ジス・ライフ ◆熱度を慣れむ歌 ◆アンダー・マイ・サム ◆ギミー・シェルター

20 FOX映画 CENTURY-FOX 映像

16 | 17

Artist John Pasche, best known for creating the Rolling Stones' tongue-and-lips logo (*see* overleaf), formally began his work with the band by handling their 1970 European tour poster, done in what has been described as an 'acid-tinged 1930s-revival style'. This was the Stones' first tour in Europe since 1967, and initiated a pattern whereby the group would play North America, Europe and the UK on a three-year rotation.

Pasche also followed up with similarly 1930s-homage artwork for the Stones' brief 1971 UK tour (they had not formally toured in their homeland since autumn 1966, and, curiously, they would soon decamp to the south of France as tax exiles, with the tour thereby for years afterwards being called the 'Goodbye Britain Tour'.

On these tours, the Stones previewed brilliant new material, including 'Brown Sugar', 'Dead Flowers', 'Wild Horses', 'You Gotta Move' and 'Bitch' which would appear on their next album, *Sticky Fingers* (1971). The male torso artwork for *Sticky Fingers* – featuring a working zipper that opened to reveal a similar man's mid-section clad in undershorts – was conceived by American pop artist Andy Warhol, photographed by Billy Name and packaged by Craig Braun. The cover's tight-jeans-wearing model was performance artist Joe Dallesandro, a regular at Warhol's studio, The Factory.

Pasche's tongue-and-lips appeared for the first time on the album's inner sleeve – a rare example of a brilliant, all-purpose graphic logo that would serve the band for decades on their albums, tours and millions of dollars of merchandise, unwittingly coupled to a sensational but albeit one-off album cover.

The *Sticky Fingers* cover art was, of course, controversial because it clearly portrayed a man's private parts rather suggestively put away in his jeans, not to mention the lewd shot of the briefs appearing when the album was zipped-down. In Spain, the male figure was replaced by an open can of 'sticky' treacle with severed fingers. In Russia, it was replaced with a female model in tight jeans.

At a party in New York in 1969, Andy Warhol casually mentioned to Mick Jagger that it would be amusing to have a real zipper on an album cover. A year later, Jagger proposed the idea for the Stones' first release on their new Rolling Stones record label.

Album packager Craig Braun had also suggested releasing the album in a clear plastic jacket with heat-sensitive liquid crystals inside '...so you could make your own little Joshua Light Show' as well as with a gatefold photo of Jagger's mammoth castle in the south of France. But Jagger was undeterred.

After the zipper's action was previewed, Braun realized there had to be an extra layer of cardboard to protect the record from the zipper. But it also turned out that during the shipment of the records in their transport boxes, the zipper would press into the album stacked on top of it, causing potentially thousands of units to be rejected by record stores upon arrival. Braun's solution: pull down the zipper before the album was shipped – that would scratch only the middle of the record label itself. The record's distributor, Atlantic, was less than thrilled, even as the cover art itself took on iconic proportions. Braun would later create the graphic package for Alice Cooper's *Schools Out* album.

BELOW

European tour poster, 1970.
Art: John Pasche

BELOW

UK tour poster, 1971.
Art: John Pasche

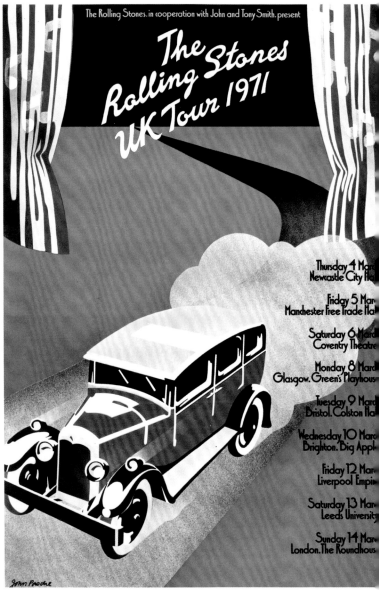

TOP
Sticky Fingers,
promo poster, 1971

BOTTOM, LEFT
Sticky Fingers, UK
press ad, 1971

BOTTOM, RIGHT
Sticky Fingers, UK
press ad, 1971

RIGHT
Sticky Fingers,
promo poster, 1971

AVAILABLE ON RSCO/AMPEX STEREO TAPES • OPEN REEL • 8-TRACK CARTRIDGE • CASSETTE

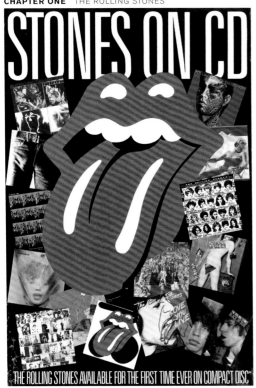

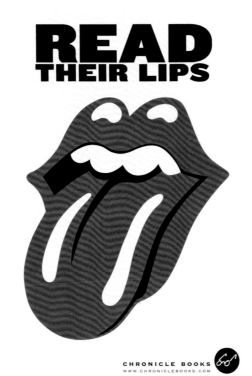

There is no rock logo more instantly recognizable. The big red mouth with its protruding tongue has been the official logo of the world's greatest (and longest-serving) rock 'n' roll band since the Rolling Stones debuted it in 1971.

It first appeared on the *Sticky Fingers* album's inner sleeve, as a very large, overprinted graphic. In quite a bit smaller version, but just as telling, it also served as the defining mark for the new Rolling Stones Records label on which *Sticky Fingers* was released.

Although the legendary American pop-art artist Andy Warhol designed the iconic jeans-and-actual-zipper cover, he did not design the tongue-and-lips logo. That was the work of London graphic designer John Pasche.

The logo combines the various elements of the band's fast-evolving worldwide image immediately following the disastrous but historically dramatic concert at Altamont Speedway in California (1969) and just before reaching one of many career peaks with the release of the double album *Exile on Main St.* (1972).

It's at once an insolent tongue stuck out at authority, a symbol of lustful panting, and a fine cartoon of Mick Jagger's distinctive mouth. It's successful as an eye-catching trademark on every level imaginable, and, just so, has been redefined a hundred times over by graphic designers working for the Stones in subsequent years, while retaining the integrity Pasche first gave it, along with its singularity of purpose.

During the period 1971-1984 the tongue appeared on the classic yellow album label of every Rolling Stones Records album except the 1975 compilation *Made in the Shade*. During that time, it also first made its way onto millions of t-shirts and hundreds of different types of tour and retail merchandise, and is still employed in both those ways – although not as completely predominant a graphic – to this very day.

Sticky Fingers followed the pivotal, bluesy *Let It Bleed* (1969) and the Stones' well-received live album, *Get Your Ya Ya's Out* (1970). *Sticky Fingers* was in the making for nearly three years, ultimately containing songs which were first heard live on stage as early as 1969, including 'Brown Sugar', 'Wild Horses', 'Can't You Hear Me Knocking' and 'Moonlight Mile'. In April, 1971, in the first

year that an original Beatles album would not be released since 1963, the Stones found themselves atop the US and UK album charts simultaneously for the first time ever. The album packaging (including both Warhol's and Pasche's contributions) has, ever since, been included in virtually every book and magazine article that chronicles the best and most influential album art of all time.

Pasche completed his BA in graphic design from Brighton College of Art in 1967, then went on to obtain his MA at London's Royal College of Art in 1970. As related in an interview published at rockpopgallery.typepad.com, here is Pasche's account of his biggest-ever gig (remember, he was fresh out of college and had been called upon to create an identity graphic for one of the biggest acts in the world, having previously designed their 1970 European tour poster):

'In 1969, Mick Jagger's office rang the Royal College of Art in London and asked if there was a suitable graphics student to come up with designs for their 1970 European tour poster,' Pasche recalled. 'I was recommended, and so on April 19, 1970 Jo Bergman, who was running the Stones' office at the time, wrote to me to confirm they indeed had commissioned me to design the poster for their forthcoming tour.

'I was in my final year of a graduate design course. I was very honoured when Mick turned up at the College to see my final degree show, as the artwork that would ultimately be used for the tour poster was on display in one of the exhibits.

'A short time later, I met Mick again, who then asked me to design a logo or symbol for the Stones' new record label. Mick showed me an image of the Indian goddess Kali, which became the starting point to our discussion regarding the design of the logo. I was paid £50 for the design, which took me about a week to complete. (Later on, in 1972, I was paid an additional £200 in recognition of the logo's success).

'The design concept for the tongue was to represent three elements: the band's anti-authoritarian attitude, Mick's mouth, and the band's now-obvious sexual connotations. I designed it in such a way that it was easily reproduced and in a style which I though might stand the

test of time. The first use of the logo was the inner sleeve for *Sticky Fingers*. The outer sleeve was designed by Andy Warhol, hence the mix-up with its credit [in many people's minds, subsequently]. I guess people just assumed he did both.

'The logo was not fully registered in all countries, and a German jeans company registered the logo in Germany for their own products. This situation – and the fact that the tongue was getting used by unauthorized manufacturers of badges, t-shirts, and suchlike – prompted the proper registration and a merchandising agreement with myself to capitalize on the success of the logo.

'The simplicity of the tongue lent itself to many variations which were done by other designers (and not myself, other than the derivative icicle-tongue graphic I created for the single 'She's So Cold'). Due to its immediate popularity, the Stones kept with it over the years and I believe it represents one of the strongest and most recognizable logos in worldwide circulation – and of course I'm proud of that! The Stones ultimately bought the copyright, but up to recently I owned the hand drawn and painted artwork.' This was to sell for more than £250,000.

Pasche created artwork for the Stones from 1970 to 1974. He later did work for Paul McCartney, the Who, and many other artists and bands.

Sticky Fingers began a string of eight consecutive studio albums that reached No 1 on the US Billboard charts. Included in that run, Pasche designed the promotional graphics for *Goats Head Soup* (1973), before heading for other pastures of plenty.

In a wonderful example of rock 'n' roll irony, the recent soundtrack for the Stones' collaboration with filmmaker Martin Scorsese yielded the *Shine A Light* deluxe edition 512 MB USB flashdrive with all the songs recorded live for the film in 2006 as audio MP3 files, with the new technology also including on the drive a tour laminate gallery, original set lists, and the full programme of marketing materials and photos.

It was furnished to the customer as a flashdrive-on-a-keyring . . . in the shape of the Rolling Stones' now, and forevermore, most distinctive and evocative logo. . . John Pasche's tongue.

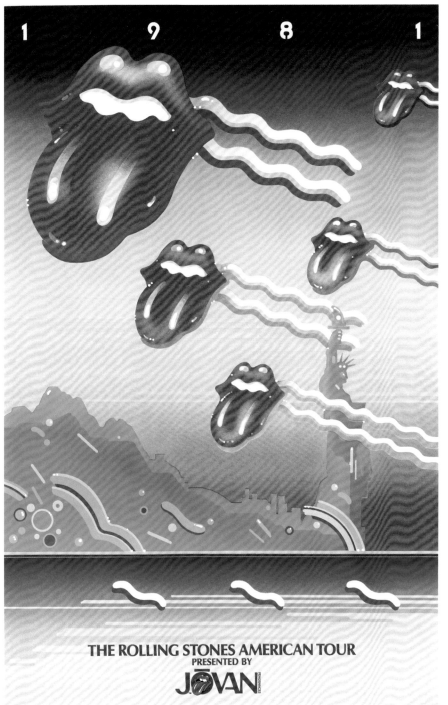

THE ROLLING STONES AMERICAN TOUR
PRESENTED BY
JOVAN

SEE THE STONES LIKE NEVER BEFORE

ROLLINGSTONES
FOUR FLICKS DVD
THE ULTIMATE LIVE 4 DVD SET

therollingstones
abiggerbang

in stores now

rollingstones.com

OPPOSITE, LEFT
Back catalogue on CD,
promo poster, 1986

OPPOSITE, MIDDLE
*According to the Rolling
Stones* book, poster, 2003

OPPOSITE, RIGHT
Voodoo Lounge tour and
catalogue, poster, 1994

ABOVE, LEFT
US tour poster, sponsored
by Jovan (cologne), 1981

ABOVE, RIGHT
Four Flicks DVD, promo
poster, 2003

RIGHT
A Bigger Bang, promo
poster, 2005

Following the release of *Sticky Fingers*, the Rolling Stones left England to avoid paying a whopping tax bill they expected to receive at any minute. They moved to France, near Nice, where Keith Richards rented the Villa Nellcote, subletting rooms to his fellow band members and their entourage.

Using the Rolling Stones' mobile studio, the band held months of all-night, every-night recording sessions in the cavernous basement. Preceded by the single 'Tumbling Dice', the completed double LP was *Exile on Main St.* (May 1972).

The album was art-directed by John Van Hamersveld. The cover shot was not a new collage but rather a 1955 photograph of a tattoo parlour wall taken by Robert Frank. The album's highly-visible billboards and promotional posters focused on one of the parlour-wall photos, a shot of a native with, absurdly, three huge rock-balls in his mouth.

'The tone of the time was one of anarchy, all defiant and distorted,' said Van Hamersveld later. The Stones' scene was notorious by this juncture – they were seen as on-the-move tax exiles, cocaine-fuelled miscreants, satyrs, and outsiders – and the album's chaotic look (along with Jagger's grease-penciled hand-lettering throughout) captured the recording quite perfectly – as did two movies that were to document the tour that followed.

The 1973 Pacific tour was to visit countries bordering the Pacific Ocean. The original intent was to play Australia and New Zealand, which had not seen the

Stones since 1966, as well as Japan, which had never seen the them at all.

Problems stemming from the band's self-inflicted high visibility created during the preceding North American Tour caused fall-back scheduling in Hawaii and the Stones ultimately being forced to cancel their Tokyo Budokan dates altogether because of prior drug convictions (despite a beautiful tour poster being printed and 55,000 tickets having been sold).

Australian promoter Paul Dainty commissioned Melbourne artist Ian McCausland to create what became the iconic image of a jet airplane winging its way into the Stones' massive lips and tongue over a stylized relief map of Australia. Original prints of the poster are among the most sought-after items by Stones fans and memorabilia collectors. McCausland also created a poster for the New Zealand leg, of a kiwi, of course. Drummer Charlie Watts then recommended that McCausland design the band's next album cover.

McCausland was paid $600 for each of his two posters and an additional $600 for the album cover. 'I felt like a millionaire,' he has said. He used the money as a deposit on his first home. 'It was the most money I'd ever made as an artist.' He mailed his album design to the Stones' London office, but was never sure it got there. 'In those naïve days, I didn't even keep a copy,' he said. 'And I never found out what happened to it. It just disappeared into the vaults, I guess.'

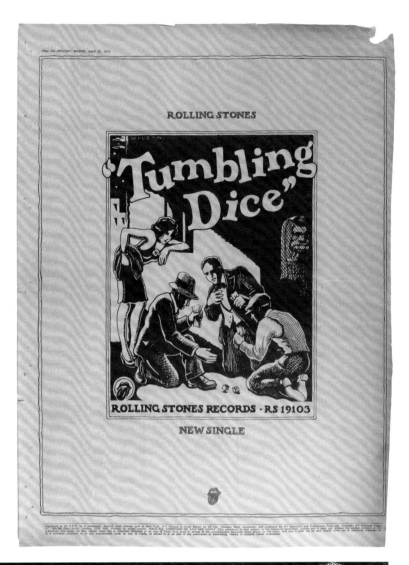

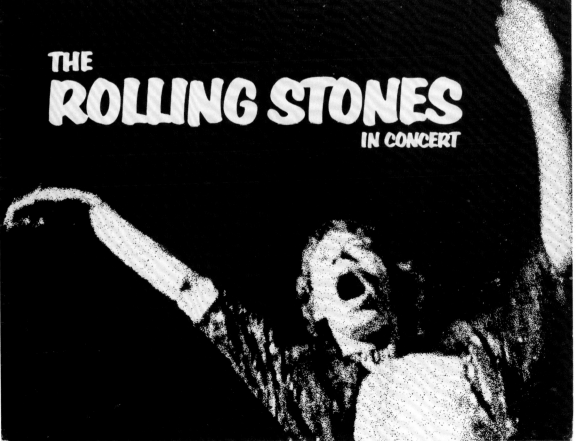

LEFT, TOP
Promo poster, 1973 (Mick in 1972 tour costume)

LEFT, BOTTOM
New Zealand tour poster, 1973. Art: Ian McCausland

BELOW
Japanese tour poster, 1973 (cancelled: Mick denied visa)

OPPOSITE
Australian tour poster, 1973. Art: Ian McCausland

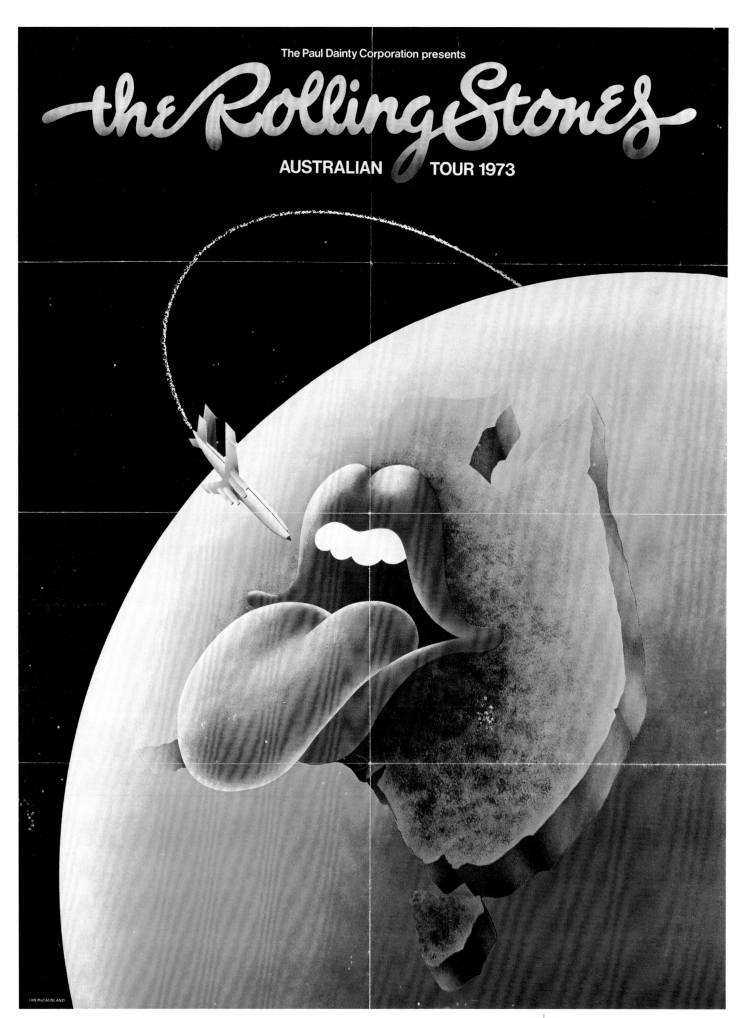

The Paul Dainty Corporation presents

the Rolling Stones

AUSTRALIAN TOUR 1973

IAN McCAUSLAND

Ladies & Gentlemen...
THE ROLLING STONES

PRESENTED BY DRAGON AIRE LTD. A SEABOARD AMERICAN COMPANY

WORLD'S FIRST QUAD FILM CONCERT.
EXCLUSIVE LIMITED ENGAGEMENT

"OUTRAGEOUS, FINE, UNSTOPPABLE—CAPTURES THE STONES AT THEIR BEST"—TIME • "...THE FIRST REALLY GOOD ROCK CONCERT FILM"—ROLLING STONE • "A PICTURE AND SOUND EXPLOSION"—N.Y. POST • "KICKS YOU IN THE ASS FROM THE WORD GO...JUST DOESN'T LET UP"—VILLAGE VOICE • "THE MOST POWERFUL ROCK FILM EVER MADE"—CASHBOX

Ladies & Gentlemen...THE ROLLING STONES

LEFT
Ladies and Gentlemen..., US movie poster, 1973

OPPOSITE, LEFT, TOP
Ladies and Gentlemen..., US movie poster, 1973

OPPOSITE, LEFT, BOTTOM
Ladies and Gentlemen..., Argentinean poster, 1973

OPPOSITE, FAR RIGHT
Ladies and Gentlemen..., New York movie poster, 1973

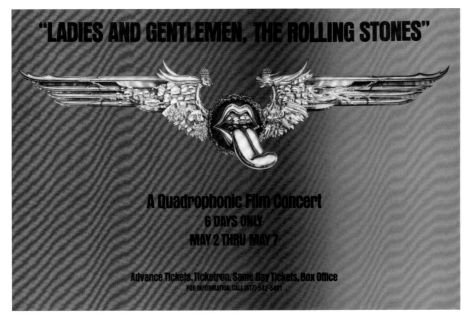

Best known for its single 'Angie', *Goats Head Soup* (August 1973), which was recorded in Jamaica, was a more polished (although rather less distinguished) production than the often ragged-edged *Exile on Main St.*

The album cover was designed and photographed by David Bailey, whose first work for the Rolling Stones was back in 1965. The head shot of Jagger on the front cover was approximately life-size in the original 12-inch LP format. The 'soup' shot was art directed by John Pasche and photographed by Phil Jude and was banned by some record stores.

The ballad 'Angie' came with a lurid picture sleeve of a painted-over but bare-breasted torso framed with long golden curls. The same artwork was used to promote the Stones' 42-show 1973 UK and European tour.

Work on *It's Only Rock 'n' Roll* (October 1974) began right after the European tour. The album would be the first to be produced by The Glimmer Twins (a pseudonym for Jagger and Richards). It was not immediately followed up by a tour, but would lead to Ron Wood's entrance as the guitarist who replaced Mick Taylor (who had himself replaced Brian Jones).

BELOW, LEFT
Goat's Head Soup,
Dutch press ad, 1973

RIGHT, TOP
Goat's Head Soup, promo
poster, 1973 (withdrawn)

RIGHT, MIDDLE
Goat's Head Soup, poster,
1973. Photo: David Bailey

RIGHT, BOTTOM
'Angie', UK press
ad, 1973

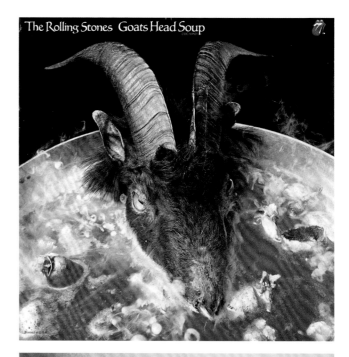

The 46-show *Tour of the Americas '75* was the Stones' first with new guitarist Ron Wood. The tour was not tied to support the compilation album that had just been issued (*Metamorphosis,* June 1975), nor the band's last studio release from seven months before, *It's Only Rock 'n' Roll*. Therefore, a new compilation album, *Made in the Shade* (June 1975) was released to capitalize on the tour's publicity.

The tour's announcement was legendary: the band drove down Broadway playing 'Brown Sugar' on the back of a flatbed truck in the middle of New York City traffic during mid-day, a gimmick that groups like U2 would emulate in future decades.

The tour's artwork featured an in-flight monster-hawk-winged-jet-engined creature that effectively symbolized the group's artistic power, efficiency and ruthlessness out on the road.

© 1975 SUNDAY PROMOTIONS INC.

ROLLING STONES
TOUR OF THE AMERICAS '75

THE BEST

THE ROLLING STONES ON TOUR

ON ROLLING STONES RECORDS AND TAPES

OPPOSITE, TOP, LEFT
Tour of the Americas,
staff pins, 1975

OPPOSITE, TOP, MIDDLE
Tour of the Americas,
tour programme, 1975

OPPOSITE, TOP, RIGHT
Tour of the Americas,
press kit, 1975

OPPOSITE, 2ND TOP, RIGHT
Tour of the Americas,
press album/tour ad, 1975

OPPOSITE, MIDDLE, LEFT
Tour of the Americas,
tour poster, 1975

OPPOSITE, MIDDLE, RIGHT
Tour of the Americas,
album/tour poster, 1975

OPPOSITE, BOTTOM
Tour of the Americas,
various cloth passes, 1975

RIGHT
Gig poster, Wales, 1973
(concert cancelled).
Artist: J. Purness.

Black and Blue (April 1976) was the band's first studio album with Ron Wood as the replacement for Mick Taylor. It was so-named for its black music influences as its tracks included strong references to jazz, funk, and reggae.

Black and Blue was given a full-on Hollywood-style promotion, replete with a controversial billboard on Sunset Boulevard. The outdoor ad graphic showcased model Anita Russell 'erotically' bruised and bound, under the header 'I'm black and blue from the Rolling Stones— and I love it!' The billboard was taken down after protests from women's rights groups complaining that the artwork encouraged violence towards women.

The same month, the Rolling Stones commenced their 41-show *Tour of Europe '76* which took them across the UK and continental Europe between April and June. The three dates at London's Earls Court were in such demand that the promoter received more than one million ticket applications in the mail. This also was the first time since 1967 that the Stones played in a communist-led country (Yugoslavia).

On 21 August, the Stones performed in front of nearly 200,000 people at the Knebworth Park Fair. The stage for their set was in the shape of a giant tongue. The show's poster of the jester in the forest has long been considered one of the holy grails of Stones poster collecting.

RIGHT
Gig poster, Knebworth
Fair, 1976

BELOW, LEFT
Gig programme, Knebworth
Fair, 1976

BELOW, RIGHT
Press ad, Knebworth
Fair, 1976

Love You Live (September 1977) was a double live album that was recorded during the Rolling Stones' 1976 European tour. Additionally, it contained tracks from the band's El Mocambo nightclub concert in Toronto in 1977. The album was the group's third official full-length live release up until that point.

This was the final album where Keith Richards' name would be spelled 'Keith Richard', with the guitarist returning to his real surname of 'Richards' on the *Some Girls* (1978) record.

Andy Warhol created the *Love You Live* album artwork; the pencil smears were added by Mick Jagger (reportedly to Warhol's great dismay).

TOP, LEFT

Love You Live, promo tote bag, 1977. Art: Andy Warhol

TOP, RIGHT

Love You Live, press conference poster, 1977

MIDDLE, LEFT

Love You Live, stickers, 1977. Polaroids: Andy Warhol

BOTTOM, LEFT

Love You Live, UK poster, 1977. Art: Warhol/Jagger

BOTTOM, RIGHT

Love You Live, press ad, 1977

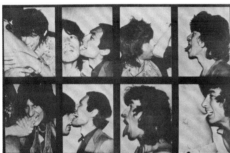

Achtung, Steinschlag, die Rolling Stones live!

C 1977 Promotone B.V.

Doppelalbum mit energiegeladenen LiveVersionen alter wie neuer Stones Hits. Die neue Stones – ein "Muß"

The Rolling Stones / Love You Live
2LP COC 89 101-A Doppel MC COC 489 101-K

Von der WEA Musik GmbH Eine Warner Communications Gesellschaft

TOP, LEFT
Love You Live, UK
two-page press ad, 1977

TOP, RIGHT
Love You Live, UK
press ad, 1977

LEFT
Love You Live, German
promo poster, 1977

ABOVE
Love You Live,
promo mobile, 1977

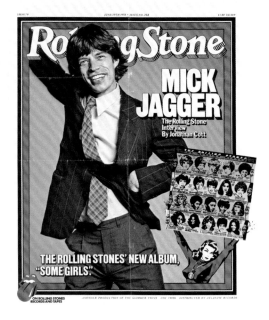

TOP, LEFT
US tour poster,
1978

MIDDLE, RIGHT
Some Girls US
promo poster, 1978

BOTTOM, FAR LEFT
'Miss You', press
ad, 1978

BOTTOM, RIGHT
'Respectable', UK
press ad, 1978

TOP, RIGHT
Some Girls, US promo poster
of *Rolling Stone* cover, 1978

ABOVE
Some Girls, promo wig
box and wig, 1978

BOTTOM, MIDDLE
Some Girls, UK
press ad, 1978

TOP ROW AND ABOVE, RIGHT
Some Girls, UK promo
poster set, 1978

LEFT
Some Girls, stand-up
display, 1978

ABOVE, LEFT
Some Girls, US boxing-style
promo poster, 1978

One of the Stones' most inspired post-*Exile on Main St.* albums, *Some Girls* (June 1978) received across-the-board plaudits upon its release. Its vitality was affected by both punk and disco, and became the band's biggest album in the US with more than six million units sold-through to date. The album yielded the band's last US No 1, 'Miss You', as well as concert favourites 'Shattered', 'When the Whip Comes Down' and 'Beast of Burden'.

Peter Corriston created the imaginative cover art (he would also design the next three Stones albums). The *Some Girls* package involved a sophisticated die-cut process, complemented by different color inner sleeves.

Corriston's concept showed the band in drag, along with select female icons (Lucille Ball, Farrah Fawcett, Raquel Welch, Judy Garland, and Marilyn Monroe), and men's magazine-style lingerie ads from the 50s, all amid a general air of salaciousness. The Stones were threatened with lawsuits by the ladies (or their estates), and the offending likenesses were removed.

The band embarked upon their summer 'back-to-basics' 1978 American tour in support of *Some Girls*. It was promoted by an unusual poster featuring a Chinese female factory worker.

The tour included a mixture of venues large and small, sometimes advertised by way of a pseudonym.

Emotional Rescue (June 1980) was the follow-up to *Some Girls.* Peter Corriston once again was the designer. He chose a theme based on shots from a thermo camera (a device invented to measure heat emission, generally for scientific projects). Perhaps the title of one of the singles from the album said what needed to be said about the work: 'She's So Cold'. An oversize poster of more thermo-shots wrapped the LP, and the package itself came wrapped in a plastic bag.

Sucking in the Seventies (April 1981) was the fourth official compilation album by the Stones. It was the successor to *Made in the Shade* (1975). The – literally – ballsy graphics were awarded high marks in the art world.

TOP, LEFT
Emotional Rescue, promo stand-up display, 1980

TOP, RIGHT
Emotional Rescue, US press ad, 1980

BOTTOM, LEFT
Emotional Rescue, promo poster, 1980

BOTTOM, RIGHT
Emotional Rescue, promo poster, 1980

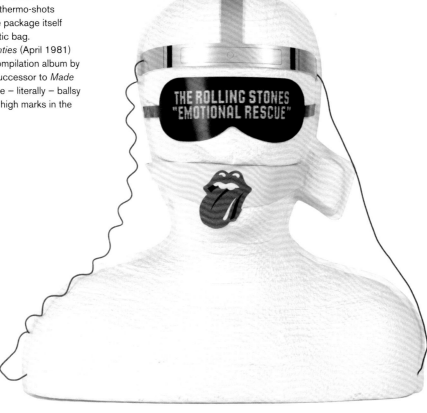

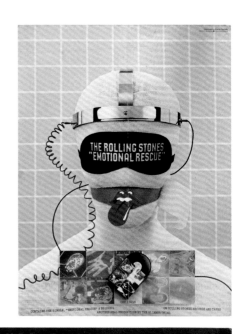

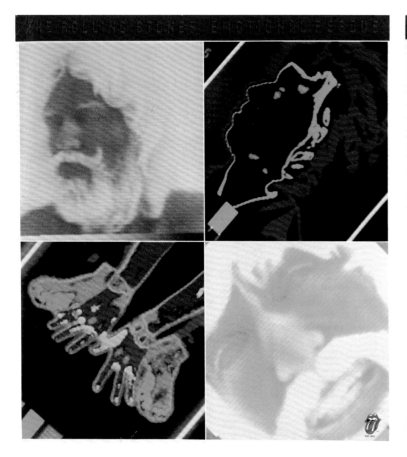

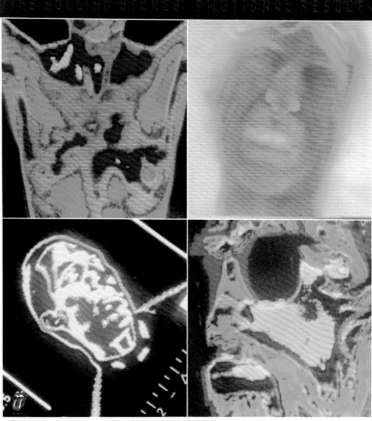

ABOVE

Sucking in the Seventies,
die-cut poster, 1981

BELOW, LEFT

Sucking in the Seventies,
press ad, 1981

BELOW, RIGHT

Sucking in the Seventies,
promo poster, 1981

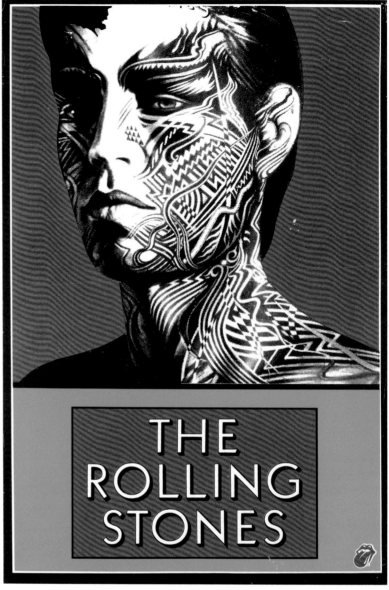

TOP, LEFT

Tattoo You, promo
poster, 1981

TOP, RIGHT

Tattoo You, promo
poster, 1981

RIGHT

Tattoo You,
die-cut poster, 1981

Tattoo You (August 1981) was composed primarily of outtakes and unfinished songs, some dating back a decade, but its singles – 'Start Me Up', 'Hang Fire' and 'Waiting on a Friend' – were to prove to be enduring classics. The album cover was again designed by Peter Corriston, who won a Grammy Award in the category of 'Best Album Package' for this release.

Tattoo You was supported by a 50-date North American tour, promoted by Bill Graham. One of its features was Kazuhide Yamazari's upbeat, colourful illustrations, incorporated into the stage design, and used on merchandising product and promotional materials.

Mick Jagger later said: 'Most outdoor concerts at that time took place during the day. So we had the idea to use bright primary colours, along with these enormous images of a guitar, a car, and a record – an Americana thing – which worked very well for afternoon shows.'

The 1981 tour was a milestone for the rock concert industry because the Stones sold major advertising rights to Jovan's Musk male fragrance (Jovan paid half-a-million dollars to put their name on Rolling Stones tickets, and distributed their own tour poster). After this breakthrough, rock-tour corporate sponsorships soon became the norm.

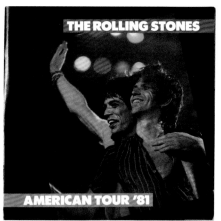

TOP, LEFT

Gig poster, Candlestick
Park, SF, 1981. Art: Kaz

TOP, MIDDLE

US tour programme,
1981

TOP, RIGHT

UK tour, laminate pass (J Geils
Band), 1981. Art: Kaz

MIDDLE

US tour poster, 1981

BELOW

Bill Graham promoter gift
poster, 1981

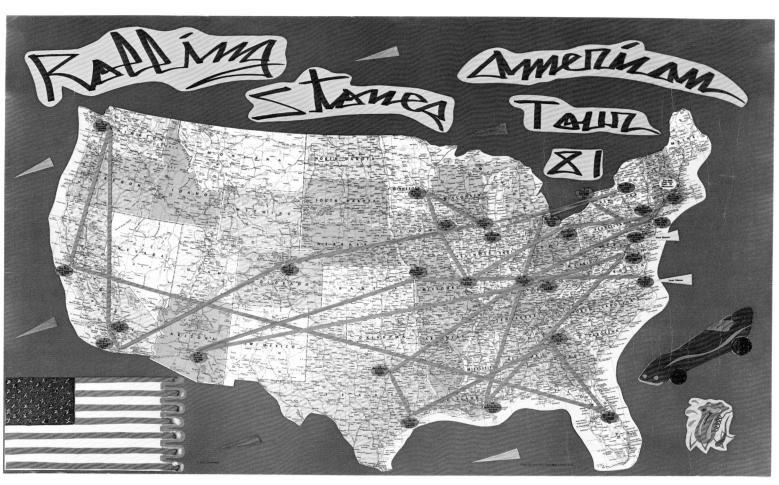

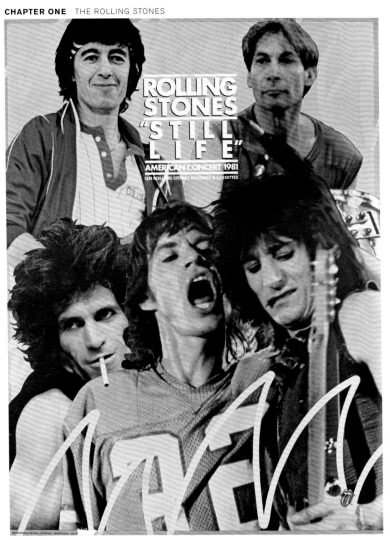

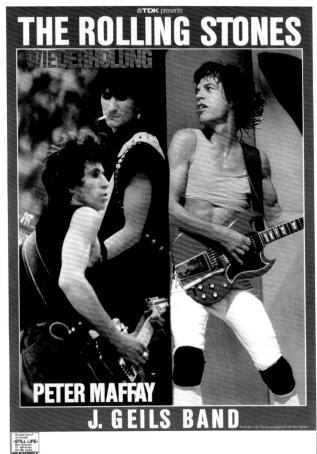

THE GREATEST ROCK 'N' ROLL SHOW IN THE WORLD...ON RECORD & TAPE

ROLLING STONES

"STILL LIFE"

(AMERICAN CONCERT 1981)

FEATURING

GOING TO A GO GO · LETS SPEND THE NIGHT TOGETHER
SHATTERED · TWENTY FLIGHT ROCK
UNDER MY THUMB · LET ME GO · TIME IS ON MY SIDE
IMAGINATION · START ME UP · SATISFACTION

Still Life (June 1982) was released in time for the Rolling Stones' European tour of 1982 and was recorded during the previous year's American tour. The distinctive album art, like the tours, was designed by Kaz.

Europe '82 would be the final Bill Graham-led Stones tour. It was an additional 36 shows added to the long and successful 1981 US tour.

LEFT
Still Life, UK promo
poster, 1982. Art: Kaz

BELOW, TOP
Still Life, promo
poster, 1982

BELOW, BOTTOM
Still Life, US promo
poster, 1982

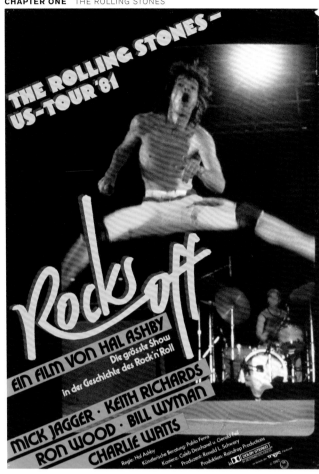

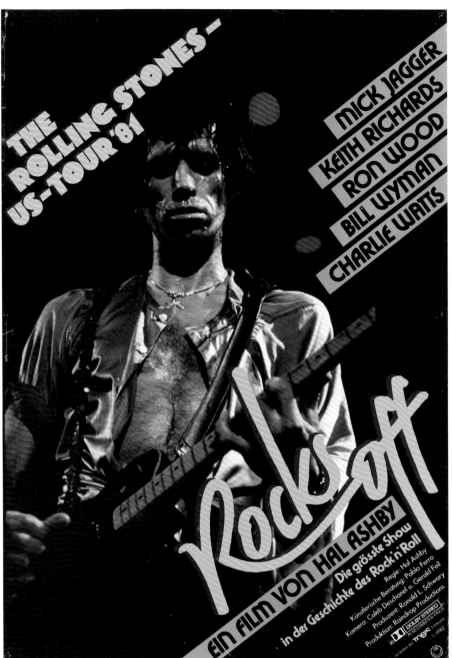

TOP, LEFT
Let's Spend The Night Together,
German movie poster, 1982

TOP, RIGHT
Let's Spend The Night Together,
German movie poster, 1982

BOTTOM, LEFT
Let's Spend The Night Together,
US movie poster, 1982

BOTTOM, RIGHT
Let's Spend The Night Together,
French movie poster, 1982

Undercover (November 1983) was the Rolling Stones' first release of material fully recorded in the 1980s. The LP's cover artwork (designed once again by Peter Corriston) included actual peel-off stickers, which when removed revealed . . . surprise! . . . no nudity but, instead, other patterned, geometric shapes.

Corriston also has worked with Billy Idol, Debbie Harry, the J. Geils Band, Jethro Tull, Led Zeppelin (Physical Graffiti), the New York Dolls, Pat Benatar, Rod Stewart and Tom Waits.

LEFT, TOP
Undercover,
press ad, 1983

LEFT, BOTTOM
Video Rewind,
promo poster, 1983

ABOVE, TOP
Undercover, promo
poster, 1983

ABOVE
Undercover, US
promo poster, 1983

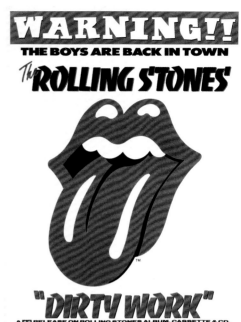

ABOVE
'Harlem Shuffle', lucite
block, 1986

ABOVE
'Harlem Shuffle', video shoot
pass, 1986. Art: Ralph Bakshi

TOP
'Harlem Shuffle',
promo poster, 1986

RIGHT, TOP
Dirty Work, promo
poster, 1986

RIGHT, BOTTOM
'Harlem Shuffle', record
store bin divider, 1986

Dirty Work (March 1986) was the Stones'
21st US-released studio album. It yielded
a major hit in 'Harlem Shuffle', the first cover
song the Stones had released as an
opening single off a new studio album since
1964. It was originally an R&B song written
and recorded by the duo Bob & Earl
in 1963 and later covered by Booker T
and the MG's.

CBS Records, distributor for the
Stones' record label, insisted on the
atypically colourful band photo on the
cover, as well as the inclusion of a lyric
sheet – a first for the Stones.

The artwork for the 'Harlem Shuffle'
picture sleeve was a collaboration between
animator Ralph Bakshi and future Ren
and Stimpy creator John Kricfalusi.

Steel Wheels (August 1989) heralded the biggest world tour of the Rolling Stones' career. It was also bassist Bill Wyman's final studio album with the Stones.

The band was inducted into the Rock & Roll Hall of Fame in February and began recording anew in March. Reviews of the first single, 'Mixed Emotions', were warm, and the singles that followed, 'Rock and a Hard Place' and 'Almost Hear You Sigh', resulted from the renewed good feelings. All the band members were determined to emulate the classic Rolling Stones' sound.

Canadian promoter Michael Cohl bought the concert, sponsorship, merchandising, radio, television, and film rights to the *Steel Wheels Tour*, launched in North America in August. It would accommodate 115 shows over three legs, and would include a jaunt to Japan in February 1990 for ten shows at the Tokyo Dome.

The European leg would follow, re-titled the *Urban Jungle Tour*, concluding the entire world tour almost exactly one year after it began.

ABOVE, LEFT
Steel Wheels tour,
laminate pass, 1989

ABOVE, RIGHT
Steel Wheels Japanese tour,
laminate pass, 1990

MIDDLE, TOP
Terrifying pay-per-view concert,
promo poster, 1989

MIDDLE, BOTTOM
Steel Wheels, North American
tour programme, 1989

RIGHT, TOP
Steel Wheels, Canadian
tour programme, 1989

RIGHT, 2ND DOWN
Steel Wheels Japanese tour,
promo poster, 1990

RIGHT, 3RD DOWN
Steel Wheels Japanese
tour programme, 1990

RIGHT, BOTTOM
Steel Wheels Japanese tour,
promo poster, 1990

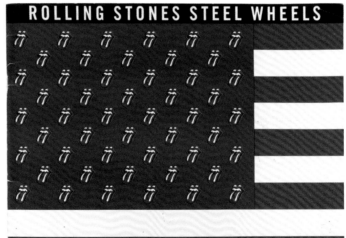

Almost a year after their founding bassist, Bill Wyman, departed after 30 years of sevice, and almost five years since their last studio album, *Steel Wheels*, the Rolling Stones released their first album under their new alliance with Virgin Records, *Voodoo Lounge* (July 1994).

It would prove to be the first album to *not* produce any significant hits in the US even while several tracks became Top 40 chart hits in the UK. Yet, it would win, in early 1995, while the *Voodoo Lounge Tour* was ongoing, the band's first Grammy, for 'Best Rock Album'. In retrospect, say many critics and fans, the sparser-sounding *Voodoo Lounge* may prove to be a better comeback for the Stones than the slicker-sounding *Steel Wheels* actually was.

Voodoo Lounge debuted at No 1 in the UK – the band's first chart-topper since *Emotional Rescue* (1980).

TOP, LEFT
Voodoo Lounge,
promo mobile, 1994

TOP, RIGHT
Voodoo Lounge tour,
promo poster, 1994

MIDDLE, LEFT
'You Got Me Rocking',
US press ad, 1994

MIDDLE, CENTRE
Voodoo Lounge,
US press ad, 1994

MIDDLE, RIGHT
Voodoo Lounge,
US press ad, 1994

BOTTOM, LEFT
'Love Is Strong', US
press ad, 1994

BOTTOM, MIDDLE
Voodoo Lounge tour
promo poster, 1994

BOTTOM, RIGHT
Voodoo Lounge, US
promo poster, 1994

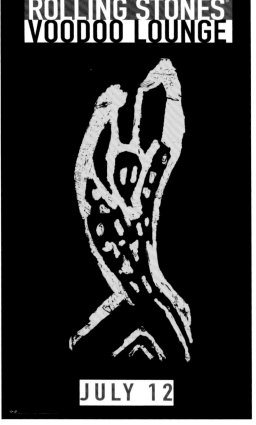

TOP, LEFT
Voodoo Lounge tour
programme, 1994–5

MIDDLE, LEFT
Voodoo Lounge, merchandise
booklet, 1994–5

MIDDLE
Voodoo Lounge, European
tour poster, 1995

ABOVE, LEFT
Premiere, promo
poster, 1995

BOTTOM, LEFT TO RIGHT
Voodoo Lounge, various
tour laminates, 1994–5

TOP, RIGHT
Voodoo Lounge, Australasia
tour poster, 1995

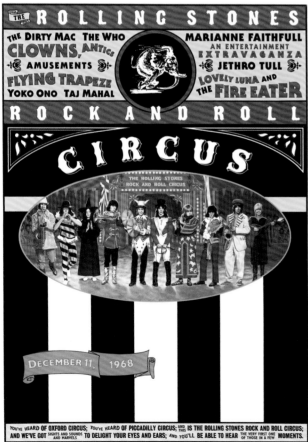

Stripped (November 1995) was an unusual live album constructed along the lines of the *MTV Unplugged* series, featuring a mix of intimate club recordings, braggadocious concert highlights, and live-in-the-studio reinterpretations of both hits and obscurities from throughout the Stones' lengthy career.

The *Rolling Stones Rock and Roll Circus* (October 1996) actually dated back to 1968, when the band taped an ill-fated television special that was never broadcast. The special was intended to promote the newly-released *Beggars Banquet* album. The Stones invited guests to perform at a rock 'n' roll extravaganza – a musical circus in effect – among whom were: John Lennon (with Yoko Ono); The Who; Eric Clapton (who'd just broken up with Cream); Taj Mahal; and Jethro Tull. In particular that night, The Who were the standouts.

The Stones felt their own performances lacked spark and so the recordings were temporarily shelved, then abandoned and nearly forgotten. Oddly, *Rock and Roll Circus* was the first Stones album not to be released on vinyl.

LEFT, TOP
Stripped, 3-D
stand-up display, 1995

LEFT, BOTTOM
Rock and Roll Circus, UK
movie poster, 1996

OPPOSITE
Rock and Roll Circus, US
stand-up display, 1996

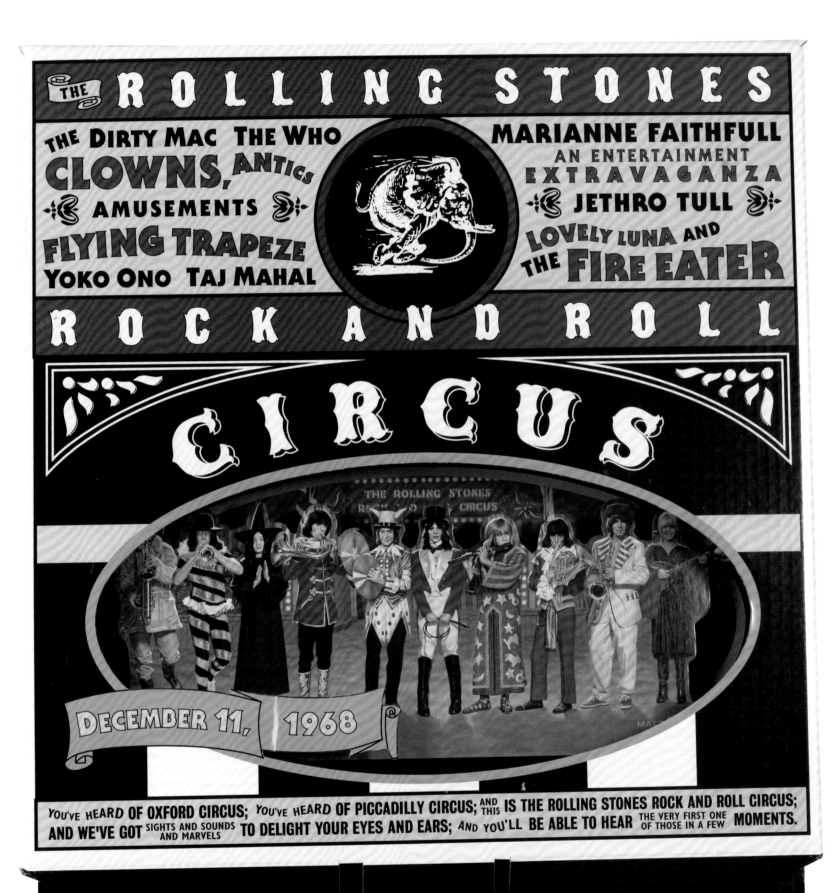

TOP, LEFT

Bridges to Babylon, UK
stand-up display, 1997

TOP, RIGHT

Bridges to Babylon,
promo poster, 1997

BOTTOM, LEFT

Gig poster,
New York, 1997

ABOVE, RIGHT

Bridges to Babylon,
various passes, 1997-8

The Rolling Stones' final studio album
of the 1990s was *Bridges to Babylon*
(September 1997), supported by
a juggernaut, year-long, worldwide tour
that featured 58 North America shows
(including two in Mexico); 37 in Europe and
the UK; six in Japan and seven in South
America (including five in Argentina)

Over 4,577,000 people attended the
108 shows in 25 countries (over two million
in Europe, two million in North America,
nearly 350,000 in Argentina/Brazil and
200,000 in Japan).

The tour's success was bested only by
the Stones' own, subsequent *A Bigger
Bang* tour.

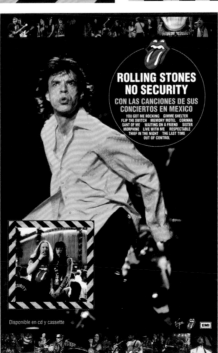

Forty Licks (September 2002) was a double compilation album, a 40-year, career-spanning retrospective. It combined the band's formative, 1960s, Decca/London era (licensed by ABKCO Records, which previously had issued many compilation albums, under many different titles, with this material over several decades) with the band's self-owned post-1970 recordings, which were distributed by Virgin Records.

Forty Licks followed the Beatles' release of a similar broad compilation, and also was inspired by an Elvis Presley package, *30 No 1 Hits*.

Concurrent with the release of *Forty Licks*, the band embarked upon a year-long international *Licks Tour*, which itself resulted in *Live Licks* (2004).

TOP, LEFT
Forty Licks, poster with embossed tongues, 2002

TOP, RIGHT
Forty Licks, promo poster, 2002

BOTTOM, LEFT
Forty Licks, promo poster, 2002

BOTTOM, 2ND LEFT
Forty Licks, promo poster, 2002

BOTTOM, LAST THREE
Forty Licks, series of three promo posters, 2002

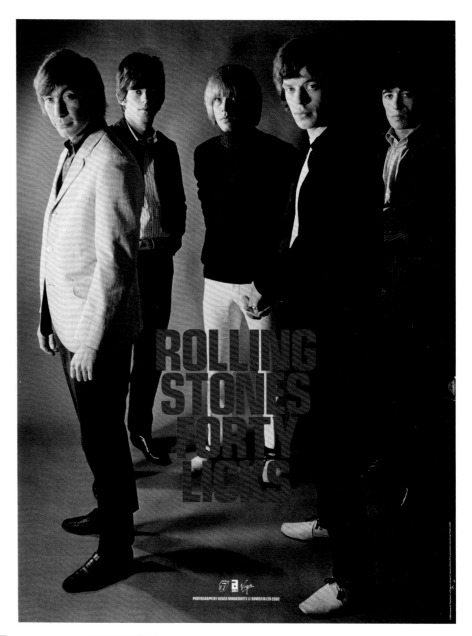

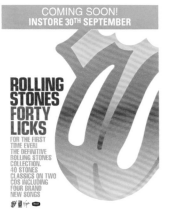

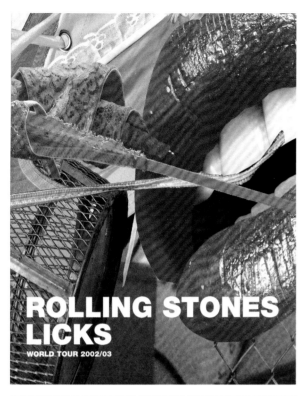

ROLLING STONES LICKS
WORLD TOUR 2002/03

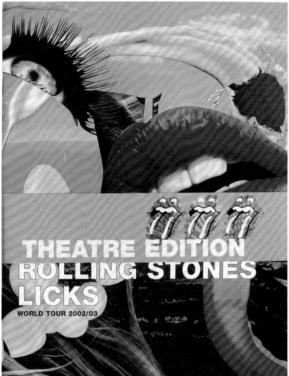

THEATRE EDITION
ROLLING STONES
LICKS
WORLD TOUR 2002/03

TOP, LEFT
Forty Licks tour
programme, 2003

TOP, RIGHT
Forty Licks tour, various
laminate passes, 2003

BOTTOM, LEFT
Live Licks, US promo
poster, 2004

BOTTOM, RIGHT
Live Licks, promo
poster, 2004

TOP, MIDDLE
Live on HBO, TV show
promo poster, 2003

MIDDLE, LEFT
Forty Licks tour programme,
'Theatre edition', 2003

BOTTOM, MIDDLE
Free concert, promo
poster, LA, 2003

The year-long 2002 – 03 *Licks Tour*
supporting their career-spanning
retrospective *Forty Licks* (2002) album, led
to the release of *Live Licks* (November
2004), the band's seventh live album.

The Stones released two subtly different
versions of the cover art for *Live Licks*.
While the concept was anime-inspired, and
both featured the Stones' tongue logo in
a suggestive context, the British version
featured the woman atop the tongue
without her bikini top.

Critics and fans alike felt that *Live Licks*
may have been the band's best live release
since *Get Yer Ya-Ya's Out* (1970).

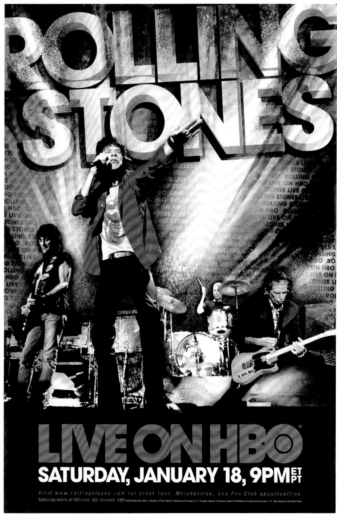

ROLLING STONES

LIVE ON HBO
SATURDAY, JANUARY 18, 9PM ET PT

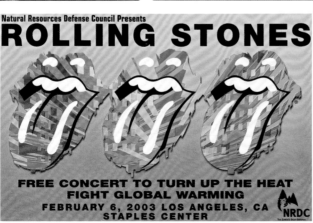

Natural Resources Defense Council Presents
ROLLING STONES
FREE CONCERT TO TURN UP THE HEAT
FIGHT GLOBAL WARMING
FEBRUARY 6, 2003 LOS ANGELES, CA
STAPLES CENTER
NRDC

ROLLING STONES
LIVE LICKS
23 live tracks including classics and rarities
from Licks 2002-2003 World Tour

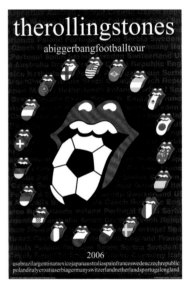

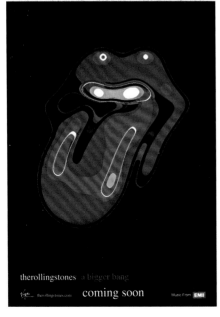

TOP, LEFT
A Bigger Bang,
promo poster, 2005

TOP, RIGHT
A Bigger Bang,
promo poster, 2005

MIDDLE, LEFT
A Bigger Bang, special
edition poster, 2005

MIDDLE, RIGHT
A Bigger Bang, World Cup-
themed tour poster, 2006

BOTTOM, LEFT
A Bigger Bang,
promo poster, 2005

BOTTOM, RIGHT
A Bigger Bang,
promo poster, 2005

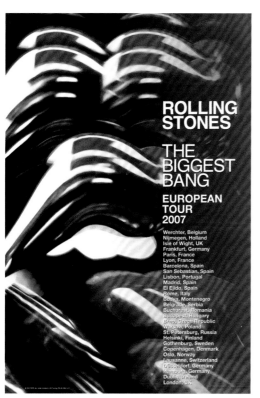

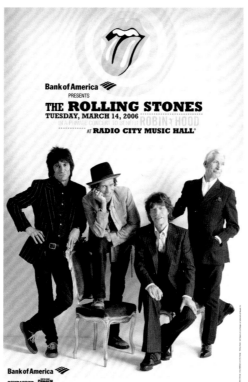

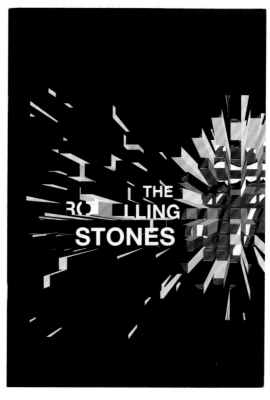

TOP, LEFT
The Biggest Bang DVD,
promo poster 2007

TOP, MIDDLE
Gig poster, benefit
concert, NY, 2006

TOP, RIGHT
A Bigger Bang tour
programme, 2006

MIDDLE, LEFT
A Bigger Bang European
tour poster, 2006

MIDDLE, CENTRE
Gig poster,
NY, 2006

MIDDLE, RIGHT
Australia/NZ tour poster,
2006. Art: Ken Taylor

BOTTOM
A Bigger Bang tour, various
laminates, 2006

2

PINK
FLOYD

PINK FLOYD

The forced retirement of the vinyl LP in the mid-1980s brought an end to a dynamic era in rock art packaging in which the marketing needs of the record industry and the renegade aesthetics of rock 'n' roll bands came together in a remarkable, often spectacular visual marriage.

Cover design was already an art, especially in the jazz field, long before the explosion of rock in the 1960s, but with the meteoric success of Pink Floyd came a power shift from the record companies to the musicians themselves, who assumed greater control over the visual presentation – packaging – of their work.

Of all the late 1960s bands that grew to great artistic prominence in the 1970s, Pink Floyd was the most adept at mastering their own image over the longest possible term (right to the present day) and Storm Thorgerson was the designer they set to work on their behalf.

Storm Thorgerson *got* Pink Floyd. To use the American vernacular, he had them *down*. Thorgerson, a prominent English graphic designer whose work has now extended over more than three decades, was a founding member of the British graphic art group Hipgnosis. Many of his most famous designs are those for Pink Floyd's album covers and their promotional campaigns. His in-the-studio collaborative design with George Hardie for *The Dark Side of the Moon* has been called one of the greatest album covers of all time.

His pioneering work with Hipgnosis went far beyond Pink Floyd; as one of the founders of the studio he also designed, photographed, and art directed projects for 10cc, AC/DC, Black Sabbath, Peter Gabriel, Genesis, Led Zeppelin, Styx and Yes.

For the solo members of Pink Floyd, Hipgnosis designed David Gilmour's *David Gilmour* (1978), Nick Mason's *Ficticious Sports* (1981) and Syd Barrett's *The Madcap Laughs* (1970). Thorgerson himself also designed Rick Wright's *Broken China* (1996).

Hipgnosis' work for Pink Floyd includes *A Saucerful of Secrets* (1968), *Ummagumma* (1969), *Atom Heart Mother* (1970), *Meddle* (1971), *Obscured by Clouds* (1972), *The Dark Side of the Moon* (1973), *Wish You Were Here* (1975), *Animals* (1977) and *A Collection of Great Dance Songs* (1981) – under the TCP pseudonym

Hipgnosis consisted primarily of Thorgerson, Aubrey Powell, and later, Peter Christopherson. The studio dissolved in 1983. Thorgerson, subsequently working on his own for Pink Floyd, then designed *A Momentary Lapse of Reason* (1987), *Delicate Sound of Thunder* (1988), *Shine On* (1992), *The Division Bell* (1994), *Pulse* (1995), *Is There Anybody Out There? The Wall Live 1980-81* (2000), *Echoes: The Best of Pink Floyd* (2001) and *Oh, By the Way* (2007).

It all began in 1968. Thorgerson and Powell were approached by their friends in Pink Floyd to design the cover for the group's second album, *A Saucerful of Secrets*. Being film and art school students, they were able to use the darkroom at the Royal College of Art, but when they completed school, they had to set up their own facilities. They built a small darkroom in Powell's bathroom, but shortly thereafter, in early 1970, rented space and built a studio.

Hipgnosis gained major international prominence in 1973 with the sleeve to *Dark Side of the Moon*. The final design was one of several versions prepared for the band to choose from, but according to drummer Nick Mason, the 'prism/pyramid' design was the immediate and unanimous group choice.

Peter Christopherson joined Hipgnosis as an assistant in 1974 and later became a full partner. The firm employed many assistants and other staff members over the years. Of particular note were freelance artists George Hardie Colin Elgie, Richard Evans and Richard Manning.

Thorgerson and Powell's elaborately manipulated photos (utilising darkroom tricks, multiple exposures, airbrush retouching, and mechanical cutting-and-pasting) were a film-based forerunner of what would, much later, lead to Photoshop computer technique. Hipgnosis used primarily Hasselblad medium-format cameras for their work, the square-film format being particularly suited to album cover design. For the inside of the gatefold to *Dark Side of the Moon*, Thorgerson literally drew the sound wave of a heartbeat. 'If the album is about any one thing, possibly it's madness – the dark side of the moon, irrationality, the other side of one's normal life,' he said. 'They had people discussing these mad little bits about their lives, and they used the heartbeat as a rhythm underneath it.'

The outside cover depicted a prism refracting white light into the visual spectrum and the back illustrated the reverse. It was Thorgerson's way of honouring another aspect of the band, namely the light shows that were fast becoming a Pink Floyd concert hallmark.

'The band developed something sophisticated in terms of trying to create a concert atmosphere with interesting light to match what they were already creating with their sound,' Thorgerson said. 'With the album, the prism was a way to talk about the fact that this band, preeminently among all bands, would do light. Light and sound.'

The full package also included two posters – one comprising shots of the band in concert, the other featuring the Egyptian pyramids, photographed by Thorgerson under a full moon. The band notably took a cut in its royalty rate so that the posters could be included without raising the cost of the record.

'That was in the days when packaging really meant something,' says Thorgerson. 'It was a present to the fans.'

ANIMALS THE WALL WISH YOU WERE HERE

PINK FLOYD
30TH ANNIVERSARY

MOMENTARY LAPSE OF REASON A COLLECTION OF GREAT DANCE SONGS THE FINAL CUT

6 ANNIVERSARY EDITION REISSUE CDS.
- REPACKAGED WITH ALL THE ORIGINAL ALBUM ARTWORK
- REMASTERED UNDER THE BAND'S SUPERVISION
ALSO AVAILABLE: THE DIVISION BELL, DELICATE SOUND OF THUNDER & PULSE

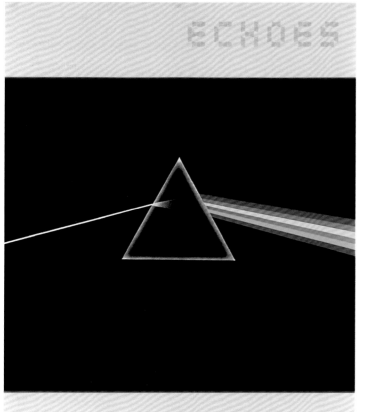

Everyone has a dark side

TOP
30th anniversary
promo poster, 1995

LEFT
Echoes, promo
poster 2007

ABOVE
Animals, UK
press ad, 1977

Pink Floyd's earliest shows were staged in 1965. The band initially focused on R&B covers, as with so many British bands of the period. Then, as they played generally unadvertised shows at the Marquee Club in London beginning in June 1966, they introduced psychedelia to their act for the first time.

In late September 1966, they were invited to play London's All Saint's Church Hall for a series of shows to raise money for the underground *International Times* newspaper.

Here they began their notable use of visual effects and started phasing out the R&B songs. In December 1966, the first of the *International Times*-associated gigs was held at the legendary UFO Club and intriguingly psychedelic advertising posters were created for them by the design group Hapshash and the Coloured Coat (which was led by Michael English and Nigel Weymouth).

The Piper at the Gates of Dawn (1967) is widely recognised as one of the most provocative debut albums ever recorded, having a huge impact on the psychedelic rock scene. Vic Singh photographed and designed the album cover, one of the few covers actually to feature all of the band members.

The album's title came from the title of chapter seven of Kenneth Grahame's *The Wind in the Willows* novel where Rat and Mole, while searching for Portly, the lost son of Otter, are drawn to a place where the 'Piper' is playing on his reed flute (the 'Piper' referred to in the title is the Greek god Pan).

Visa problems caused cancellation of several shows heralded by beautiful and highly collectible posters designed by promoter Bill Graham's wife Bonnie MacLean for October shows at the Fillmore Auditorium in San Francisco, but the November show at Winterland arena, advertised by a poster by Nicolas Kouninos, was apparently held.

In late 1967 the band put out the word that they were in need of an extra guitarist and David Gilmour was brought in. For the first four shows of 1968, Pink Floyd was a five-man live act, but then, while they were on their way to a gig at Southampton University in late January, they decided to leave Syd Barrett at his home. His deteriorating mental state was making it increasingly difficult for him to perform with the band.

Despite the significant change in band personnel, Pink Floyd actively toured throughout 1968, supporting their second album (released in 1968, the last that Barrett worked on) with the official *Saucerful of Secrets* Tour beginning in July headed up by a memorable two-month North American leg.

There are images of two Marvel Comics characters included in the album cover collage (designed by Storm Thorgerson) for *A Saucerful of Secrets* (1968): The Living Tribunal in the upper left corner, and Doctor Strange along the right edge.

The album name *Ummagumma* (1969) allegedly refers to a slang word for sexual intercourse made up by Pink Floyd roadies (although that never was quite corroborated by the band).

Longtime art director Storm Thorgerson created a suitably perplexing concept for the album cover using a similar scene involving each of the bandmembers against an outside wall, switching positions in and out of the format's frame to create what is termed a continued "recursive" effect (where each recursion further shows another bandmember's exchanged position). After four recursive variations of the scene, the final picture-within-picture is the cover of the previous Pink Floyd album, *A Saucerful of Secrets*.

On the album's back cover, roadies Alan Stiles and Peter Watts are shown with the band's considerable array of sound equipment carefully spread across a runway at Biggin Hill Airport in England. This was a concept proposed by drummer Nick Mason who would later house his legendary collection of vintage racecars at an airport location.

RIGHT
UK press ad for
charity gig, 1972.

BELOW
Gig poster, Shrine, LA,1968.
Art: Van Hammersveld/Fried

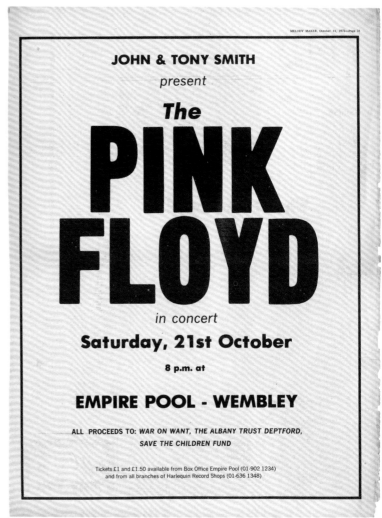

MELODY MAKER, October 14, 1972—Page 31

JOHN & TONY SMITH

present

The
PINK
FLOYD

in concert

Saturday, 21st October

8 p.m. at

EMPIRE POOL - WEMBLEY

ALL PROCEEDS TO: WAR ON WANT, THE ALBANY TRUST DEPTFORD,
SAVE THE CHILDREN FUND

Tickets £1 and £1.50 available from Box Office Empire Pool (01-902 1234)
and from all branches of Harlequin Record Shops (01-636 1348)

The original LP cover for *Atom Heart Mother* (1970) showed a cow looking round in an open pasture without any explanatory text, nor any other hint as to what kind of music might be on the record. Neither was there any band name or album title, although later editions had the title and band name added.

As the world has learned with respect to Pink Floyd, from their earliest days the band wanted no limitations put on their music at all, or any hint at their intentions. They advised their friend and associate, graphic designer Storm Thorgerson, that they wanted "something plain" for the album cover, which, famously, became the deliberately unremarkable cow.

Thorgerson, said to be inspired by Andy Warhol's equally impish "cow wallpaper", later told the story that he simply drove his car out 18 miles north of London to a rural area where he himself was born – near Potters Bar – and "photographed the first cow he saw." The cow's owner later identified the animal as "Lulubelle III."

Thorgerson put more cows on the back cover (also with no text or titles) and more on the inside gatefold.

The release of the compilation album *Relics* (1971) was sparked by the success of *Atom Heart Mother* in the UK The *Relics* cover art was initially a black-and-white sketch by drummer Nick Mason, later rendered in various colourful 3-D forms.

TOP, LEFT

UK press ad, Crystal Palace Bowl, 1971

TOP, RIGHT

Gig poster, Japan, 1972

BOTTOM, LEFT

Atom Heart Mother, UK press ad, 1970

BOTTOM, RIGHT

Relics, promo poster, 1971

Storm Thorgerson once again played a significant role in helping Pink Floyd create a concept for their next album, *Meddle* (1971). He recalls suggesting a close-up shot of a baboon's characteristically colourful anus as the album cover photograph. But the band, then on an autumn tour in Japan, informed him via a memorable inter-continental telephone call that they would instead prefer an "ear underwater". That difficult-to-imagine concept became the final design.

The album's interior gatefold featured four superimposed black-and-white photographs of the individual band members – their final appearance together on one of the band's album sleeves.

The new Pink Floyd album is like throwing a party for your ears when all your ears were expecting were a few friends over for pinochle.

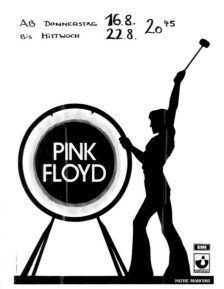

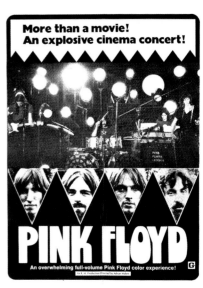

The first live performance of *The Dark Side of the Moon* was at the Dome in Brighton, Sussex, England on 20 January, 1972 (although there are reports that it was on the next night, January 21 at the Guildhall in Portsmouth).

The album, *The Dark Side of the Moon* (1973), would not be released until 17 March, 1973.

The album was originally released utilizing a gatefold LP sleeve that was a collaboration by the Hipgnosis design studio (led by Storm Thorgerson) and George Hardie, then of Nicholas Thirkell Associates. After some experimentation, the final version incorporated Hardie's iconic refracting prism on the cover.

Inside were two posters, one featuring pictures of the band live in concert and the other showing a psychedelicized image of the Great Pyramids of Giza in Egypt photographed on infra-red film. As an added bonus, also included was a sheet of stickers of the Pyramids.

In a 1991 issue of *Rolling Stone*, the refracting prism cover was No 35 on the magazine's list of the 100 greatest album covers of all time. Other more contemporary surveys consistently rank it much higher, in the top 15 of the most graphically significant album artworks.

At the time of writing, *The Dark Side of the Moon* remains the third best selling album of all time worldwide.

RIGHT, TOP
The Dark Side of the Moon,
UK press ad, 1973

RIGHT, MIDDLE
The Dark Side of the Moon,
UK press ad, 1973

RIGHT, BOTTOM
The Dark Side of the Moon,
UK album/tour press ad, 1973

BELOW
The Dark Side of the Moon,
UK tour programme, 1973

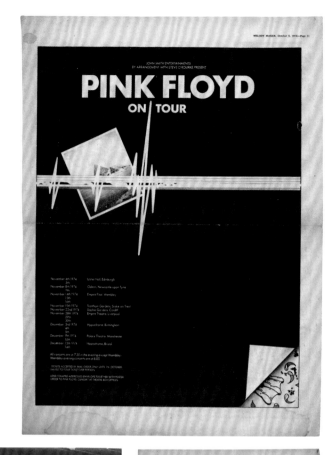

A Nice Pair (1973) was a compilation album, re-issuing Pink Floyd's first two albums, The Piper at the Gates of Dawn and A Saucerful of Secrets in a new gatefold sleeve.

The album cover is by Storm Thorgerson's Hipgnosis design studio. Thorgerson and his associates came up with two displays each showing nine small pictures of apparently proposed but previously rejected album cover designs.

Some of the images cleverly depict a clever phrase or saying in the form of a visual pun, one image featuring "a fork in the road", while another represents "a different kettle of fish." There is also "a nice pair", illustrated by a picture of a woman's breasts. Naturally, this was censored in various ways around the world.

A controversial aspect for the U.K. release was the inclusion of a sign depicting "Mr. W.R. Phang's dental surgery business," which was deemed objectionable on the grounds that advertising for business was not something dentists were permitted to do. The picture was temporarily replaced by one of a "gargling monk."

In the US the censored photos were restored in the 1980s, but the LP itself went out of print due to the worldwide reissue of the original two albums on CD.

BELOW

A Nice Pair,
press ad, 1973

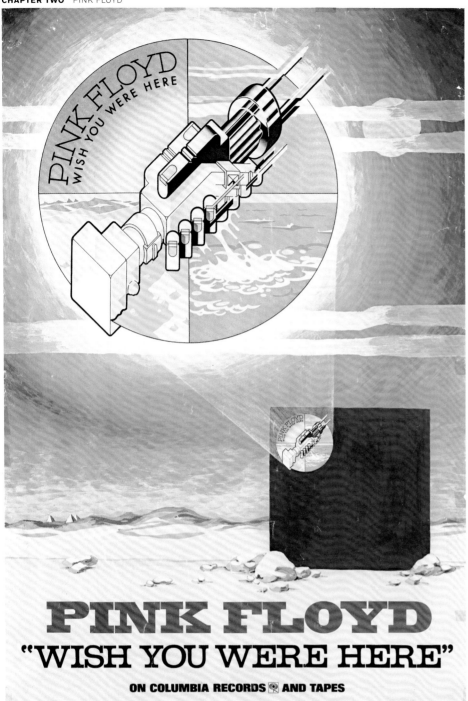

Pink Floyd toured France in June and England in November 1974, then performed at sold-out stadiums and arenas across North America in April and June in 1975 before headlining at the second Knebworth Festival in July 1975. The Knebworth Festival was then, between 1974 and 1979, an ongoing UK institution annually featuring top acts including the Rolling Stones, Led Zeppelin and Genesis, among many others.

Pink Floyd put on a memorable show that year which along with some great special effects featured a fly-by with a pair of historic Spitfire warplanes intended to synchronize with the start of the song 'Breathe' (frustratingly, the band had some tuning difficulties and the planes flew over prematurely). Knebworth was the last time the band would perform *Echoes* and the entire *Dark Side of the Moon* with Roger Waters.

Then, in September, the band released another of their most significant albums, *Wish You Were Here* (1975). The grand, ambitious (but no less honest and poignant) production shot to No 1 on both sides of the Atlantic. To date, the album has sold more than ten million copies worldwide.

Hipgnosis' artwork reflected the group's surprisingly minimalist self-evaluation. The album came shrinkwrapped – initially hiding, in effect, the album from public view – in opaque black cellophane, with only a colourful sticker showcasing four new elements and a handshake and revealing the album name. This also made the album's promotion a major challenge for the record label to get it sold-through in the stores.

Underneath the wrapper, a cover photo appeared of 'two movie studio execs' on a 'movie studio back lot' shaking hands – with one of them on fire.

This was wonderfully surreal, leaving the explanation for what it could mean in each album purchaser's own head, once they tore off the plastic and stared at it for a while.

The photo simply left a lot to the imagination, but one explanation (later provided by designer Storm Thorgerson) is that, in effect, a robotic businessman obtaining a handshake from a flaming businessman is as empty (or absent) a gesture as you can get.

Further accentuated by the cartooned robotic handshake on the sticker, graphically this did tie into Roger Waters'

typically discomforting and challenging anti-music-establishment lyrics.

The two men are stuntmen Danny Rogers on the left and Ronnie Rondell (on fire) on the right. Under his cloth business suit, Rondell wore asbestos protection that extended over his head, where a wig was attached. The first attempt at setting him on fire was in the wrong wind direction, and the flames were blown back and ignited his moustache for an instant . . a close shave, Thorgerson later drolly commented.

There were two different versions of the flaming photo. Some fans used to think it was guitarist David Gilmour on the left and keyboardist Rick Wright on the right. The UK version (the one with the flaming man leaning forward) became the version used on all of the CD releases.

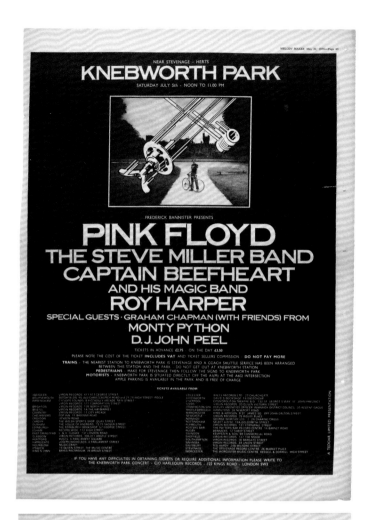

LEFT

Animals, promo
mobile, 1977

BELOW

Animals, promo
poster, 1977

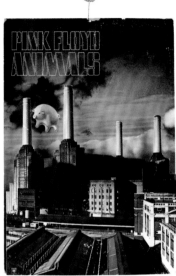

Animals (1977) is Pink Floyd's concept album conceived to rail against the evils of capitalism. Even in the prog rock-hating punk era, *Animals* proved to be a huge success, reaching No. 2 on the UK album charts as well as No. 3 in the US.

The iconic, helium-filled pig made its debut flight for the album cover when it took to the air over London's 1930s-era Battersea Power Station (on the south bank of the River Thames) during the December, 1975 photo shoot under the direction of Hipgnosis Studio head Storm Thorgerson.

On the first day of shooting, a marksman was on hand in case the tethered pig broke free. However, according to Thorgerson, this was considered "only a problem for the insurance agency," and the marksman was not hired for the second day.

On December 3 (the second day) a sudden gust of wind wrenched the giant pig free of its moorings between two of the four classic smokestacks. Because there was no one to shoot the inflatable down, it simply floated away.

A passenger plane reported seeing the free-flying piggy, causing all the flights at London's Heathrow Airport to be delayed for nearly a half hour.

A police helicopter was immediately dispatched to track the pig, but was forced to return after following it to an altitude of 5,000 feet. A warning was sent out to all commercial pilots that a giant, soaring pink pig was loose in the area.

The British Civil Aviation Authority lost radar contact with the big boar near Chatham in Kent, heading east at a height of 18,000 feet. At this point it was listed as a "significant airborne hazard."

The Pink Floyd pig eventually came back to earth, virtually undamaged, in a farmer's field. Thorgerson's crew then re-secured the cable clips, returned the pig to the scene of the crime, and flew it once again.

Unfortunately, the resulting pictures were not deemed sufficiently evocative as the clear blue sky from day three was thought to be much less dramatic. The final album image was skillfully created as a composite of the Battersea Power Station picture from day one and the tethered pig from day three.

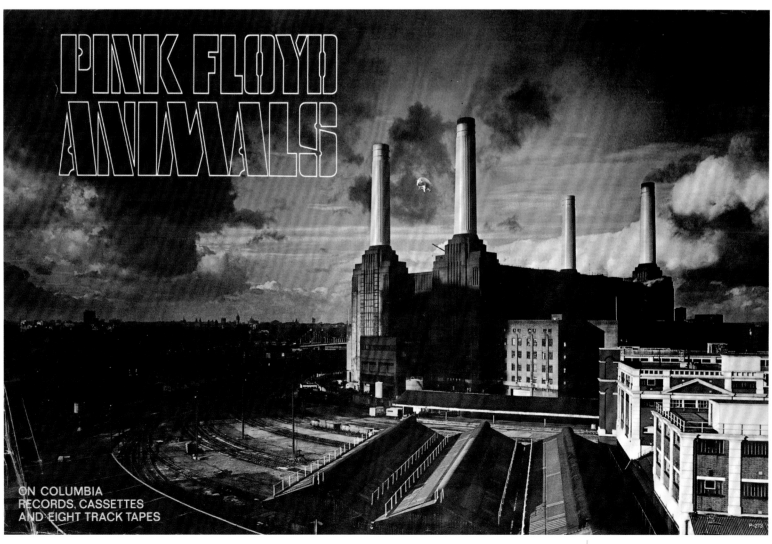

The final major worldwide tour with Roger Waters was the *Pink Floyd – In the Flesh Tour* of 1977. Audiences were treated to the now-famous inflatable character-puppets, a stupendous pyrotechnic waterfall, and the band performed on one of the biggest and most elaborate stages ever built for a rock band. It incorporated umbrella-like canopies that would rise quite dramatically from the stage if the band needed protection from inclement weather.

The band enjoyed an intense promotional campaign for the *In the Flesh Tour* with major advertisements in both the *New York Times* and *Billboard* magazine. Their prestigious tour venues included a four-night run at Madison Square Garden in the heart of New York City.

RIGHT
Animals, promo sun visor, 1977

BELOW
Animals, European tour poster, 1977

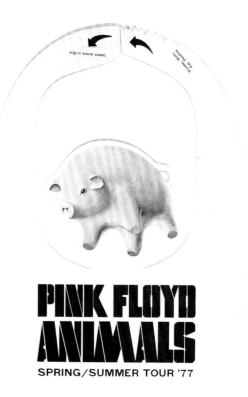

PINK FLOYD ANIMALS

SPRING/SUMMER TOUR '77

PINK FLOYD ANIMALS EUROPEAN TOUR 1977

© Brockum International Ltd

RIGHT
Animals US tour,
press ad, 1977

FAR RIGHT
Animals tour
programme, 1977

BELOW
Animals German tour,
poster, 1977

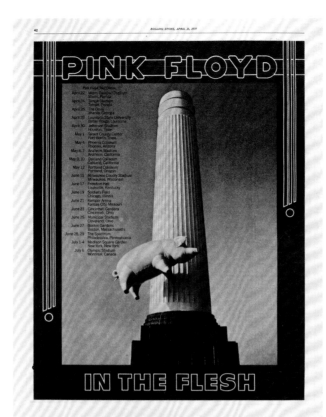

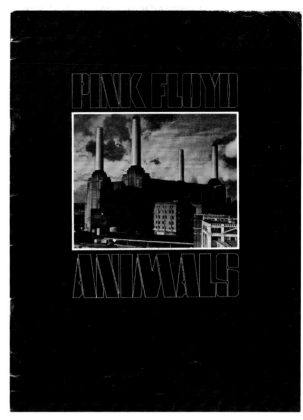

The Wall (1979) was a double-album rock opera subsequently briefly performed live and later made into a dark musical film.

The album was inspired in part by an incident that occurred on Pink Floyd's 1977 *Animals Tour*, when Roger Waters spat in the face of a fan who broke free from the crowd in Montreal, Canada and began climbing the netting. This led Waters later to question why such separation had to exist at all. His anger provided *The Wall* with its central focus on the subjects of isolation and exclusion.

The LP's defiantly brittle sleeve art by Gerald Scarfe ties in with the album's concept. Scarfe is a cartoonist, stage designer, live-action film maker and animator. Born in 1936, he is one of the greatest British cartoonists of the second half of the 20th century. He has depicted the highs and lows of the British political and cultural scene through his work as one of the political cartoonists for the *Sunday Times*, in his drawings of the Beatles and his depictions of the Vietnam War.

Scarfe began work for Pink Floyd in 1973, and was responsible for the *Wish You Were Here* tour videos and cartoon comics in the 1974 – 75 tour programmes.

Scarfe says: "When Roger wrote *The Wall* he came to me at that point, to my house here in London, and played me the tapes. He knew even at that point that it was going to be a new kind of rock show for the band – an opera for them – and then a film . . . hopefully.

'He had a clear picture of what he was aiming at. We spent a certain amount of time together at first talking it through and played a lot of snooker!

'Sketching out the visions for the album art and everything else, it was all quite back and forth. I got the tapes from him, and then I got his lyrics. It was up to me, really, to interpret them, as I thought, that was my job . . . to visualize what was literal or audible to me, so I put onto paper what the characters did and how they should do it and so on.

'I used to show Roger a whole wall of my drawings here in Chelsea. Sometimes he'd get further ideas from my drawings, or sometimes it wasn't working.'

At which point, presumably, they played more snooker.

RIGHT
The Wall, UK
press ad, 1979

BOTTOM, LEFT
The Wall, US promo
poster, 1979

MIDDLE, RIGHT
The Wall, US promo
stand-up display, 1979

BOTTOM, RIGHT
The Wall, press
ad, 1979

OPPOSITE
The Wall, US promo
poster, 1979

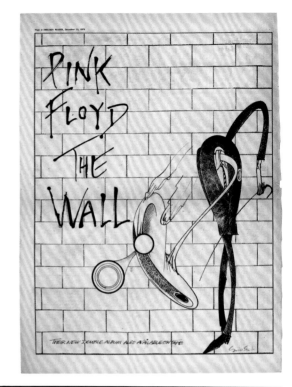

Pink Floyd performed seven *The Wall* concerts at the Sports Arena in Los Angeles in early February, 1980, followed by five more at the Nassau Coliseum on Long Island, New York. In August, there were six *Wall* shows at Earls Court in London. In February 1981, came eight shows at the Westfalenhalle in Dortmund, West Germany, with a final five again at Earls Court in June.

The Wall was a most elaborate staging. Inflatables reached their peak of brilliant absurdity during the shows, several of the Gerald Scarfe characters from the album being brought to life in the form of fully mobile puppets with menacing spotlights for eyes. A 160-foot long, 35-foot high wall made from 340 white bricks was built between the audience and the band during the first half, the final brick being placed as Roger Waters sang "goodbye" at the end of the song 'Goodbye Cruel World.'

For the second half, the band was largely invisible, except for a hole in the wall that simulated a hotel room where Waters acted out the story of Pink, and an appearance by David Gilmour to perform the climactic guitar solo in 'Comfortably Numb.' Other parts of the story were told by Scarfe animations projected onto the wall itself. The animations were later integrated into the film *Pink Floyd: The Wall*. At the finale of the concert, the wall was totally demolished amidst terrifying sound effects and a spectacular light show.

The tour costs were estimated to have reached $1.5 million even before the first performance.

LEFT
The Wall LA show,
press ad, 1980

BELOW, LEFT
The Wall London show,
press ad, 1980

BELOW, RIGHT
The Wall Dusseldorf show,
promo poster, 1981

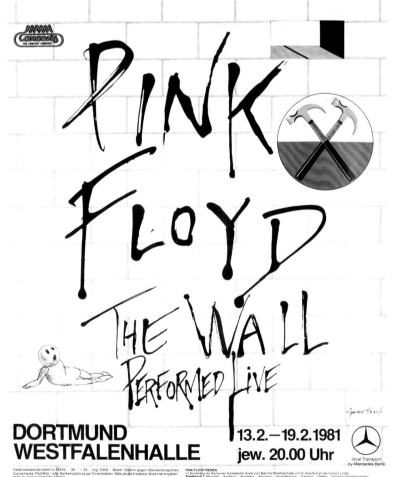

Pink Floyd: The Wall is the 1982 movie by British film director Alan Parker, based on the 1979 Pink Floyd album of the same name. Roger Waters wrote the screenplay for the movie which, in many respects, is more akin to an extended music video than a traditional filmed musical.

One dramatic aspect of the movie is its 15 minutes of enthralling animation sequences by Gerald Scarfe, parts of which show disturbing images forming his interpretation of the German World War II 'blitz' bombing raids over Britain, set to Pink Floyd's 'Goodbye Blue Sky'.

Scarfe's graphics were also the basis for the film's promotional posters, which were recreated in many different forms throughout the world.

TOP, LEFT

Pink Floyd The Wall, UK 'quad-size' poster, 1979

TOP, RIGHT

Pink Floyd The Wall, Japanese poster, 1979

BOTTOM, LEFT

Pink Floyd The Wall, Korean poster, 1979

BOTTOM, MIDDLE

Pink Floyd The Wall, Polish poster, 1979

BOTTOM, RIGHT

Pink Floyd The Wall, Japanese poster, 1979

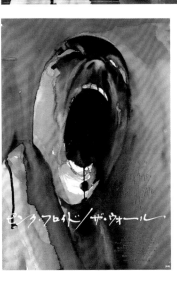

Was there ever more a facetious album title than Pink Floyd's *A Collection of Great Dance Songs* (1981)?

The cover art, handled once again by the Hipgnosis design team (working under the pseudonym TCP after a falling out with Roger Waters several years earlier), utilized a photograph of two ballroom dancers outdoors in a field guy-wired to the ground. The promotional photography chosen was similarly tongue-in-cheek.

The album itself is a compilation album, apparently released against Waters' will, containing alternative mixes and a variety of tracks and edits.

TOP, LEFT

A Collection of Great Dance Songs, promo poster, 1980

TOP, RIGHT

A Collection of Great Dance Songs, promo poster, 1980

BOTTOM, LEFT

A Collection of Great Dance Songs, promo poster, 1980

BOTTOM, RIGHT

A Collection of Great Dance Songs, promo poster, 1980

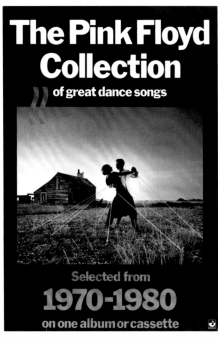

TOP

The Final Cut, stand-up
display, 1983

BOTTOM

The Final Cut, cassette
stand-up display, 1983

The final Pink Floyd album to feature the band's bassist and primary songwriter Roger Waters was, appropriately enough, *The Final Cut* (1983). Indeed, it was predominantly the work of Waters, being the only Pink Floyd album on which the composers' credit on every track was given to Waters alone.

None of the album's songs has ever been performed live by Pink Floyd, although some have been performed live by Waters during his solo tours. Of note is the inscription on the back cover which reads: *The Final Cut: A Requiem for the Post-War Dream – by Roger Waters, performed by Pink Floyd.*

The front cover was designed by Waters himself, featuring a Remembrance Day poppy and four World War II medal ribbons, which were:
• 1939 – 45 Star (for at least six months service between 1939 – 45
• Africa Star, for service in the North African Campaign
• Defence medal, for three years' service
• Distinguished Flying Cross, for acts of courage, valour, or devotion to duty while flying.

TOP, LEFT
A Momentary Lapse of Reason, staff tour pin, 1987

TOP, RIGHT
A Momentary Lapse of Reason, press ad, 1987

MIDDLE, LEFT
A Momentary Lapse of Reason, display unit, 1987

MIDDLE, RIGHT
A Momentary Lapse of Reason, Italian poster, 1987

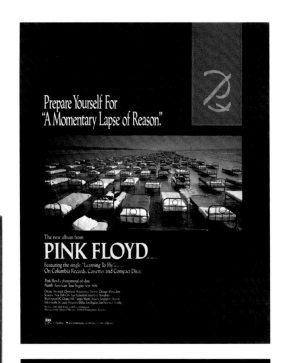

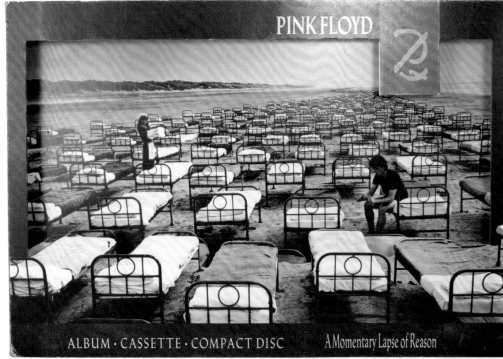

BOTTOM, LEFT
A Momentary Lapse of Reason, US display unit, 1987

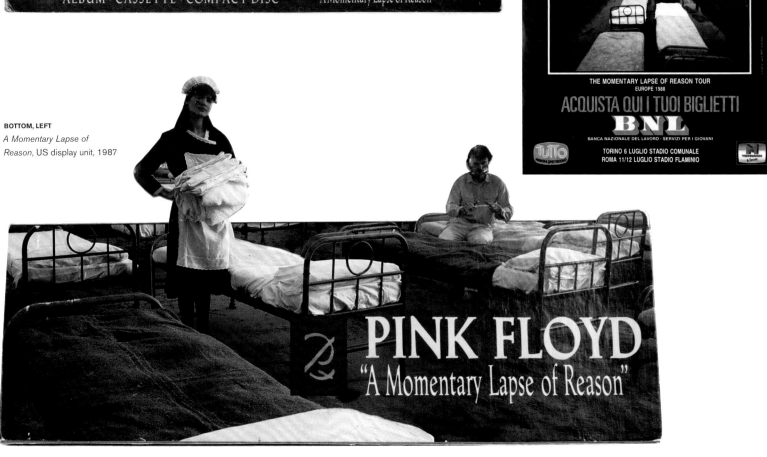

TOP, LEFT

A Momentary Lapse of Reason, promo sponge, 1987

TOP, RIGHT

A Momentary Lapse of Reason tour laminate,1987

TOP, MIDDLE

A Momentary Lapse of Reason tour laminate,1987

BELOW

'On The Turning Away', stand-up display, 1987

A Momentary Lapse of Reason (1987) was Pink Floyd's first album following the departure of Roger Waters from the band in 1985. A very uncomfortable dispute with Waters then erupted, but David Gilmour and Nick Mason eventually settled out of court, obtaining the right to continue using the name Pink Floyd without interference.

The *Momentary* album art involved 700 hospital beds placed by hand on the Saunton Sands beach on the North Devon coast near Braunton, a popular longboard surfing location.

No slight-of-hand hocus-pocus was involved. The design studio team led by Storm Thorgerson personally hauled the wrought-iron beds using several trucks, driving over three hours from London to Devon to make a preferable tide, and arranging the beds to create the

perspective realized in the finished design.

When the team realized that the photoshoot would take a second day to complete, they packed up temporarily but left a single bed on the beach to see if the very active sea would alter the position of that bed overnight. When they returned the following morning, the bed was nowhere to be found.

David Gilmour and Nick Mason appeared on the inside gatefold sleeve, the first time that band members had been seen on an album cover since 1971's *Meddle*, although a poster of the band playing live was given away with vinyl versions of 1973's *Dark Side of the Moon*.

The Saunton Sands beach also was used by Pink Floyd as a location for the World War II Anzio landings sequences in the 1982 film *The Wall*.

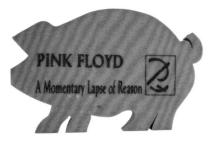

The first live double album from Pink Floyd's David Gilmour era was *Delicate Sound of Thunder* (1988), recorded at the Nassau Coliseum on Long Island, near New York City, in August 1988.

Storm Thorgerson once again provided a provocative cover and, as usual with Thorgerson, there was more going on than first met the eye. The important question he asked himself was: 'What was the most impressive thing about Pink Floyd live?' This was, after all, to be a live album.

Thorgerson's answer was that the band presented the world's very best rock & roll audiovisual experience live – a combination of overwhelming sound and stunning light-and-visual effects. In other words, for Thorgerson, a Pink Floyd concert was where 'Mr Light' met 'Mr Sound'.

Therefore, for the album cover, Mr Light wore a suit of light bulbs (après Salvador Dali) and Mr Sound was surrounded by a halo of flying birds (as in 'birdsong'). Numerous eye hooks were used to hang the many unlit lightbulbs on the suit, the attaching all done on site in central Spain, not far from Madrid. The birds were released from behind a rock, behind far figure, at the moment of shooting. There was literally no room for error in capturing the moment Thorgerson had imagined.

Delicate Sound of Thunder became the first classic rock album to be played in outer space when Soviet cosmonauts took a cassette tape aboard the Soyuz TM-7. Pink Floyd were present at the launch in November 1988.

TOP, LEFT

Delicate Sound of Thunder, cassette display unit, 1988

TOP, RIGHT

Gig poster, Stockholm, 1988

MIDDLE, LEFT

Delicate Sound of Thunder, stand-up display, 1988

MIDDLE, RIGHT

Gig poster, Cologne, 1988

BOTTOM, LEFT

Delicate Sound of Thunder, promo display, 1988

BOTTOM, RIGHT

Delicate Sound of Thunder video, promo poster, 1989

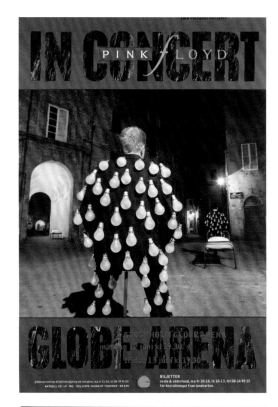

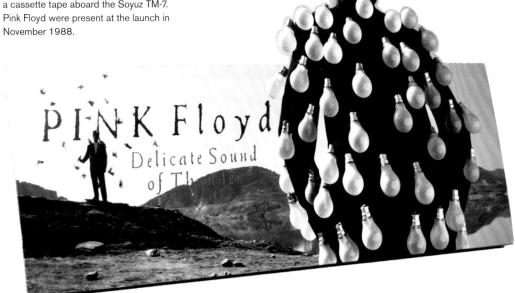

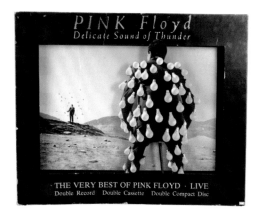

Pink Floyd celebrated their 25th anniversary as a recording and touring rock band by releasing *Shine On* (1992) a nine-CD box set, characteristically thorough and uber-intelligent.

The previously-released albums were redesigned to achieve a complete, unified presentation for the set rather than simply packaging the old designs together. By aligning the black CD cases in the correct order you could create the image of *The Dark Side of the Moon* prism.

The box set also featured a hardcover book detailing the band's history from the very beginning right up to the 1980s.

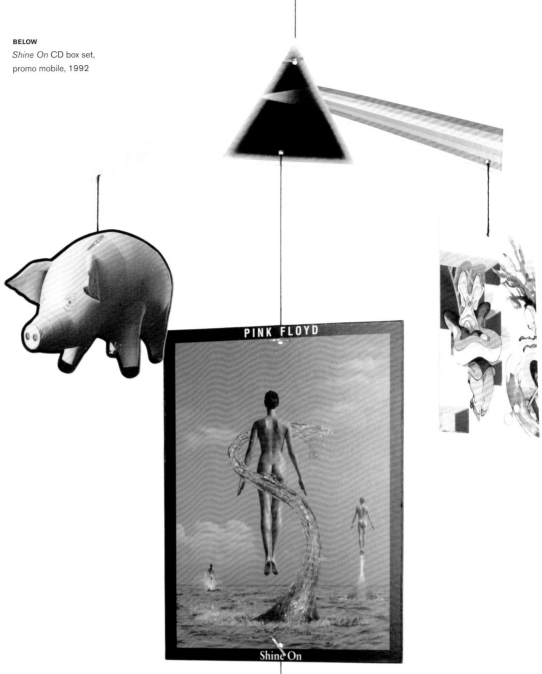

Pink Floyd Shine On

8-CD BOXED SET OF NEWLY-REMASTERED RELEASES.
AVAILABLE IN THE BOXED SET SECTION OF THIS STORE.

A Saucerful Of Secrets • Meddle • The Dark Side Of The Moon • Wish You Were Here
Animals • The Wall (Part One/Part Two) • A Momentary Lapse Of Reason

INCLUDES A 112-PAGE HARD COVER BOOK,
BONUS CD DIGIPAK OF EARLY SINGLES AND B-SIDES...
AND MORE.

COLUMBIA

The final studio album (so far) by Pink Floyd is *The Division Bell* (1994). It was recorded at several studios including David Gilmour's houseboat studio, *The Astoria.*

The title of the album derives from a bell of the same name that is rung in the British House of Commons to signal the commencement of a vote by Members of Parliament.

The album's cover concept was the work of (who else?) Storm Thorgerson, who used two metal sculptures of giant heads devised by Keith Breeden and built by John Robertson to the height of a double decker bus (each the size and bulk of a small house, like the Aku Aku totems on Easter Island).

The metal statues weighed a ton, literally. They were taken by flatbed truck to a field near Cambridge, Pink Floyd's hometown, close to Ely Cathedral.

Clever positioning made each appear to be even taller than it really was and they were placed in a complementary posture in their field to be shot under all weather and lighting conditions over a two-week period. Sometimes visual effects such as unusual background lighting or interesting objects in the distance were introduced. Ely Cathedral is visible in the background in one photo set, while in another set a line of lights are seen beyond the sculptures' mouths, although they could be regarded as 'travelling' from one mouth to the other.

The sculptures present the idea of two heads in profile, facing or talking to each other, making up a third face, facing front. Storm Thorgerson later noted, 'The single eyes of the two faces looking at each other become the two eyes of a single face looking at you, the viewer. It was intended that the viewer should not see both at the same time.

'The point was, a person would see the single face of the two profiles. If one saw both it was alternating, like an optical illusion, which was even better because it meant that the viewer was interacting, or communicating, with the image directly, viscerally.'

The third or facing head is implied, not defined, more ghostly than real, and may reference either or both Roger Waters and Syd Barrett, the 'departed saints of Pink Floyd', one possible underlying theme of the new album.

The sculptures were eventually removed and shipped across the Atlantic for display at the Rock & Roll Hall of Fame in Cleveland, Ohio.

ABOVE, LEFT
The Division Bell, promo rotating display, 1994

ABOVE, RIGHT
The Division Bell, promo rotating display, 1994

BELOW, LEFT
The Division Bell, UK stand-up display, 1994

BELOW, RIGHT
The Division Bell, US stand-up display, 1994

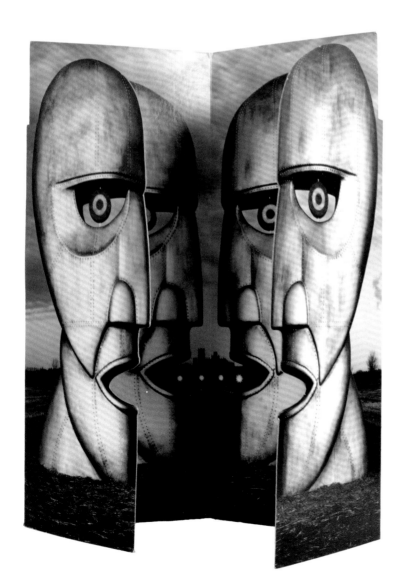

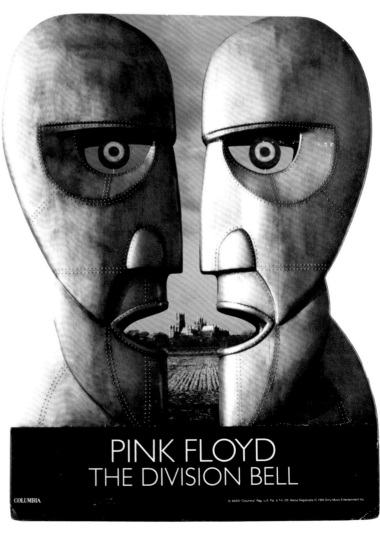

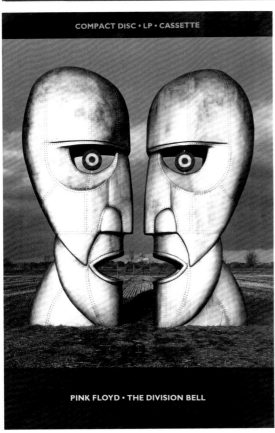

TOP, LEFT
The Division Bell, European
tour programme, 1994

TOP, RIGHT
Gig poster,
Cologne, 1994

BOTTOM, LEFT
The Division Bell, US
promo poster, 1994

BOTTOM, RIGHT
The Division Bell, UK
promo poster, 1994

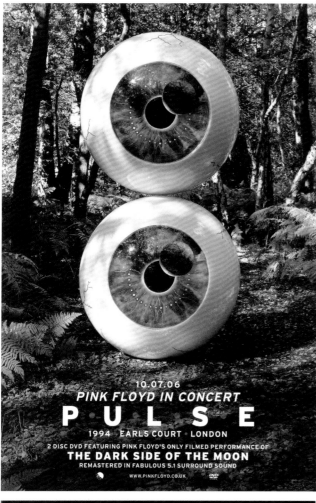

Pulse (1995) was recorded during Pink Floyd's 1994 Division Bell tour – specifically the UK and European legs which ran from July to October.

The album included a complete live version of *The Dark Side of the Moon* and featured a booklet with many photos from the tour.

The original CD cover featured 'eye-like' artwork with symbology portraying a complex evolutionary process.

An art gallery exhibiting Storm Thorgerson's artwork for this album noted: 'The "eye" design on the front of the *Pulse* CD box comprised about 36 separate photographs, moulded and vignetted together. Not only does the design reflect, in the viewer's actual eye, elements of the live Pink Floyd concert circle of lights, it is stylistically a mixture of old semi-psychedelic ideas and modern technology – to echo the variety of material in the concert. The circularity of the eye, pupil and iris, the circularity of the film screen at a Pink Floyd show, the circularity of the approaching moon, even the circularity of time embodied in the wide range of songs on *Pulse* – all these were carried through the entire package. Closer inspection of the front art reveals symbols and images that refer to Pink Floyd songs (for example, a bike for Syd Barrett) and various elements only lately discovered by the cognoscenti. The designer, Storm Thorgerson, advises us to "Look more deeply and you will find further visual connections that link and refer to Pink Floyd, some of which were never even intended".'

TOP, LEFT
Pulse DVD, UK promo
poster, 2006

TOP, RIGHT
Pulse DVD, UK double-sided
promo poster, 2006

MIDDLE, LEFT
30th anniversary, double-sided
promo poster, 1995

MIDDLE, RIGHT
Pulse, UK promo
poster, 1995

BOTTOM, RIGHT
30th anniversary, inflatable
chair display, 1995

As of 2009, *The Dark Side of the Moon* ranked as the third best-selling album of all time worldwide (not counting compilations and soundtracks) and the 20th-best-selling album in the US.

Though it held the No 1 spot on the US album charts for only one week, it spent a total of 741 consecutive weeks – or about 14 years –on the list until 23 April, 1988, the longest duration of any album in history, only to be removed by a rule change.

In 1988, after considerable research by the recording industry certifying authority, *The Dark Side of the Moon* was certified at 15 x platinum. On the week of 5 May, 2006 it achieved a combined total of 1,500 weeks on the *Billboard 200* and *Pop Catalogue* charts.

It's estimated that one in every 14 people in America under the age of 50 owns, or has owned, a copy of *The Dark Side of the Moon*.

According to the *Wall Street Journal*, the album continues to sell 9,600 units per week in the US, continuously on average.

BELOW, LEFT
The Dark Side of the Moon,
press ad, 1998

BELOW, RIGHT
The Dark Side of the Moon,
press ad, 1998

RIGHT
The Dark Side of the Moon,
promo poster, 1998

OPPOSITE
The Dark Side of the Moon,
press ad, 1998

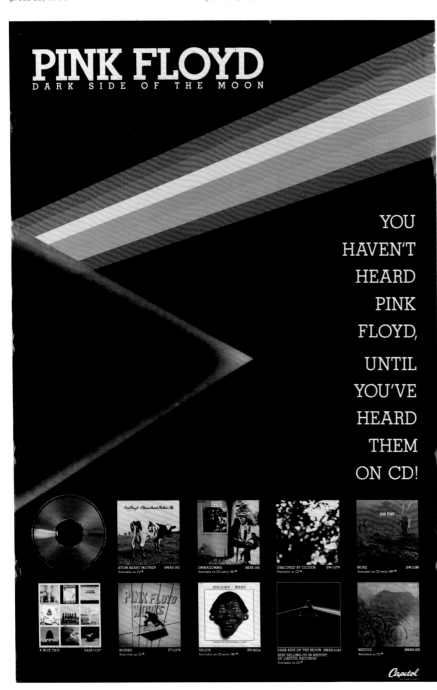

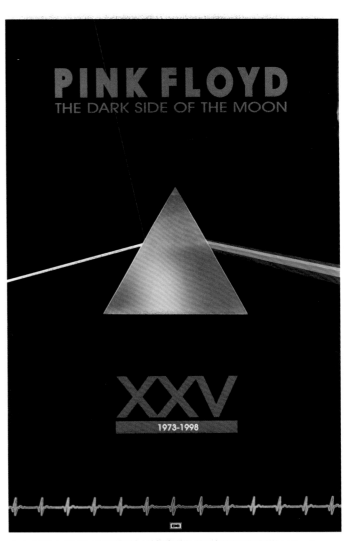

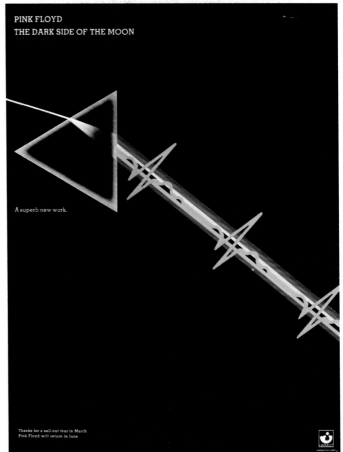

Is There Anybody Out There? The Wall Live 1980 – 81 (2000) is a live recording of *The Wall*, taken from the August 1980 and June 1981 performances by Pink Floyd at Earls Court in London.

The shows involved the construction of the band's iconic white-brick wall on stage during the first half. Once it was fully mounted, members of the band performed on top of the wall and through gaps in the wall as well as in front of and behind it.

The album cover showed the masks, cast from the band members' own faces, that were worn by the four 'imposters' who opened the show pretending to be Pink Floyd.

TOP, LEFT
Is There Anybody Out There?
promo poster, 2000

TOP, RIGHT
Is There Anybody Out There?
promo poster, 2000

BOTTOM, MIDDLE
Is There Anybody Out There?
promo poster, 2000

TOP, MIDDLE
Is There Anybody Out There?
promo poster, 2000

BOTTOM, LEFT
Is There Anybody Out There?
UK promo poster, 2000

BOTTOM, RIGHT
Is There Anybody Out There?
press ad, 2000

In general, Pink Floyd have maintained control of all their promotional graphics. While these two Swedish catalogue promotions are unusual, they are also unusually clever.

OPPOSITE, TOP
Back catalogue, Swedish
promo poster, 2006

OPPOSITE, BOTTOM
Back catalogue, Swedish
promo poster, 2006

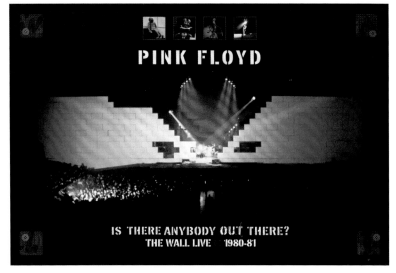

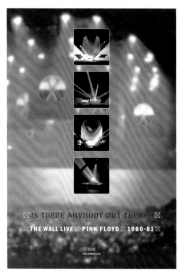

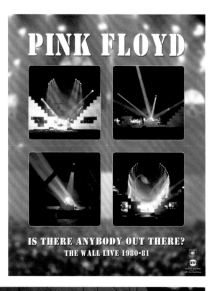

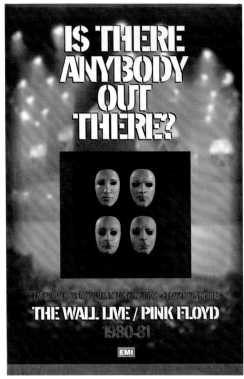

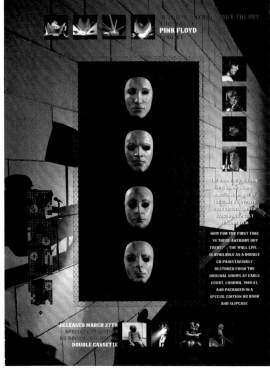

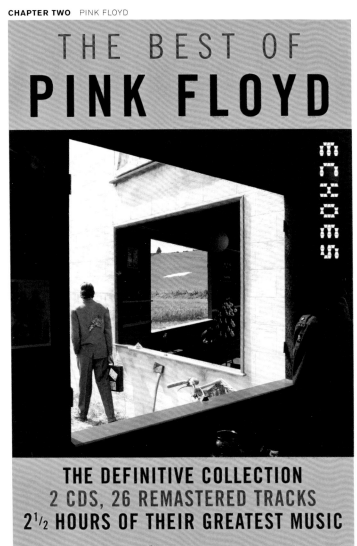

THE BEST OF
PINK FLOYD

THE DEFINITIVE COLLECTION
2 CDS, 26 REMASTERED TRACKS
2¹/₂ HOURS OF THEIR GREATEST MUSIC

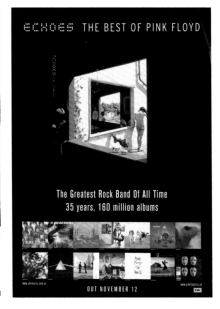

The Greatest Rock Band Of All Time
35 years, 160 million albums

OUT NOVEMBER 12

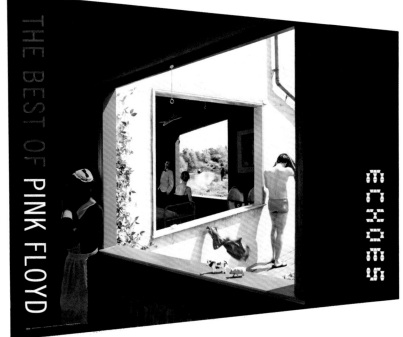

Storm Thorgerson worked with the band Dream Theater on their 1997 album *Falling into Infinity* and submitted to them two sketches for possible covers.

One became the cover that was used on their release. The second, rejected by Dream Theater, ended up being used by Pink Floyd for *Echoes* – a compilation album – four years later.

The compilation spans the career of Pink Floyd from their first single 'Arnold Layne' (1967) through to 'High Hopes' (1994), from their studio album *The Division Bell*.

Each of the 26 tracks fades from one to the next with no break in the music, helping to recreate a concept-album feel of the band's mid-period work, and they are not sequenced in any chronological order.

The artwork is a collage of well-known images from previous album covers. These include:

• A burning man (from *Wish You Were Here*)
• A porcelain pig and cow (from *Animals* and *Atom Heart Mother*)
• A sheep (from *Animals*)
• Several pyramids (from *The Dark Side of the Moon*)
• A man in a light-bulb suit (from *Delicate Sound of Thunder*)
• An iron bedstead (from *A Momentary Lapse of Reason*)
• A white brick wall (from *The Wall*)
• A crossed-hammer insignia (from the film *The Wall*)
• A bike (from *The Piper at the Gates of Dawn*)
• An axe (from the song 'Careful With That Axe, Eugene')
• A *Piper at the Gates of Dawn* poster
• A fishbowl (from the song 'Wish You Were Here')
• A man in military attire (from *The Final Cut*)
• A mirror ball (from the song 'Comfortably Numb')
• An aeroplane model (from the *Pulse* DVD)
• A rowing boat (from *A Momentary Lapse of Reason*)
• Two metal statues (from *The Division Bell*)
• A *Shine On* DVD poster
• Four masks (from *Is Anybody Out There?*)
• A picture of an ear (from *Meddle*)
• A swimmer drying off (from *Wish You Were Here*)
• A couple of dancers (from *A Collection of Great Dance Songs*)
• A maid (from *A Momentary Lapse of Reason*)
• A sitting man with his briefcase (from *Wish You Were Here*)
• A picture of a lake shaped like a pig (from *Animals*)
• Multiple windows in an infinite-like passage (from *Ummagumma*)

TOP, LEFT
Echoes, promo poster, 2007

TOP, MIDDLE
Echoes, promo poster, 2007

TOP, RIGHT
Echoes, promo poster, 2007

BOTTOM
Echoes, trapezoid promo poster, 2007

As well as containing the historic albums packaged together as mini-vinyl replicas, along with more extra material, *Oh, By The Way* (2007), a Pink Floyd compilation box set, comes with a special 40th Anniversary poster by Storm Thorgerson, featuring 40 Pink Floyd images.

The box set title references a satiric couplet in the song "Have a Cigar" from *Wish You Were Here*:

"The band is just fantastic
That is really what I think
Oh by the way
Which one's Pink?"

The idea for the cover of the box set involves an intriguing kind of 'spot the difference' puzzle that plays homage to the *Ummagumma* 'altered recursion' cover created in 1969. Here, one side of the box set depicts a room with a red-framed mirror as its centerpiece while the reverse has a blue-framed mirror. The main band members are in photographs hung on the walls, although these change in position and framing. Subtle changes abound throughout the two rooms, a cricket bat becoming a tennis raquet, for example, and a glass of white wine becoming red.

Keyboardist Richard Wright, Pink Floyd's 'quiet one', died of cancer in London on 15 September, 2008. He played on every Pink Floyd release except *The Final Cut*.

3 THE WHO

THE WHO

The Who often cloaked themselves in the Union Jack (perhaps the best-known English rock band to do that so consistently) as well as in clothing sporting the roundels of the Royal Air Force (concentric rings of blue and white with a red disc center). Although these colours and patterns represented their Mod roots — and their early persona was further established though photography — the band did not seek a key interpretive graphic arts image for one of their works until their rock opera *Tommy* (1969).

Author and Who historian Richard Barnes points out that, strictly speaking, *Tommy* is not an opera since it has no staging, scenery, acting, or recitative: 'In fact, it would be more accurately described as a cantata or a song cycle.' However categorized, *Tommy* remains The Who's best known and most influential work and one of the most celebrated creative works of the rock era.

Tommy was originally released as a two-LP set with a 12-page booklet of lyrics and artwork tucked into the triptych-style fold-out package. All three of the outer panels of the triptych were spanned by a single Pop Art painting by Mike McInnerney, earlier a psychedelic poster artist whose work was distributed by the pioneering Osiris Art Agency. He also was art editor for the underground *International Times*, and a member of the UFO Club (from which Pink Floyd would emerge). McInnerney's *Tommy* drawing was of a sphere with diamond-shaped cutouts and and a faint-to-bold overlay of clouds and seagulls all rendered in figure-ground dis-equilibrium.

Mike McInnerney met Pete Townshend at the Alexandra Palace in April 1967; both were attending the '14-Hour Technicolour Dream' event benefiting the *International Times*. Not long after, Townshend and his wife Karen would attend McInnerney and his wife Katie's wedding in Hyde Park (a hippy event that made all the British papers).

The many ideas for *Tommy* coalesced between late 1968 and early 1969 (when the album was recorded, arduously, over many months and when Townshend

commissioned McInnerney to do the album's cover). One theme seemed to prevail throughout, according to Townshend, who later explained: 'There was a parallel to the world of an autistic child, so the hero had to be deaf, dumb, and blind; seen from our already limited point of view, his limitations would be symbolic of our own.' But McInnerney had to procede with his own intuition, graphically speaking.

McInnerney: 'It was 1968 and the world was full of messages. Everyone was promoting some kind of message: feminism, expanded consciousness, meditation, revolution, God, drugs, love, the environment. Rock was doing its usual up-to-the-minute job of transmitting them; if rock could do it, I thought, so should illustration.'

'The project started off as a double-album cover job and grew into a triptych with a 12-page booklet. I chose to do images that acted as symbols for key moments in the story. I hoped the images would be viewed like painting and sculpture are viewed — that is, in a contemplative way, with a long look at images layered with references.

'I liked the "idea" of the Tommy character. Rather than trying to portray him, I wanted to picture his experience of being in a world without conventional senses. I thought it would be limitless and unbounded, yet trapped in an environment made for people who have all of their senses.

'The outer and inner covers seemed to be the appropriate places for this statement. The outer cover has its globe (Earth/self) hanging in an endless infinite space

that can never be touched, only imagined. The inside cover has its wall and wall lights, a symbol of domestic space (the room we all live in). The light from these lamps, however, does not fix things as in our sighted world — it shifts and changes for Tommy.

'The work took nearly three months to complete. During that time, I had the feeling that I was working on a special project. That's why it kept expanding.

'I have this memory snapshot, back in mid-1969, sitting in Pete Townshend's kitchen, showing him the finished artwork for the *Tommy* cover and both of us trying to find a way to bring God into the cover copy. The Indian word for God is "Avatar" and, for us, his name was Meher Baba and the cover credit list was where we put him.

'Somehow, giving God a job description on the album, juxtaposing the ordinary with the extraordinary, seemed appropriate to the project. It was a contrast that wove its way throughout the opera.'

With God overseeing the project or not, executives at The Who's record label insisted on having the band members pictured on the cover for marketing purposes, so McInnerney's finished art was further adapted to include small images of their faces inserted into the gaps in the central sphere. That was not McInnerney's — or Townshend's — desire or intention.

McInnerney and Townshend commentary found in 1990 essays in a descriptive text accompanying limited-edition prints then published by Record Art, New York.

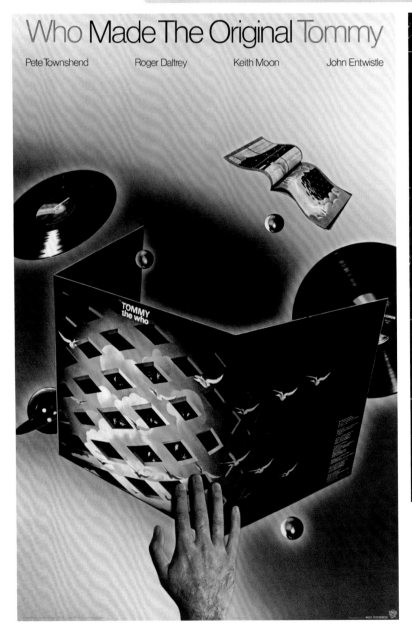

Who Made The Original Tommy

Pete Townshend   Roger Daltrey   Keith Moon   John Entwistle

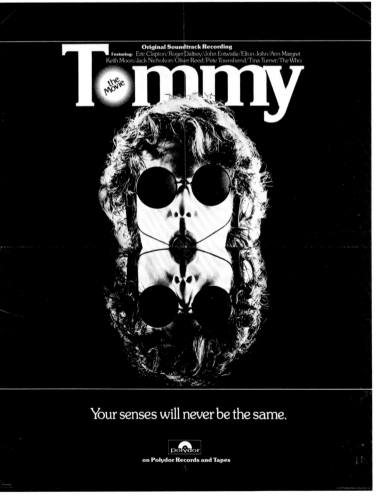

Original Soundtrack Recording
Featuring: Eric Clapton/Roger Daltrey/John Entwistle/Elton John/Ann-Margret
Keith Moon/Jack Nicholson/Oliver Reed/Pete Townshend/Tina Turner/The Who

Your senses will never be the same.

on Polydor Records and Tapes

TOP, LEFT
Tour programme,
1968

TOP, RIGHT
Tour programme,
1971

BOTTOM, LEFT
Tommy, promo
poster, 1969

BOTTOM, RIGHT
Tommy movie soundtrack
album, promo poster, 1975

Roger Daltrey, John Entwistle and Pete Townshend first played together as the Detours in 1962 in small venues, clubs and pubs. On 22 December 1963, the Detours played support to the Rolling Stones. It was here, just before the Stones went on stage, that Townshend saw Keith Richards swing his arm in a wide arcing motion, a gesture that inspired Townshend's trademark windmill strum.

They were introduced to their fans as The Who in February 1964. In May, Keith Moon, then aged 17 and working as a plaster salesman, sat in with the band for the first time. Keith impressed Pete, Roger, and John considerably and was asked along to the next gig. 'Nobody ever said "You're in,"' recalled Moon. 'They just said, "What are you doing next Monday?"'

During the summer and autumn of 1964 they were the High Numbers. In July they met their (first) manager, Kit Lambert, who recalled: 'There was one very scruffy-looking pub in Harrow where there was this great cluster of scooters outside, and I went in and there were The Who. They were playing in this room with just one red bulb glowing and an extraordinary audience that they had collected. They were the *loudest* group I'd ever heard.

'It just seemed to me that this had to be the face of the late 1960s. There was Keith Moon, the drummer, raised on a high stool dominating the group, battering away. The rest of the group was playing on a stage made out of beer crates. And the ceiling came right down on top of them, so that when Pete Townshend – the lead guitarist – was playing, he'd bang the guitar neck against the ceiling, and one night he physically poked a hole through it because it was getting in his way. Since the ceiling was only made of plasterboard he went straight through it.

'This went down tremendously with the audience, and that's how the whole instrument destruction thing started.'

Lambert took out a display ad in the 7 November issue of *Melody Maker* with bold white lettering on a black background announcing 'The Who: Maximum R&B' with a vertical arrow extending from the letter O.

On 24 November, 1964, now as The Who once more, they began their legendary residency at the Marquee Club, in Soho, London. They were set to run for 16 weeks but were extended for another seven weeks as they eventually broke house attendance records established by Manfred Mann and The Yardbirds. The Marquee poster advertising The Who, based on Lambert's newspaper ad, became an enduring classic.

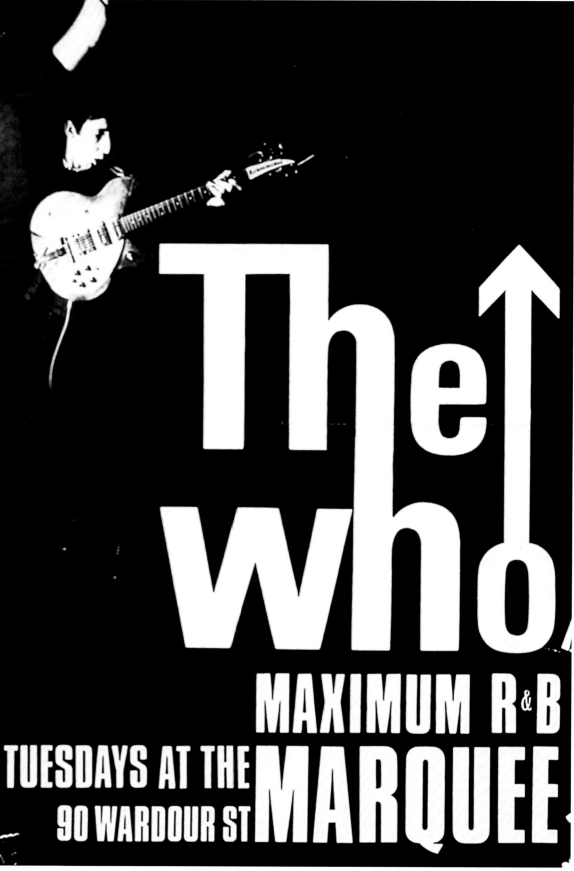

ABOVE
Gig poster, The Marquee, London, 1964

OPPOSITE, LEFT
Tommy (Tomi) film poster, 1975

OPPOSITE, MIDDLE, TOP
Gig poster, Shrine Auditorium, LA, 1968. Art: Victor Moscoso

OPPOSITE, MIDDLE, BOTTOM
Print ad for *Who's Next*, featuring Keith Moon in drag, USA, 1971

OPPOSITE, RIGHT, TOP
'Magic Bus' press ad, 1968

OPPOSITE, RIGHT, BOTTOM
'Squeeze Box' print ad for single from *The Who By Numbers*, USA 1976

The Who began 1965 with a new single, 'I Can't Explain', that would put them in the charts for the first time. Although they were still playing cover songs almost exclusively in their live set, it was the original material that Townshend began submitting to the group that was to provide them with a future. Their first album, *My Generation* (1965), would contain an even split between covers and Townshend originals.

With a record in the charts they were able to play further afield and command higher fees. They played their first Scottish tour in early May and went on to make their debut on the Continent. They played their first outdoor events and made their first appearance in the prestigious Richmond National Jazz & Blues Festival. Then they played Scandinavia for the first time. 'My Generation' – the quintessential rock song of the 1960s – followed.

A Copenhagen newspaper described The Who's arrival: 'They're part of a new wave of girl-follower groups. Their music is so-called Pop Art. They've created their own style which is expressed both in their clothing and by way of the instruments they smash on stage. They use the English flag

to make jackets, and on the back of the jackets are big "one-way-street" signs.'

The band had hoped to open their US campaign in 1966, but among other things the constant destruction of their instruments left them short of funds. Instead, they concentrated on recording their second album. Two return Scandinavian tours were a smash – literally.

Melody Maker reported about the UK gigs of that time: 'The Who have a kind of bizarre science-fiction appeal – electronically violent, deafeningly strident, all rather removed from reality. There is no other group on the current scene remotely like them, with the melodies themselves blasted out of existence. The Who enjoy themselves thoroughly, smashing footlights, kicking over amplifiers, breaking guitars, demolishing drums, throwing buckets of water at the audience, and managing to squeeze in 'Barbara Ann', 'Heatwave' and 'My Generation' in between. Each night, the stage is left in utter chaos when they finish.'

Then, the singles 'Substitute', 'Happy Jack' and 'Magic Bus' began garnering some US airplay, thanks to the autumn 1966 release of the EP *Ready Steady Who*

and the album *A Quick One*. The latter was the band's first foray into rock opera, with the title track 'A Quick One, While He's Away' clocking in at nine minutes, a suite of song snippets telling the story of infidelity and reconciliation. It set the stage for the full scale rock operas *Tommy* (1969) and *Quadrophenia* (1973) to follow.

In America, The Who's reputation was spread by word of mouth, not as much through radio play or record sales. They made four trips across the Atlantic in 1967 in little more than eight months, and within just a few years after that, their exposure in America would cause them to become one of the highest grossing attractions in the entire world.

During 1967, the Who played in more countries than ever before – or since. They made their concert debut in March in New York City, the closing act in nine straight shows (the line-up included Wilson Pickett, Eric Clapton and Cream and ten others) at the RKO 58th St Theater.

The Who's first dates for America's pre-eminent rock promoter, Bill Graham (with whom they would continue a close working relationship right up through the

1989 *The Kids Are Alright Tour*), took place at the San Francisco Fillmore Auditorium in June, supported by the Carlos Santana Blues Band.

Their first major North American tour began in July, opening for Herman's Hermits, the Manchester pop group which had enjoyed 11 US top 10 hits in three years. They played auditoriums, high schools, clubs, arenas, and fairgrounds, concluding in Honolulu.

In November they commenced a fourth tour of America, this time headlining, and ended a bravura year with the release of their third album, *The Who Sell Out* (December 1967).

Poster art during this period was commissioned by the concert promoter, very often Bill Graham, who established a tradition for that at his Fillmore Auditorium, Fillmore West, and Winterland venues in San Francisco and his Fillmore East hall in New York. Graham's poster artists whose work portrayed the Who included his wife Bonnie MacLean, Lee Conklin, Alton Kelley, and Rick Griffin. One of Victor Moscoso's masterpieces was created for the Shrine Auditorium concert.

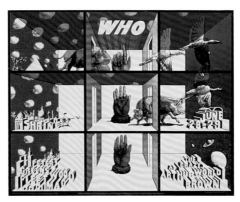

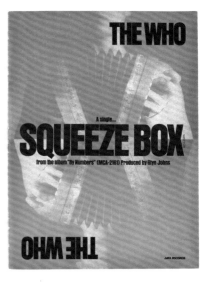

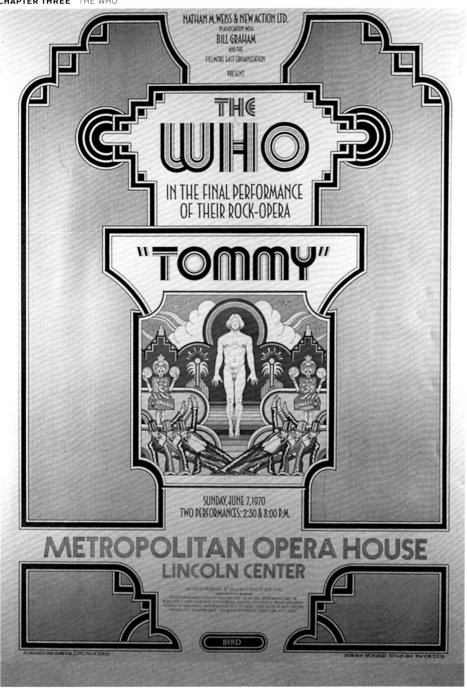

ABOVE
Gig poster, Metropolitan, NY
1970. Art: David Byrd

RIGHT, TOP
Gig poster, Chicago, 1969.
Artist: Mark Behrens

RIGHT, BOTTOM
Gig flyer, Detroit, 1969.
Art: Carl Lundgren

The years 1969 and 1970 were dominated by the release of *Tommy* and the tours backing the work – virtually in its entirety – in front of rapt audiences throughout the UK, North America, and Europe.

The album received overwhelming critical acclaim. *Life* wrote: 'For sheer power, invention and brilliance of performance, Tommy outstrips anything which has ever come out of a recording studio.' *Melody Maker* declared, 'Surely The Who are now the band against which all others are to be judged.' And so it was, in conjunction with constant touring, that The Who achieved its superstar status.

1969 was the year of The Who's greatest triumph. No rock band in the world was performing better. No rock band in the world dared follow them on stage. For at least the next three years they became the greatest of Britain's rock bands – at a level of greatness beyond even the Rolling Stones – and were legitimate contenders to be the most exciting live act in the world.

Tommy was originally released as a two-LP set with a thin booklet of lyrics and artwork in a triptych-style foldout cover. All three of the outer panels are spanned by a single magnificent Pop Art painting by Mike Mclinnerney.

In February 1970 The Who recorded *Live at Leeds*, their first live album. In 2003,

the album was ranked No 170 on *Rolling Stone's* list of the 500 Greatest Albums of All Time. It was also included in *Q*'s list of the loudest albums of all time!

The album cover art was deliberately fashioned to look like the cover art of a bootleg LP. The original LP came with facsimiles of various memorabilia including a photo of the band from the *My Generation* photoshoot, handwritten lyrics to the 'Listening to you' chorus from *Tommy*, a receipt for smoke bombs and the early black 'Maximum R&B' Marquee poster showing Townshend windmilling his Rickenbacker guitar.

Carl Lundgren and Gary Grimshaw both

did posters for Detroit's Grande Ballroom that portrayed The Who. One of Rick Griffin's masterworks was created for a Who show at the Hollywood Palladium. David Byrd, who did much of the advertising work for Bill Graham's Fillmore East, became graphically associated with *Tommy* in New York over a period of two years, on the basis of handbills, posters, and show booklets.

David Singer was entrusted by Graham to handle pieces in the latter part of his classic series that included Who performances, with his defining Who work made for the well-remembered 1973 Cow Palace show.

TOP, LEFT
Press ad, Isle of Wight
festival, 1970

TOP, RIGHT
Gig poster, Isle of Wight
festival, 1970

BOTTOM, LEFT
Gig flyer, Boston, 1969.
Art: Engstrom

BOTTOM, LEFT
Gig poster, Hollywood,
1969. Art: Rick Griffin

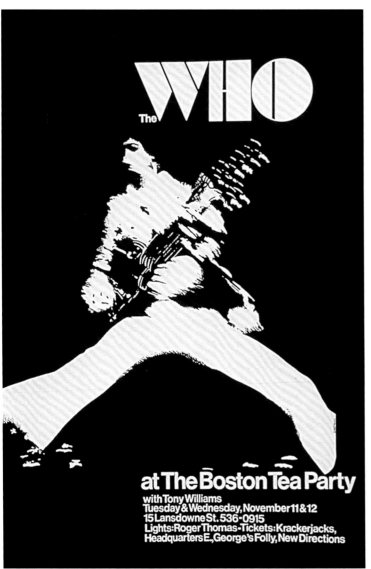

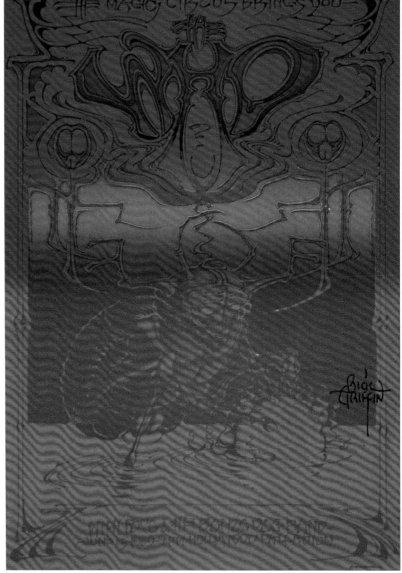

Who's Next (1971) was the fifth album by The Who. It emerged from a second, futuristic Pete Townshend rock opera called *Lifehouse*. The new rock opera never actually came to be, but some of the songs from *Lifehouse* ended up on *Who's Next*, giving the album a somewhat eclectic feel, although this did not detract from its commercial success.

Easington Colliery in County Durham (remembered in England for its 1951 mining disaster) was the site chosen for Ethan A. Russell's startling cover photo for *Who's Next*, the band apparently having just urinated on a large concrete piling set in a coal-slag hillside. According to Russell, most of the band were unable to urinate on cue, so rainwater was scooped up in an empty film canister and sloshed on the piling instead. The use of the concrete structure in the iconic photo has been said to take its inspiration from the famous space monolith from Stanley Kubrick's film *2001: A Space Odyssey* (1968).

In 2003, VH1 declared *Who's Next's* front cover to be the second greatest album cover ever. Alternative cover designs had featured photos of grotesquely obese naked women or Keith Moon wearing a wig, black lingerie and weilding a whip. Although they didn't make it onto the album cover, a few of the shots from those photo sessions were used by Decca in the USA for promotional purposes.

Meaty Beaty Big and Bouncy (1971) is one of many 'Greatest Hits' albums by The Who and for several years was regarded as the best, including as it does singles that were absent from the band's previous LPs.

The Railway Hotel, on the bridge next to the Harrow and Wealdstone railway station in northwest London, was the subject of the panoramic photo seen on the album's inside gatefold cover. Mods – who numbered significantly in The Who's early audiences – regularly gathered at the hotel pub from the time that The Who first played there in June, 1964. Legend has it that it was here that Pete Townshend first stuck his guitar head through the ceiling, then smashed it to pieces, egged on by the crowd. He would continue to destroy guitars (and the band the rest of their equipment) on stage for years afterwards.

BELOW, LEFT
Who's Next,
promo poster, 1971

BELOW, RIGHT
Who's Next, UK
press ad, 1971

TOP, LEFT
Quadrophenia, UK
press ad, 1973

LEFT
Gig ad, Charlton Athletic FC,
London, 1974

TOP, RIGHJT
Quadrophenia, US
press ad, 1973

BOTTOM, LEFT
UK tour press
ad, 1973

The Who released *Quadrophenia*, their sixth album, in autumn 1973. It was the group's second official rock opera. Set in London and Brighton in 1964 and 1965, the story revolves around the lifestyle of a mod at a time when mods and rockers clashed in mass brawls on the Brighton beaches. Specifically, it covers about five days in the life of Jimmy Cooper, the son of simple working-class parents.

The title is meant to reflect four distinct personalities of Jimmy, each of which was said to represent the personality of one member of The Who. The album's liner notes fleshed out this concept:
• 'A tough guy, a helpless dancer' (Roger Daltrey)
• 'A romantic, is it me for a moment?' (John Entwistle)
• 'A bloody lunatic, I'll even carry your bags' (Keith Moon)

• 'A beggar, a hypocrite, love reign o'er me' (Pete Townshend)

The title also referenced the Quadraphonic sound systems then being introduced to many concert venues.

Quadrophenia was originally released as a two-LP set containing a thick booklet with lyrics, a text version of the story, and photography illustrating the tale.

Photographer Ethan Russell (*Who's Next*) provided the art direction, which included his supervising the creation of an iconic photo of a mod astride a multi-mirrored scooter while wearing a Who cape.

Townshend was to look back on *Quadrophenia* with much pride: 'That music is the best music I've ever written, I think, and it's the best album that I will ever write.'

Bassist John Entwistle was assigned the task of creating a new compilation album, *Odds & Sods* (1974), from various archived tapes in response to the live audio bootlegging that was taking place at most of The Who's concerts. His work in the fall of 1973 took place while the others were preparing for their roles in the *Tommy* film.

Only one *Odds and Sods* album was released even though Entwistle collected enough material for a second. The tongue-in-cheek football-esque album cover was the work of Graham Hughes.

In 1974, The Who also delivered four back-to-back concerts at New York's Madison Square Garden and in 1975 continued with 14 UK concerts, 8 European shows and 20 more North American gigs. John Pasche, who created the Rolling Stones' tongue logo, handled the UK tour poster featuring the classic bulldog Winston Churchill figure.

TOP, LEFT
Odds & Sods, US press ad, 1974

TOP, RIGHT
UK tour poster, 1975.
Art: John Pasche

BOTTOM, RIGHT
Odds & Sods, US promo poster, 1974

RIGHT
Odds & Sods-era tour programme, 1974

BELOW
Odds & Sods, UK album and tour promo poster, 1974

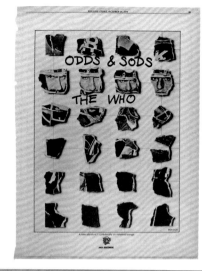

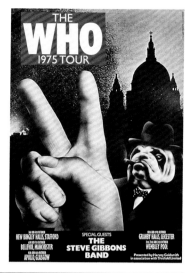

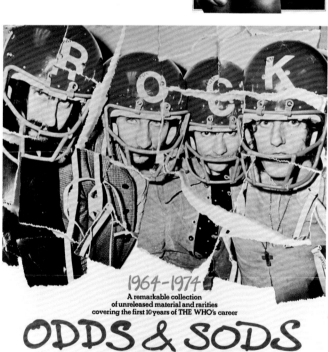

The Who By Numbers (1975) is The Who's seventh album. It was largely sparse and surprisingly dark, without the synthesizers and overdubbing present on the previous releases.

Townshend's themes address alcoholism, lust, self-loathing, advancing middle age, and the fear of irrelevance. Despair and cynicism creeped into many of the songs, although 'Squeeze Box' was playful and lighthearted.

The cover art was illustrated by John Entwistle, who was at the time drawing a cartoon history of the Who.

TOP, LEFT
US and Canada tour,
promo poster, 1976

TOP, RIGHT
UK tour poster,
1976

BOTTOM, RIGHT
The Who By Numbers,
promo poster, 1976

MIDDLE, LEFT
'Slip Kid' and tour dates, US
press ad, 1976

MIDDLE, CENTRE
Gig poster, Munich, 1976.
Art: Gunther Kieser

BOTTOM, LEFT
'Squeeze Box',
UK press ad, 1976

Three years went by between the release of *The Who By Numbers* (1975) and *Who Are You* (1978), during which time punk and prog-rock gained in popularity and significance. The Who were determined to remain relevant but, in part due to the bandmembers' concentration on their own solo projects, The Who's internal unity was beginning to fray.

Keith Moon in particular was in difficulty. Alcohol and drug abuse, coupled with weight gain and general exhaustion from the grueling tour schedule the band had endured over the previous ten years, was catching up with him. He only managed to come into the recording studio during the last few weeks of the *Who Are You* sessions, and was unable to play consistently in time on several songs.

Moon died just three weeks after *Who Are You* was released in August 1978. On the album cover, Moon is sitting backwards in a portable chair, the back of which reads 'Not to be taken away'.

LEFT

Who Are You, promo mobile, 1978

RIGHT

Promo poster, 1976

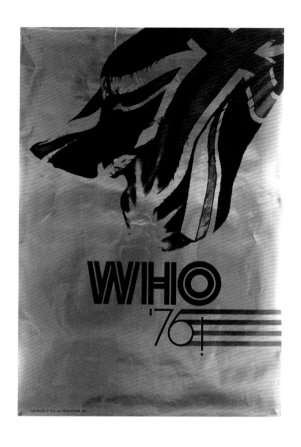

BELOW

Who Are You, promo poster, 1978

BELOW

Who Are You, US press ad, 1978

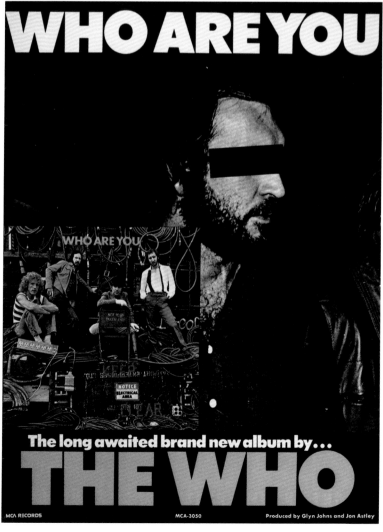

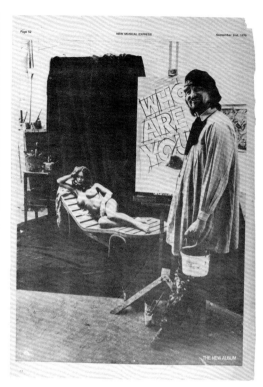

TOP, LEFT
Who Are You,
UK press ad, 1978

TOP, MIDDLE
Who Are You,
UK press ad, 1978

TOP, RIGHT
Who Are You,
UK press ad, 1978

BOTTOM, LEFT
Who Are You,
UK press ad, 1978

BOTTOM, RIGHT
Who Are You,
UK press ad, 1978

On 15 December, 1977, in front of a select invited audience at the Gaumont State Theatre in Kilburn, north London, the who gave a live performance to record material for director Jeff Stein's film, *The Kids Are Alright* (1979). It was one of Keith Moon's last public appearances with the band before his death in 1978 and one of the group's greatest performances. It was later released as *Kilburn 1977* on DVD in 2008.

Over the years, footage of this 1977 show has become a much sought-after holy grail for Who fans because only a few minutes of the concert ended up in the final cut of the movie. The full performance shows Moon in fiery form – one of the drummer's very finest hours.

Live performances, promo films and interviews spanning the period between 1964 and 1979 form the basis for Stein's movie. He was an American fan who had no previous film-making experience, but his passion for the documentary convinced the band to lend him their support.

Stein had learned that filmed recordings of many of the band's most memorable moments had been lost or discarded. For over two years he scoured TV and movie company archives and even acquired film footage from fans, his research extending from the US to Britain, Scandinavia, Germany, France, Australia and even Finland. He got to some of the material in the nick of time, rescuing it from the trash.

THE WHO 1981

Drummer Kenney Jones replaced Keith Moon and was in the studio to help The Who record their ninth album, Face Dances (1981).

Some derided the album but it also received some encouraging reviews, helping it to reach No 4 in the US, with strong competition from AC/DC's Dirty Deeds Done Dirt Cheap sitting at No 3, REO Speedwagon's Hi Infidelity at No 2, and Styx's Paradise Theatre at No 1.

The single 'You Better You Bet' was the last release by The Who to reach the Top 20 on the Billboard Hot 100. It was also their last single to hit the Top Ten in the UK, peaking at No 9.

Face Dances was art directed by Peter Blake, who had previously designed the cover of the Beatles' Sgt. Pepper's. The paintings of the band members that formed the cover were specially commissioned by Blake, who also contributed his own art, and included top British artists such as Tom Phillips, Richard Hamilton, Allen Jones, David Hockney, Clive Barker, R.B. Kitaj, Howard Hodgkin and Patrick Caulfield.

The It's Hard (1982) album cover, designed by Richard Evans and Graham Hughes, features a kid playing an arcade game. This was a reference to Tommy, with Tommy's pinball machine brought up to date. Townshend was not keen on this cover as he felt the band should have been more involved in its design.

TOP, LEFT
Face Dances tour programme, 1981

TOP, RIGHT
Face Dances, promo poster 1981

BOTTOM, LEFT
Face Dances, promo poster 1981

BOTTOM, MIDDLE
It's Hard, promo poster 1982

BOTTOM, RIGHT
'You Better You Bet', press ad, 1981

Has there ever been a band as significant as The Who that released as many greatest hits packages as they did in the 1980s and 1990s? Between those releases and the band's indefatigable touring – and notwithstanding the loss of band members – The Who managed to keep their profile high through two decades when they hardly recorded a new song.

They played only one show from 1990 to June 1996 but then recommenced touring in earnest, with an outdoor show in London's Hyde Park followed by six sold-out shows at Madison Square Garden in New York. In 1997 they revisited Europe, playing 16 shows before flying across the Atlantic for 20 more North American shows. The Who were back and ready for action.

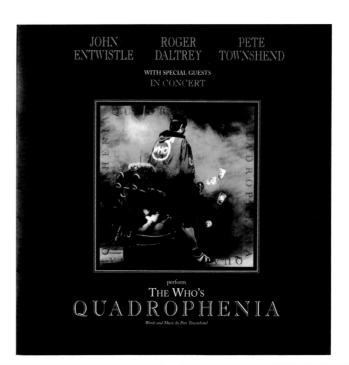

TOP

Quadrophenia, revival tour programme, 2000

BOTTOM, LEFT

Tommy deluxe edition CD poster, 2003

MIDDLE, RIGHT

Who's Last, promo poster, 1984

BOTTOM, RIGHJT

Tommy, Radio City, NY, programme, 1989

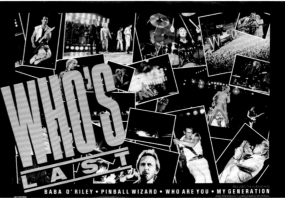

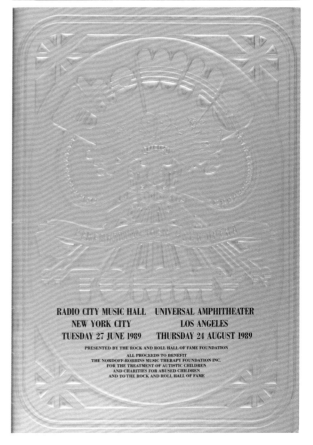

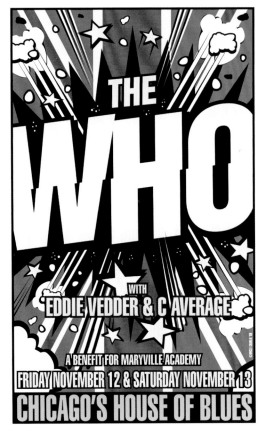

The Who's big news in the new millennium was the release of *Endless Wire* (2006), their eleventh album.

It was their first new album of original material in 24 years following the release of *It's Hard* (1982).

The design and art direction were by Richard Evans, utilizing elements created with the Visual Harmony software designed by Dave Snowdon and Lawrence Ball.

A new concert poster artist had appeared in The Who's orbit in the late 1990s: the prolific Charlie Hardwick, aka Uncle Charlie, based in Houston, Texas.

Hardwick had a serious daytime job as a senior graphics artist for a food-packaging firm, but had a long time high regard for

The Who along with punk and heavy metal bands.

His vibrant, beautifully silk screened art both reflected and defined the times. Luckily for Hardwick, The Who continued to tour relentlessly.

To open the new decade, The Who seemingly would play one year on, one year off. In 2000, they played 27 shows in North America (including four in a row at Madison Square Garden), then returned to the UK for another eleven. Only one show followed in 2001.

Then, tragically, John Entwistle died unexpectedly on the eve of The Who's proposed 2002 tour of the US.

TOP, LEFT
Gig poster, Atlantic City, 2008. Art: Charlie Hardwick

TOP, RIGHT
Tour programme, 2006

BOTTOM, LEFT
Gig poster, Houston, 2006. Art: Charlie Hardwick

BOTTOM, 2ND LEFT
Gig poster, Chicago, 2002. Art: Charlie Hardwick

BOTTOM, 3RD LEFT
Gig poster, Dallas, 2006. Art: Charlie Hardwick

BOTTOM, RIGHT
Gig poster, Chicago, 1997. Art: Charlie Hardwick

4 LED ZEPPELIN

LED ZEPPELIN

Only a handful of rock bands can boast a career's worth
of iconic album covers. Led Zeppelin may head that list.

The story goes that designer George Hardie first
approached Led Zeppelin's guitarist Jimmy Page with an
idea for *Led Zeppelin I* (1969) involving the Hindenburg,
perhaps the most iconic rigid airship in history. Page then
asked Hardie to refer directly to a public domain
photograph he had found showing the 1937 Hindenburg
disaster in New Jersey, where the zeppelin caught fire
as it landed. Hardie then spent hours with 'his finest
rapidograph' printing dots on top of a tracing paper copy
of the famous photo, all to create an iconic treatment that
would anchor the band's merchandising for decades.

Hardie, subsequently a designer in the famed Hipgnosis
studio, now is Senior Art Lecturer at the University of
Brighton in Sussex, England.

David Juniper's design for *Led Zeppelin II* (1970) was
based on a old photo of the Jasta Division of the German
Air Force during World War I. After the photo was tinted,
the faces of the four members of the band were airbrushed
on, using a 1969 promo photo. Two out of two, then, in the
iconic imagery stakes.

The artwork to *Led Zeppelin III* was an innovation in
sleeve design, incorporating a rotating wheel that revealed
different icons and shots of the band members in the ten
circular windows on the front cover. Zacron, the cover
artist, had been working on the development of books with
moving inserts. Jimmy Page would later tell *Q*: 'I knew the
artist and described what we wanted (a variation on crop
rotation calendars). He got very personal with this artwork
and disappeared off with it.'

Houses of the Holy (1973) presented altogether new
challenges for Aubrey Powell, who – with his partner in
Hipgnosis, Storm Thorgerson – came up with an

eye-opening photo-tint concept for the album cover. 'I'd
heard lots of interesting things about Led Zeppelin, and
I was slightly nervous about the prospect of working with
them,' said Powell, known as 'Po' to his friends and clients.
'They asked us to meet them and talk about ideas. Jimmy
Page and Robert Plant were there with their manager,
Peter Grant, who was a very big, overpowering man.'

Powell, who hadn't heard the music or even been given
a title for inspiration, presented two concepts. One
featured a shoot in Peru; the other involved photographing
children on the Giant's Causeway, an eccentric rock
formation in Northern Ireland.

'The idea came from a science-fiction book called
Childhood's End,' said Powell. 'At the end of the book,
all the earth's children gather together to be lifted off into
space. I suggested the children climb the octagonal steps
there so it would look like they were climbing to the
to-be-taken away point.' They said, "We like either of these
ideas, so do what you like." I said, "Well, both are extremely
expensive." And Peter Grant said, "Money? We don't
fucking care about *money*. Just fucking *do it*."'

So, Powell ventured forth to Northern Ireland with the
children and a crew that included talented make-up artists.
'It promptly rained for ten days straight,' foiling his plans to
shoot the photo in colour. Though the cover appears to be
one wide-frame photograph, it is actually a collage of 30
different shots; only two children posed for the shoot.

'Originally,' said Powell, 'I'd intended the children to be
gold and silver. Because I shot in black and white and it
was a grey day, the children turned out very white. So when
we hand-tinted it, the airbrush artist, by accident, put a kind
of purple tinge onto them. When I first saw it, I said, "Oh,

my God!" Then we looked at it, and I said, "Hang on a
minute – this has an otherworldly quality." So, we left it.'

The deliberately iconic *Physical Graffiti* (1975), besides
delivering on enormous commercial expectations, would
bring countless rock fan tourists to St Mark's Place
on New York's Lower East Side to view the two adjoining
tenement buildings featured on the cover. Artist Peter
Corriston (also responsible for three of the Rolling Stones'
great album covers) worked with designer Mike Doud at
AGI to convince the highly sceptical Peter Grant that the
art concept was a good one.

A rogues' gallery of celebrities and icons inhabited the
album's die-cut/interchangeable image artwork, including
Lee Harvey Oswald, Neil Armstrong, Elizabeth Taylor, King
Kong, Charles Atlas, Queen Elizabeth, Laurel and Hardy,
and the Virgin Mary. The building is still standing today;
in the basement is a second-hand clothes shop named,
naturally, Physical Graffiti.

David Juniper would be nominated for a 'Best Recording
Package' Grammy in 1970 for his work on *Led Zeppelin II*.
Hipgnosis would earn a Grammy nomination for *Houses of
the Holy* in 1974; AGI for *Physical Graffiti* in 1976;
Hipgnosis and Hardie for Presence in 1977; and Hipgnosis
for *In Through the Out Door* in 1980.

Led Zeppelin's many box sets and packages would,
over time, come to include hundreds of iconic photos shot
by luminaries who included Robert Alford, Dick Barnatt,
Richard Cremer, Jim Cummins, Ian Dickson, Chris Dreja,
Carl Dunn, Robert Ellis, Bob Gruen, Ross Halfin, Janet
Macoska, Terry O'Neill, Barry Plummer, Neal Preston,
Michael Putland, Peter Simon, Pennie Smith, Laurens Van
Houten, Chris Walter, Baron Wolman and Neil Zlozower.

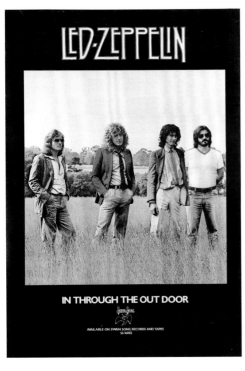

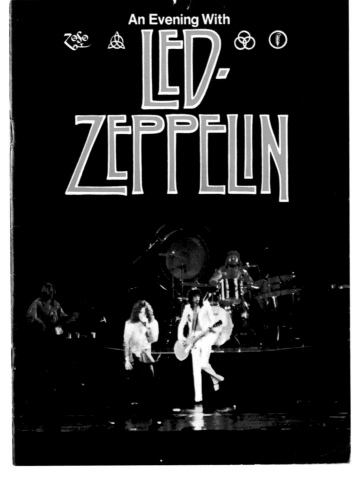

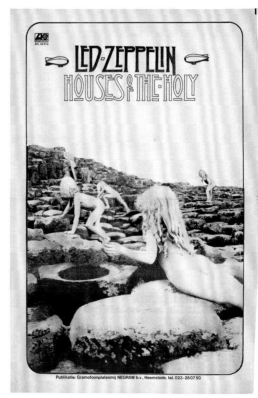

TOP, LEFT
In Through The Out Door,
press ad, 1979

TOP, MIDDLE
In Through The Out Door
songbook, poster, 1979

TOP, RIGHT
US tour, promo
poster, 1977

BOTTOM, MIDDLE
US tour programme,
1977

MIDDLE, RIGHT
Physical Graffiti, Canadian
promo poster, 1975

BOTTOM, RIGHT
Houses of the Holy,
press ad, 1973

BOTTOM, LEFT
The Song Remains The Same,
Australian movie poster, 1976

Led Zeppelin I was released in January 1969 during the band's first US tour. Its signature blues-rock fusion had folk and eastern influences, but the key feature of the group's sound lay in the full-on amplified distortion. The album would become one of rock's most pivotal achievements in the path towards establishing heavy metal music as a genre. *Led Zeppelin I* took only 36 hours in the studio to create; it cost less than $2,500 to produce. By 1975, the album had grossed over $7 million.

Jimmy Page chose the cover artwork, featuring a public domain photograph of the German airship *Hindenburg* famously exploding in flames at the end of its transatlantic voyage in May 1937 in New Jersey. In rock 'n' roll terms, the historical drama was a good omen; the cover artwork was unquestionably iconic. *Rolling Stone* said: 'The image did a pretty darn good job of encapsulating the music inside: sex, catastrophe, and things blowing up.'

Designer George Hardie, with whom the band also would also work on future album art, coordinated the packaging. He says that he originally suggested a design based on an club sign he'd seen in San Francisco (an image of a phallic-looking airship up in the clouds), but he was unable to persuade Page. The concept was saved nevertheless, and modified for the back cover logos on Led Zeppelin's first two albums, as well as being used for several early advertisements.

From the very beginning, collectors focused on rarities involving Led Zep album sleeves. When *Led Zeppelin I* was released in the UK, the sleeve had the band's name and the Atlantic record label logo printed in turquoise. When it was changed to the orange print, the turquoise version became an acknowledged holy grail.

What Led Zeppelin had in spades, according to *Rolling Stone*, was 'The potential for a mass audience'. Having first performed live at the University of Guildford

in England on 25 October, 1968, Led Zeppelin played 13 shows in the UK before their US concert debut the day after Christmas in Denver. Initially they would play as support act for bands such as Vanilla Fudge, Iron Butterfly, and Country Joe & the Fish. However, as the tour progressed, it was apparent that Led Zeppelin were easily outshining the headlining acts.

Over their career, the bulk of Led Zeppelin concerts were performed in the United States, which their management saw as the primary foundation for their success. Even as early as 1969 all but 33 of the band's 139 shows were performed in the US.

By April of that year, the band had assumed top billing (they were also was one of the first groups to perform without any opening act) although on 25 May Led Zeppelin received second billing in support of The Who, the only time these two

English bands ever performed on the same bill. During this leg, the band also took time out at various recording studios to record tracks for *Led Zeppelin II*.

On Led Zeppelin's third tour of North America, they were headliners at the Schaeffer Music Festival in New York City's Central Park, and appeared at another eight major outdoor festivals that summer. On the fourth leg, Led Zeppelin were the first rock act to perform at New York's Carnegie Hall since the Rolling Stones in the mid-1960s.

Another significant US concert took place at Boston Garden on 25 June. Performing to an audience of 15,000, Led Zeppelin netted $45,000, an indicator of the jaw-dropping pay scale the band would achieve on future tours where they regularly filled the largest venues.

Peter Grant, the band's manager, later commented: 'That Boston show made me realize Zeppelin can be bigger than the Stones and the Beatles.'

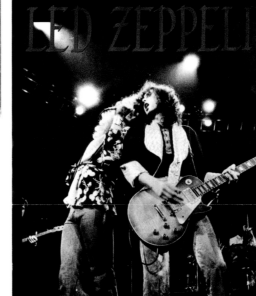

TOP, LEFT
UK tour programme, 1969

TOP, RIGHT
Promo poster, Japan, circa 1973

BOTTOM, LEFT
Gig poster, Santa Barbara, 1969. Art: Bettencourt

BOTTOM, MIDDLE
Gig flyer, Rose Palace, Pasadena, 1969

BOTTOM, RIGHT
Atlantic Records promo poster, Japan, circa 1976

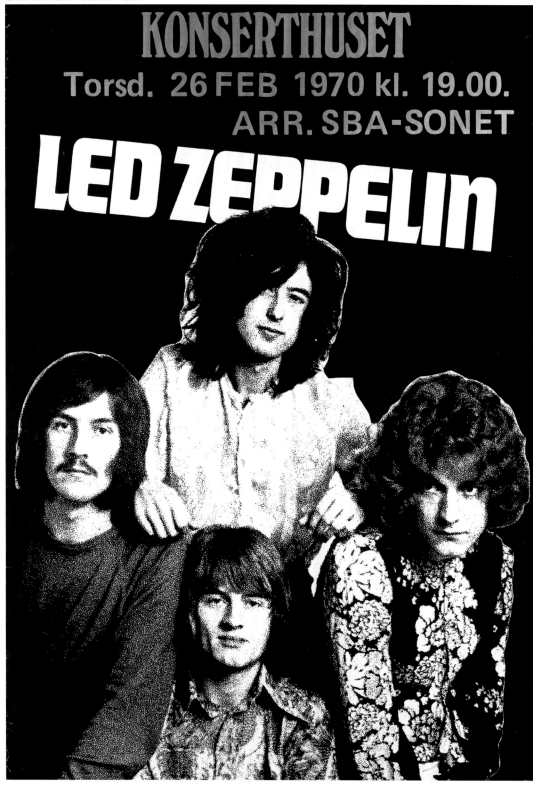

While the band rolled through the UK and Europe (three times), and North America (four times) on an impressively hectic schedule in 1969, they managed to take just enough time to record a distinguished second album, *Led Zeppelin II* (1969).

Robert Plant would tell historians Dave Lewis and Simon Pallett, 'It was crazy, really. We were writing the numbers in hotel rooms and then we'd do a rhythm track in London, add the vocal in New York, overdub the harmonica in Vancouver, then come back to finish mixing in *New York*.'

Recording engineer Eddie Kramer's earlier work with Jimi Hendrix had impressed the band greatly, and their collective creative juices were really flowing during the *Led Zeppelin II* production.

Kramer would later confide to Dave Lewis, 'The famous "Whole Lotta Love" mix, where everything is going bananas, is a combination of Jimmy Page and myself just flying around on a small console, twiddling every knob known to man.'

This album is generally considered the foundation for heavy metal music and a huge source of inspiration for bands like Van Halen and Guns N' Roses.

It was also the first Led Zeppelin album to feature Page playing a 1959 Gibson Les Paul, the guitar he helped to make famous.

Led Zeppelin told designer David Juniper to 'come up with an idea that was *interesting*.' He chose an archived photograph of the Jasta 11 Division of the German Air Force during World War I (the famed Flying Circus led by 'The Red Baron', ace pilot Manfred von Richthofen). The Germans had used zeppelins as fear-inducing, nearly silent bombers over military and civilian targets in Britain.

Juniper proceeded to tint the picture and then airbrush in the band's faces (using their 1969 promo photo), along with the faces of manager Peter Grant, tour manager Richard Cole, a woman named Glynis Johns (the mother from the movie Mary Poppins, whose inclusion was a humorous play on the name of their recording engineer Glyn Johns) and also bluesman Blind Willie Johnson.

The album package was nominated for a 1970 graphic package Grammy — as were many subsequent Led Zeppelin albums.

It's also known as the 'Brown Bomber' by fans and collectors.

Bron-Yr-Aur, an 18th century cottage in Gwynedd, Wales, situated on a hilltop overlooking the Dyfi Valley, was where the band laid the groundwork for *Led Zeppelin III* (1970). Robert Plant and Jimmy Page discovered the remote location on a vacation following their 1969 North American summer tour. Oddly, it had no running water or electric power, and the stripped-down setting was said to be an influence in moving the band towards a more mellow musical sound that included the featured use of acoustic instruments.

Page later explained to writer Dave Lewis, 'It was the tranquility of the place that set the tone of the album. Obviously we weren't crashing away at 100-watt Marshall stacks. Having played acoustic, and being interested in classical guitar anyway, being in a cottage without electricity, it was acoustic guitar time. After all the heavy, intense vibe of touring which is reflected in the raw energy of the second album, this was just a totally different feeling.'

The album's original LP edition was packaged in a gatefold sleeve with a clever cover designed by Zacron, a multi-media artist introduced to Page in 1963.

The cover and interior gatefold art included images on a white background, many of them connected thematically with flight or aviation. Behind the front cover was a rotatable laminated card disc, or *volvelle*, covered with more images, including photos of the band, which showed through holes. The images moved to different holes as you rotated the disc. The concept of the *volvelle* was based on crop rotation charts, with which Jimmy Page was familiar. Curiously, since 1965, Zacron himself had been working on graphics that rotated.

LEFT, TOP
Led Zeppelin I, II , III,
UK press ad, 1970

LEFT, BOTTOM
Led Zeppelin III,
US press ad, 1970

RIGHT
Led Zeppelin III,
promo poster, 1970

After the critics' generally unenthusiastic reaction to *Led Zeppelin III*, Jimmy Page determined that, to spite the critics, the next Led Zeppelin album (generally referred to as *Led Zeppelin IV*) would not have a title. Instead, it would feature four calligraphic symbols on the inner sleeve and record label, each one chosen by the band member it represented.

Page explained to interviewer Dave Schulps, 'After all this crap we had with the critics, I put it to [the band] that it'd be a good idea to try something totally anonymous. We decided that on the fourth album we would deliberately play down the group name and there wouldn't be any information whatsoever on the outer jacket. Names, titles, and things like that do not mean a thing.

'At first I wanted just one symbol [representing us], but because there were four [in the band], we could each choose our own symbol. I designed mine and everyone else had their own reasons for using the symbols they did.'

Page's symbol was generally referred to as 'ZoSo', although the symbol is a pictograph and not a word intended to be pronounced. He designed it himself by altering a symbol he found in a book on ancient mythology – and since then a huge debate has sprung up across the internet concerning the mythological origins.

John Paul Jones' symbol was a single circle intersecting three *vesica pices* (a 'triquetra').

John Bonham's symbol, three interlocking rings, represented the trinity of mother, father and child. It also was seen to depict an overhead view of a drum kit. Years later, former Nirvana drummer and current Foo Fighter frontman Dave Grohl had Bonham's symbol tattooed on his right wrist.

Robert Plant's symbol was the feather of the Egyptian goddess Ma'at, representing truth, justice, fairness and writing, inside an unbroken circle of life.

The painting on the front of the album, showing an old man carrying a bundle of sticks, was said to have been purchased from a junk shop in Reading, Berkshire by a Led Zeppelin roadie. On the album, it was depicted affixed to a peeling, papered wall inside a partly demolished house.

The album's inside illustration was 'The Hermit', credited to Barrington Colby Mom, influenced by the design of the tarot card of the same name.

Page has subsequently explained that the cover of the fourth album was further intended to bring out a city/country dichotomy that had initially developed during the making of *Led Zeppelin III*, representing an ongoing change in the band's musical balance between hard electric and acoustic sounds.

TOP, LEFT
Japanese tour programme, 1972

TOP, MIDDLE
London gig, 1971, press ad

TOP, RIGHT
'Black Dog', 1971, US press ad

BOTTOM, LEFT
Led Zeppelin IV, UK promo poster, 1971

BOTTOM, MIDDLE
Florida show, celebratory UK press ad, 1973

BOTTOM, RIGHT
Japanese gig poster, 1972

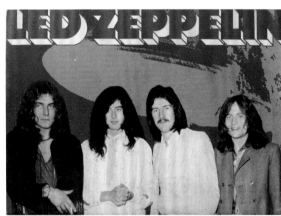

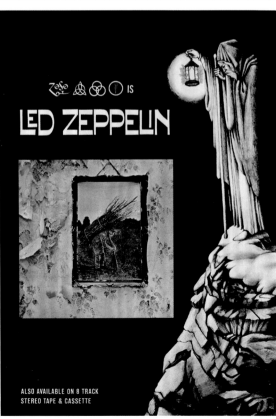

During the middle of Led Zeppelin's 1972 North American tour, the band stopped in New York to mix tracks that had been earlier recorded at several locations in the UK for their forthcoming fifth album, *Houses of the Holy* (1973). The album's title is said to be a sincere acknowledgement by the band of their fans, who dubbed the band's concert venues 'houses of the holy'.

The stunning ending to Arthur C. Clarke's novel *Childhood's End* was the inspiration for *Houses of the Holy's* cover art. It is an engineered composite of several photos taken by Hipgnosis dessign's Aubrey Powell. The photos were shot at the Giant's Causeway rock formation in County Antrim in Northern Ireland, a location Powell selected after also considering a similar setting in Peru. Young siblings Stefan and Samantha Gates were the two nude children (seen from the back only) who posed for the cover. Powell aimed to capture the best light at dawn and at dusk but constant rain and clouds made the shooting very frustrating.

The collage created the effect of eleven nubile youths scrambling over the rocks and an accident in post-production tinting created an unexpected image colouration.

The inner gatefold photo was taken at Dunluce Castle near the Causeway.

As with *Led Zeppelin IV*, the band's name and the album title did not appear printed on the sleeve. However, Atlantic Records added a wrap-around band with that information, also used to hide the children's buttocks. Nevertheless, the LP was banned in Spain and some parts of the Southern US for years afterwards.

Page later explained that the cover was actually a second version submitted by Hipgnosis. The first, by Storm Thorgerson, utilized the theme of an electric green tennis court. Apparently angry that Thorgerson implied that Led Zeppelin's music sounded like a racquet/racket, the band ditched him and used Powell instead. Nevertheless, Thorgerson did go on to produce the album artwork for Led Zeppelin's *Presence* 1976) and *In Through the Out Door* (1979).

TOP, LEFT
Houses of the Holy,
promo mobile, 1973

MIDDLE, LEFT
Houses of the Holy,
UK press ad, 1973

MIDDLE, RIGHT
Houses of the Holy,
UK press ad, 1973

BOTTOM, RIGHT
Formation of Swan Song
Records, press ad, 1974

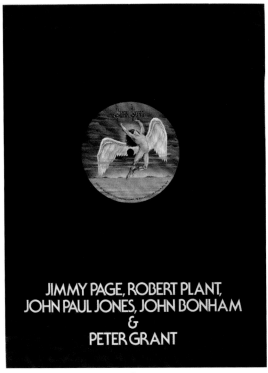

The sleeve design for Led Zeppelin's sixth album, *Physical Graffiti* (1975) was based on a photograph of a New York City tenement block, with interchanging insert images showing through. Musically and graphically, it is one of the band's most defining works.

The album's art director, Peter Corriston, was looking for a symmetrical building that was at once funky and cool, was not obstructed by other objects such as trees, and would re-proportion nicely to fit the square album cover dimensions.

Corriston later told the *New York Times*: 'We walked around New York for a few weeks looking for the right building. I'd come up with a concept of a band living in a tenement building, with people moving in and out. So, the original LP featured the building with die-cut windows on the outer sleeve and four sides of inner sleeves showing many different images through the cut-outs.'

The adjoining two buildings at 96 and 98 St Mark's Place in the Greenwich Village district ultimately were selected. It was the same exterior where, in 1981, Keith Richards and Mick Jagger would film the music video for the Rolling Stones' 'Waiting on a Friend'.

TOP, LEFT
Physical Graffiti, promo stand-up display, 1975

TOP, MIDDLE
US tour programme, 1975

TOP, RIGHT
Celebratory press ad after winning US awards, 1975

BOTTOM
Physical Graffiti, US promo poster, 1975

LED ZEPPELIN
1975 U. S. TOUR

BEST GROUP:
LED ZEPPELIN
BEST MALE
VOCALIST:
ROBERT PLANT
BEST SONGWRITER:
JIMMY PAGE,
ROBERT PLANT
BEST ALBUM
PRODUCER:
JIMMY PAGE
BEST GUITAR:
JIMMY PAGE*

*Based on the results of the 8th Annual Circus/ Hype Music Awards Poll.

As if you didn't know

Designed by Peter Cranley Graphics, Bournemouth

TOP

Earls Court gigs,
promo poster 1975

ABOVE

Earls Court gigs,
press ad, 1975

RIGHT

Earls Court gigs,
programme, 1975

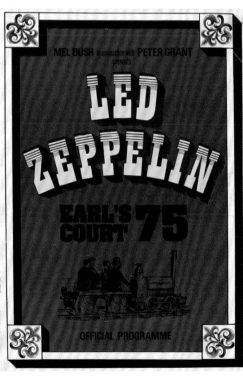

Earls Court 1975 were five memorable concerts performed by Led Zeppelin at Earls Court Arena in London in May 1975. Over 85,000 tickets were sold.

Earls Court took place less than two months following the last show of the band's 1975 North American tour. The entire stage and all the components for the light show were skylifted from America especially for these concerts.

A huge Ediphor screen erected above the stage showed the performances as they were being filmed for in-house projection – thought to be one of the first instances when such a soon-to-be-key piece of equipment (for most top bands) was used for a rock show in the UK.

The inspiration for the event's poster was George Stephenson's first modern British locomotive, the Rocket (1829).

Each show exceeded three hours in length, and the final show clocked in at just under four hours.

The set list for these concerts was (with some variation on the order):

1. 'Rock and Roll'
2. 'Sick Again'
3. 'Over the Hills and Far Away'
4. 'In My Time of Dying'
5. 'The Song Remains the Same'
6. 'The Rain Song'
7. 'Kashmir'
8. 'No Quarter'
9. 'Tangerine'
10. 'Going to California'
11. 'That's the Way'
12. 'Bron-Yr-Aur (Stomp)'
13. 'Trampled Under Foot'
14. 'Moby Dick'
15. 'Dazed and Confused'
16. 'Stairway to Heaven'
encores:
17. 'Whole Lotta Love'
18. 'Black Dog'
19. 'Heartbreaker'

Three nights of concerts at Madison Square Garden in New York, shot at the end of Led Zeppelin's 1973 North American tour, were the basis of the film *The Song Remains the Same* (1976).

Its release was accompanied by a soundtrack album of the same name, but was not entirely synched to the movie's song sequence. It also was criticized at the time for not offering up the best live sound or material available from the tour.

Promotional materials stated that the film was 'The band's special way of giving their millions of friends what they had been clamouring for – a personal and private tour of Led Zeppelin'. When finally released, it was 18 months behind schedule and grossly over budget.

Some of the live sequences were recreated at London's Shepperton Studios in August 1974 on a mock-up of the Madison Square Garden stage, as there were crucial holes in the original live concert footage.

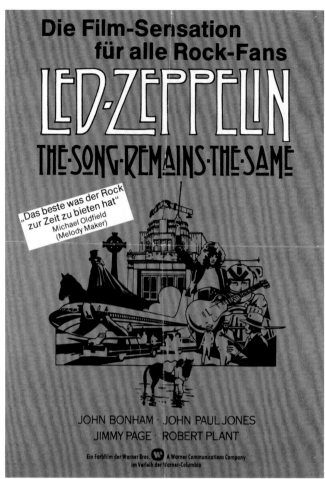

TOP, LEFT

The Song Remains The Same, stand-up display, 1976

TOP, RIGHT

The Song Remains The Same, German promo poster, 1976

MIDDLE, LEFT

The Song Remains The Same, Boston premiere ticket, 1976

BOTTOM

The Song Remains The Same, UK promo 'quad' poster, 1976

Presence (1976), according to rock historian Dave Lewis, was 'Led Zeppelin with their backs against the wall'. It was conceived after Robert Plant sustained serious injuries from a car accident while on holiday with his wife Maureen (who nearly died) on the Greek island of Rhodes in August 1975, causing the band to cancel a world tour due to begin the same month.

The album's title was thought to convey a powerful force and 'presence' that the band members felt surrounded the group, especially as, arguably, Led Zeppelin were at the very peak of their popularity. The Hipgnosis design studio created the iconic cover and inside sleeve that featured a well-dressed family in the presence of a black obelisk-type object. In fact, ever since, the item has been referred to simply as 'The Object.'

In the liner notes of *Led Zeppelin Remasters* (1990), Page explained, 'There was no working title for *Presence*. The record jacket designer said, "When I think of the group, I always think of power and force. There's a definite presence there." That was it. He wanted to call it *Obelisk*. To me, it was more important what was behind the obelisk. The cover is very tongue-in-cheek, to be quite honest. Sort of a joke on [the film] *2001, A Space Odyssey*. I think it's quite amusing.'

RIGHT
Presence, 'The Object' promo mobile, 1976

BELOW
Presence, stand-up display, 1976

ABOVE
Presence, US press ad, 1976

RIGHT
'The Object' and box, 1976. Only 1,000 were ever made

RIGHT
Gig poster, Oakland, 1977.
Art: Tuten/Bostedt

BELOW
US tour laminate
pass, 1977

Led Zeppelin's eighth studio album *In Through the Out Door* (1979) was the last recorded before drummer John Bonham died from the effects of alcoholism. The group itself would disband, as a result, in 1980. It was the band's sixth and final album to reach No 1 on the American *Billboard* pop album charts – and it did so within one week of its release, a first for a rock band. Once again, with its release, the entire Led Zeppelin album catalog re-entered the *Billboard Top 200*.

Why the curious name? It was so titled because of the taxation exile the band took from the UK, resulting in the band's inability to tour in their homeland for over two years. Trying to return to the embrace of their UK fans was like 'trying to get in through the "out" door.'

The original LP edition of *In Through The Out Door* featured an unusual graphic hook. Its outer wrapper looked like a plain brown paper bag with a small overstamp. There also were six different inner covers featuring a different pair of photographs, and the plain external wrapper meant it was near impossible for record buyers to tell which inner cover they would be getting.

The pictures all depicted variations on a scene in a bar in which a man burns a 'Dear John' letter. Each photo was taken from the separate viewpoint of someone who appeared in the other photos.

The album's graphic concept was the work of the Hipgnosis design studio.

TOP
In Through The Out Door, stand-up display, 1979

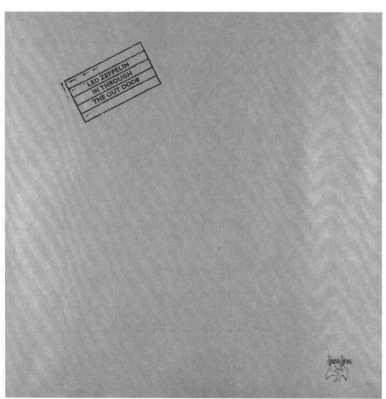

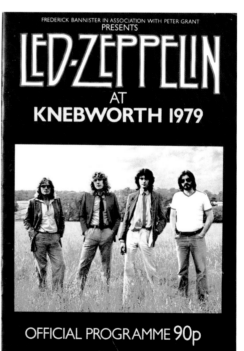

MIDDLE, LEFT
In Through The Out Door, promo poster, 1979

MIDDLE, RIGHT
Gig poster, Knebworth, 1979

BOTTOM, LEFT
In Through The Out Door, promo poster, 1979

BOTTOM, RIGHT
Gig poster, Knebworth, 1979

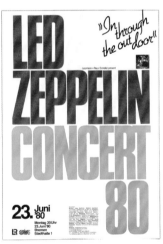

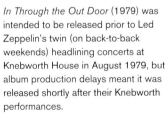

TOP
Tour over Europe,
promo poster, 1980

LEFT
Gig poster,
Bremen, 1980

RIGHT
Tour over Europe,
promo poster, 1980

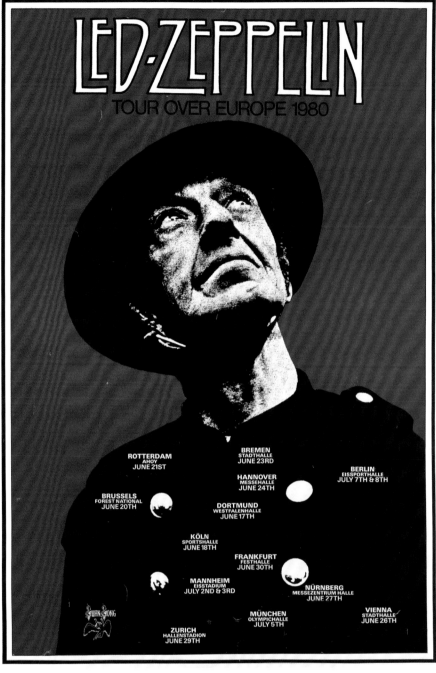

In Through the Out Door (1979) was intended to be released prior to Led Zeppelin's twin (on back-to-back weekends) headlining concerts at Knebworth House in August 1979, but album production delays meant it was released shortly after their Knebworth performances.

Beginning in 1974 and for five years afterwards, the grounds of Knebworth House near the village of Knebworth had been converted to a major outdoor rock concert site. When Led Zeppelin signed up to perform, they had not been heard live for two years, ever since the death of Robert Plant's son at the conclusion of the band's 1977 North American tour.

Also, due to self-imposed taxation exile, they had not performed in the U.K. for over four years. It was said that as many as 125,000, possibly closer to 200,000, people showed up for each show, with noise complaints were received from as far as seven miles away.

The band's performances were criticized for being sluggish and rusty, not surprising in the wake of their long layoff (the Knebworth shows were only preceded by two, low-key, warm-up shows in Copenhagen).

Furthermore, in the midst of the ongoing punk rock explosion, which was especially prominent in the UK, Led Zeppelin were nearing a form of irrelevance, according to some commentators.

The promotional photograph that was used was taken on the fields at Knebworth prior to the one of the performances.

Tour Over Europe 1980 was the final Led Zeppelin concert tour. The bulk of the 14 shows took place in Germany with the exception of one show each in Brussels, Rotterdam, Vienna and Zurich.

This was Led Zeppelin's first concert tour since their two Knebworth shows nearly a year before. Manager Peter Grant elected to schedule a relatively short European leg, hoping that going live would rejuvenate Robert Plant's appetite for touring, prior to the band's return to their lucrative stomping grounds in the US.

While the tour poster indicated a second concert in Berlin on 8 July, the final full-length rock concert Led Zeppelin ever played was on 7 July, 1980. 'Whole Lotta Love' was the final song performed at the final gig.

Coda (1982), a collection of outtakes from various sessions during Led Zeppelin's career, was released two years after the group called a halt to their colourful adventure. The decision followed the death of beloved drummer John 'Bonzo' Bonham on 25 September 1980, aged 32, after an all-day drinking binge.

The word 'coda', suggested by John Paul Jones that in effect meant 'an ending tailpiece that follows the main body of a musical work', was therefore appropriate to the band's career accomplishments. The graphic treatment on the album cover also reflected the group's equally four-part musical partnership.

RIGHT, TOP
Coda, promo
poster, 1982

RIGHT, BOTTOM
Coda, promo
poster, 1982

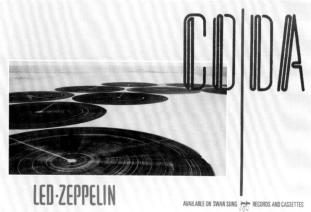

LEFT, TOP
Coda, promo
poster, 1982

LEFT, BOTTOM
Coda, promo
poster, 1982

LED ZEPPELIN
B B C   S E S S I O N S

Live Album In Stores November 11

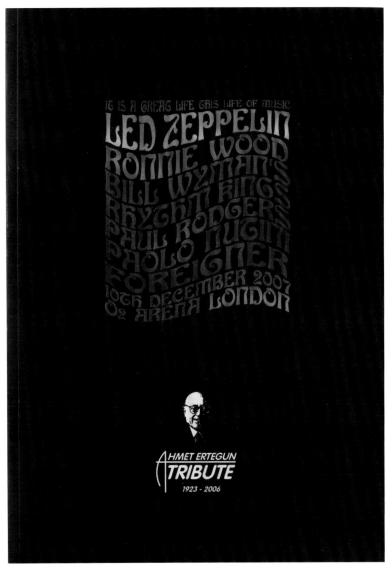

LEFT, TOP
BBC Sessions,
promo poster, 1997

LEFT, MIDDLE
Mothership, promo poster,
1997. Art: Shepherd Fairey

RIGHT, TOP
Ahmet Ertegun Tribute concert,
London, programme, 2007

LEFT, BOTTOM
Mothership, promo poster,
1997. Art: Shepherd Fairey

Collectively, Led Zeppelin's nine studio albums have gone 86 times platinum, with, of that number, *Led Zeppelin IV* (1971) alone having achieved 23x platinum sales. As a result, following the band's breakup, and over the past 20 years, Led Zeppelin have issued many music sets that both capitalized and expanded upon the band's considerable market-friendly legacy.

In many cases, the accompanying well-crafted promotional artwork continues to be attractive to fans and collectors.

On *Mothership* (2007) – a compilation album representing 24 selections from all the studio albums, released on the same day that Led Zeppelin's entire catalogue became available as digital downloads – the cover art was the work of Shepard Fairey, who would become well known

for his streetwise 'obey' campaign and his 2008 election campaign posters for US President Barack Obama.

On 13 July, 1985, Page, Plant, and Jones reunited for the US segment of the Live Aid concert, although they refused to allow footage from their performance to be used, feeling it was not up to their usual standard. The three members reunited again in May 1988 for the Atlantic Records 40th Anniversary concert, with Jason Bonham – John's son – on drums, again with some technical difficulties.

Then, on 10 December, 2007, the surviving members of Led Zeppelin reunited again (along with Jason Bonham) for the Ahmet Ertegun Tribute Concert at the O_2 in London. Fans converged from across the globe and the show was widely acclaimed.

5

DAVID BOWIE

DAVID BOWIE

David Bowie not only writes and performs music, he paints and sculpts in his spare time and has been extremely encouraging to young graphic artists. Throughout his career he has adapted his performance art to his own changing tastes, much as a painter or sculptor would. Many of Bowie's stage characters have in turn become iconic images; some are reflected in the choices of art or photography that are the album covers.

In many respects Bowie's transformative process began with the cover art to *Space Oddity* (1969), initially released on the Philips label in the UK as *David Bowie*, and by Mercury in the US as *Man of Words, Man of Music*.

The original UK LP cover showed a close-up portrait of Bowie by his childhood friend George Underwood floating atop a painting by Victor Vasarely with blue and violet spots on a green background. The same portrait was used on the companion US release, but this time it was on a plain blue background.

The original UK LP cover showed a close-up portrait of Bowie by George Underwood (the childhood friend of Bowie who was responsible for Bowie's eye damage) hovering atop a Victor Vasarely painting with blue and violet spots on a green background. The same portrait was used on the US release but on a plain blue background.

When they were both about 15 years old, Underwood smacked Bowie in the left eye while attempting to settle a dispute over a girl. Underwood was wearing a ring on his finger when his punch was thrown, and the blow caused potentially life-changing damage. For nearly eight months, Bowie was at home, unable to attend school while receiving treatment to repair his nearly blinded eye. But the doctors were not successful in fully repairing the damage, leaving him with a permanently dilated pupil.

The result was that Bowie developed faulty depth perception; he can see out of his injured eye but the color vision was also impaired. The colour of the damaged eye also often looks 'different' to observers. The two remained good friends despite the fight, and Underwood worked on artwork for several of Bowie's early albums.

When *David Bowie* was re-released in 1972 as *Space Oddity*, because of the enormous, continuing success of Bowie's Apollo-moon-landing-era single of the same name, a contemporary portrait by Mick Rock from the *Ziggy Stardust* period was displayed.

Next, Bowie would famously explore androgyny. On the original cover of *The Man Who Sold the World* (1970) Bowie appeared wearing a 'man's dress' created by British fashion designer Michael Fish. Bowie also wore it, rather strangely, during promotional interviews on his first US tour. Mercury rejected the cover for the US release, replacing it with a cartoon drawing by Michael J. Weller, an artist friend of Bowie's, featuring a bizarre-looking cowboy in front of the Cane Hill mental asylum.

The Rise and Fall of Ziggy Stardust and the Spiders from Mars (1972) launched the first of Bowie's many characters, Ziggy (a visiting Martian, who was on a mission to save the world with sex, drugs and rock 'n' roll, only to be torn apart by his fans in the end).

The photograph that serves as the basis for this cover image shows Bowie-as-Ziggy standing on London's trendy Heddon St in front of what was actually (then) K. West Furriers. Many Bowie fans still seek out this spot on trips to London (although the phone booth shown in the back cover background was removed many years ago).

In the words of album cover artist Terry Pastor: 'I was given a black and white photograph printed on matte paper – David Bowie's management wanted some colour put into it. (I also did the cover for his previous LP, *Hunky Dory*.

That was also a black-and-white photo that I coloured up in the same way. Perhaps this is why the record label decided that the Ziggy cover would be similar). I applied the colour using photo-dyes with an airbrush (a DeVilbiss Super 93). The lettering for the front cover was done with *lettraset* (rub-down transfer lettering) – a very hands-on way of doing things, but in 1972 that was the way things were done. There were no Mac computers in those days!'

Bowie's *Aladdin Sane* (1973) referenced both Ziggy Stardust and Bowie's own hot-and-cold reaction to stardom in America; thus the album was conceptually 'split down the middle'. This schizophrenia was conveyed on the Brian Duffy art-directed album cover with its glittery lightning bolt bisecting the singer's face.

The mixed-up nature of reality would build on *Diamond Dogs* (1974) with Guy Peellaert's iconic canine-satyr portrayal of Bowie on the cover. Brian Duffy would continue to play a major packager's role for Bowie, through *Scary Monsters (and Super Creeps)* (1980). Its cover art featured Bowie in the Pierrot costume he wore in the 'Ashes to Ashes' video, rendered in a combination of Duffy's photos and a painting by Edward Bell.

Packaging for tour promotion and merchandising purposes would hit its high mark with *Let's Dance*, Bowie's single best-selling album. Released in 1983, the title track became a No 1 worldwide hit, and the subsequent *Serious Moonlight* tour swept the globe. As late as 1990, Bowie's work would be enhanced by significant art direction with Roger Gorman winning the Grammy for 'Best Recording Package' for Bowie's *Sound + Vision* box set.

TOP, LEFT

Stage, stand-up
display, 1978

TOP, RIGHT

Rock Style, art show
poster, Barbican, 2000

BOTTOM, LEFT

Back catalogue, record
store bin divider, 1974

BOTTOM, MIDDLE

'Diamond Dogs',
UK press ad, 1974

BOTTOM, RIGHT

*Scary Monsters and Super
Creeps*, press ad, 1980

The cliché about David Bowie is that he is a musical chameleon, adapting himself to both the latest fashion and his own – brilliant – self-invented trends. While there's no denying that Bowie saw a great light beginning with *The Rise and Fall of Ziggy Stardust* (1972), his prior four albums largely hinted at that genius.

Prior to the Ziggy breakthrough, he debuted with an eponymous ode to psychedelia and music hall stylings, *David Bowie* (No 1) (1967). He followed it with the haunting folk-rock *David Bowie* (No 2) (1969). Then came the proto-metal fantasy *The Man Who Sold the World* (1970) and the experimental pop-art *Hunky Dory* (1971), which introduced the enduring classic 'Changes'.

David Bowie (No 1) was released in the UK on 1 June, 1967, the same date

as the Beatles' *Sgt. Pepper's Lonely Hearts Club Band* and perhaps, by immediate comparison, Bowie's first efforts were destined to be commercial failures at the time.

Bowie did catch the eye and ear of the public in the autumn of 1969 with the introspective lost-in-space melodrama of Major Tom in 'Space Oddity', a UK top 5 single.

The eerie tones on this riveting masterpiece were created on Bowie's Stylophone, a pocket electronic organ, but here he also established his signature baritone voice.

The title and subject matter of 'Space Oddity' were inspired by filmmaker Stanley Kubrick's *2001: A Space Odyssey*, and its release was timed to coincide with man's first moon landing. Major Tom

is for most fans as iconic a conceptual figure as Bowie's own recording and performance personae to come – Ziggy Stardust and then the Thin White Duke.

When Bowie gained much-deserved recognition with *Ziggy*, *David Bowie* (No 2) (originally issued in the US as *Man of Words, Man of Music*) was re-issued as *Space Oddity* in 1972 and re-promoted with much edgier LP cover and poster art.

The Man Who Sold the World was Bowie's first album with the nucleus of what would become the 'Spiders from Mars', the backing band made famous by the upcoming Ziggy.

Many critics feel *The Man Who Sold The World* is where Bowie's full story really starts. It has elements comparable to Led Zeppelin and Black Sabbath's efforts from the same period.

The Man was written and rehearsed at Bowie's home in Haddon Hall, Beckenham, an Edwardian mansion converted to a block of flats described by one visitor as entering 'Dracula's living room'.

The album's tone was borrowed from the horror/fantasy of HP Lovecraft and backed by Mick Ronson's heavy metal guitar, and has been cited as influencing the goth rock of Siouxie & the Banshees, The Cure, Gary Numan, and in due course Nine Inch Nails and Nirvana (who later performed the title song live).

The British cover of *The Man* showed Bowie reclining in what Bowie himself called a 'man's dress', an early indication of his interest in exploring and exploiting androgyny. In the US, the album was originally released with a cartoon cover that did not show Bowie.

LEFT
The Man Who Sold The World,
promo poster, 1970

BELOW
'Life On Mars',
press ad, 1970

RCA Records and Tapes

I love you ZIGGY

Bowie X

Thanx to all OUR people for making ZIGGY

BOWIE'S BACK!

Dec. 24 Rainbow Theatre, London
,, 28 Manchester, Hard Rock
Jan. 5 Green's Playhouse, Glasgow
(Matinee & Evening)
Jan. 6 Empire Theatre, Edinburgh
,, 7 Newcastle City Hall
,, 9 Preston Guild Hall

SPACE ODDITY
LSP 4813
PK 2101 cassette
P8S 2101 cartridge

THE MAN WHO
SOLD THE WORLD
LSP 4816
PK 2103 cassette
P8S 2103 cartridge

Hunky Dory
SF 8244
PK 1850 cassette
P8S 1850 cartridge

Ziggy Stardust
SF 8287
PK 1932 cassette
P8S 1932 cartridge

HIS LATEST SINGLE "THE JEAN GENIE" RCA 2302 RCA Records and Tapes

---

OPPOSITE
Ziggy Stardust, UK 'thank you' press ad, 1972

LEFT, TOP
Ziggy Stardust, promo poster © RCA

LEFT, BOTTOM
Ziggy Stardust, UK 'thank you' press ad, 1972

RIGHT
Ziggy Stardust, album and tour UK press ad

The Rise and Fall of Ziggy Stardust and the Spiders from Mars (1972) was a fully-realized concept album that has enjoyed tremendous critical admiration since it was first conceived.

The album presented the story of the androgynous character Ziggy Stardust, who was said to be 'The human manifestation of an alien being, attempting to present Earth's citizens with a message of hope in the last five years of their existence'.

More simply, Ziggy was a Martian rock star (the real-life inspiration apparently being British musician Vince Taylor), sexually promiscuous, a wild and excessive partaker in drugs, but nevertheless conveying peace and love. He was destroyed by his own abuses and by the people he attracted. Bowie further explained the full, complex plot of Ziggy in an interview with William S. Burroughs, as having to do with 'a star-tribe of anti-matter "Infinites" who travel from universe to universe, black-hole jumping, with Ziggy believing he is a prophet of future starmen, come to save Planet Earth'.

Bowie always claimed he found the name 'Ziggy' on an advertising display above a London tailor's shop. Some promotional graphics for *Ziggy* included Bowie with a saxophone, based on his pioneering and original use of the instrument on the album's 'Soul Love'.

There are many influences on Bowie's music from this time, including the Who, the Beach Boys, T. Rex, the Kinks' Ray Davies, the Small Faces, the Velvet Underground, and his growing friendship (and musical and business partnership) with Lou Reed and Iggy Pop among them.

But as the singular achivement that it is, every rock poll from the 1970s on includes *Ziggy Stardust* high among the Top 100 best rock albums of all time. Between 1972 and 1973, Bowie would have four top 10 albums and eight top 10 singles in the UK and even give away a top 10 song, 'All The Young Dudes', to Mott the Hoople. The *Ziggy Stardust Tour* of 1972 – 73 (Bowie's first venture into ultra-theatricality, featuring bold songs like 'Suffragette City') delivered 182 performances throughout the UK, North America and Japan. Here, with a three-piece band led by Ronson, Bowie presented the Ziggy character by donning flaming red hair and wearing impossibly wild outfits.

A concert film, *Ziggy Stardust: The Motion Picture*, directed in conjunction with Bowie by famed cinematographer D. A. Pennebaker (*Don't Look Back* with Bob Dylan (1967), *Monterey Pop* (1968) and many others) was released in 1983. It documented the final *Ziggy* show (at London's Hammersmith Odeon on 3 July, 1973). Just before the final track, Bowie announced: 'Not only is it the last show of the tour, but it's the last show that we'll ever do. Thank you.' Many in the audience believed that Bowie himself was retiring – but it was only Ziggy.

Bowie's title for his *Aladdin Sane* (1973) album that immediately followed *Ziggy Stardust* was a pun on 'A Lad Insane'. It was the first UK No 1 album that Bowie wrote and released as a bona fide rock star. It yielded the No 3 UK hit 'Drive-In Saturday' and the No 2 UK 'The Jean Genie' that would be one of the songs Bowie has played in concert throughout his entire career.

Although regarded as either 'uneven' or 'urgent and compelling' depending on the whims of the critic, it eventually became one of six Bowie entries in *Rolling Stone*'s list of the 500 greatest albums of all time (at No 277).

Famous British fashion photographer Brian Duffy here surfaced as an artistic collaborator with Bowie. He would later help create the graphic treatments for *Lodger* (1979) and *Scary Monsters* (1980).

Characterized by Bowie as 'Ziggy goes to America', all the new songs on *Aladdin Sane* were written on ships, buses, or trains during the first leg of his US *Ziggy Stardust* tour. The album's cover, featuring Bowie shirtless with Ziggy hair and a red, black and blue lightning bolt across his face, has been called 'as startling as rock covers ever got'.

Pin Ups (also 1973) was a covers album featuring Bowie's favourite songs, primarily those recorded in the 1960s. It was the last studio album with many members of the Spiders from Mars backing band from his *Ziggy Stardust* period. The bands whose songs were covered included the Pretty Things, Pink Floyd, the Who, the Kinks and Bruce Springsteen, among others.

Pin Ups successfully charted over many weeks, peaking at No 1, then repeatedly re-entered the charts in a somewhat unusual fashion. The woman who featured on the cover with Bowie and in many of the graphics promotions was famous 1960s British supermodel Twiggy.

ABOVE
'Drive-In Saturday',
UK press ad, 1973

BELOW
Bowie Pin-Ups US TV special,
promo poster © RCA

RIGHT
UK tour,
press ad, 1973

Guy Peellaert, a Belgian painter-collagist whose fervid imagination also produced surreal album covers for John Lennon and Mick Jagger, illustrated the cover art for Bowie's *Diamond Dogs* album (1974).

A reviewer for Britain's *Independent* newspaper was later to describe Peellaert's images as rock iconography: 'This was the pornography of rock, and also its stained-glass window – almost as thrilling as the music itself.'

Peellaert's work for Bowie featured the singer as a grotesque dog-man and sparked a censorship war in 1974 when the record company erased the dog's genitalia from the reprinted original painting. At the time the album was released, only a very few copies of the original non-retouched cover made their way into mass circulation. These have become among the most hard-to-find LP collectibles, and pricey too, changing hands at several thousand dollars.

Later, in what some critics saw as aesthetic vindication, the controversial erased area reappeared on CD versions of the album.

Peellaert was notable for publishing the book *Rock Dreams* (portraits in the style of the *Diamond Dogs* cover) which sold more than a million copies in the 1970s. He died aged 74 in November 2008.

Diamond Dogs featured 'Halloween Jack', a character who lived in the decaying, post-apocalyptic 'Hunger City'. It was as if Bowie was setting George Orwell's *1984* novel to music (licensing issues prevented Bowie from doing exactly that).

Yet the previous Bowie character, *Ziggy Stardust*, was still alive in spirit, evident in Bowie's haircut as painted by Peellaert, and in the glam-trash stylings of the first single, 'Rebel Rebel'.

The album's raw lead guitar tracks (handled uncharacteristically by Bowie himself) coupled to its vision of urban chaos, in some respects anticipated the punk revolution that would take place in the following years simultaneously in the UK and the US.

Diamond Dogs would become his first major commercial success in the US, peaking at No 5.

RIGHT, TOP
Diamond Dogs re-release, promo poster, 2004

RIGHT, MIDDLE
'Rebel Rebel', UK press ad, 1974

LEFT
Diamond Dogs, promo poster, 1974. © RCA/Main Man Ltd

RIGHT, BOTTOM
Diamond Dogs, promo poster, 1974. © RCA

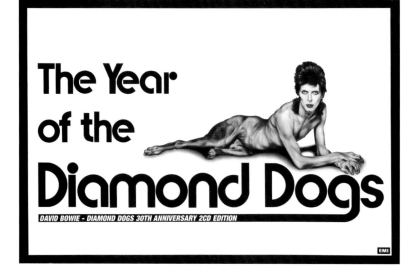

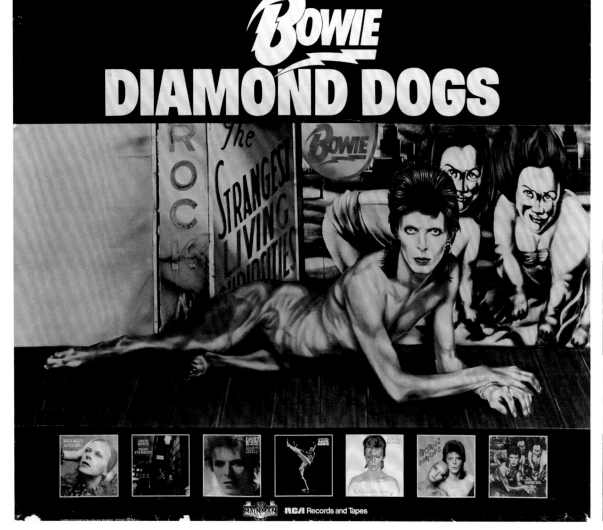

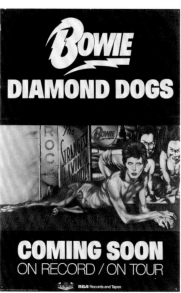

DAVID LIVE

The first 'live'
BOWIE
single
"KNOCK ON WOOD"
FROM HIS FORTHCOMING ALBUM

THE THEATREGOER

MCA Inc presents Amphitheatre '741

BOWIE

SEPTEMBER 2-8   UNIVERSAL AMPHITHEATRE

LEFT
David Live, US promo
poster, 1974. © RCA

RIGHT, TOP
'Knock On Wood',
US press ad, 1974

RIGHT, BOTTOM
Gig programme,
LA, 1974

Bowie played nearly all of the *Diamond Dogs* songs on his massive 1974 US tour, recorded and released as *David Live* (1974). Originally the album was titled *David Bowie at the Tower, Philadelphia*.

This North America-only tour started off promoting *Diamond Dogs* but the end of the tour, now called the *Soul Tour* or sometimes the *Philly Dogs* tour, also included songs from Bowie's next album, *Young Americans* (1975).

The full tour was 73 shows, from June to December, with many repeat nights including four at Philadelphia Tower Theatre, seven at the Universal Amphitheater in Los Angeles, five at Detroit's Michigan Palace and seven at Radio City Music Hall in New York.

David Live caught Bowie in transition from the *Ziggy Stardust/Aladdin Sane* personae to what Bowie himself described with some irony as the 'plastic soul' of *Young Americans*.

The dichotomy of meshing the two eras on one live album (his first) could be seen in the cover photo that featured a picture of Bowie in contemporary soul threads but also wearing a striking pompadour haircut and much glam-style make-up (a juxtapose he was said to be uncomfortable with, in retrospect).

The *Diamond Dogs* tour was exciting and ambitious, utilizing a giant set imagined as the album's 'Hunger City' urban decay setting. While performing 'Space Oddity', Bowie elected to use a microphone

disguised as a telephone. He also soared into the air, being raised and lowered above the stage by a stinger-style crane in early anticipation of similarly flamboyant concert-mechanics to come from Peter Gabriel, the Rolling Stones and U2.

After the opening leg, however, Bowie mostly jettisoned the elaborate sets. When the tour resumed after a summer break to record new music, the *Diamond Dogs* sound no longer seemed in keeping with his new musical direction. Bowie cancelled some dates, made changes to the band, and returned to the road in October as the *Philly Dogs*.

Despite concerns about the album's uneven sound quality, it made No 2 on the UK charts and No 8 in the US.

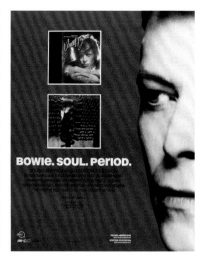

With *Young Americans* (1975) Bowie achieved major crossover success, shedding glam rock for Philadelphia-style soul. The album – termed 'plastic soul' by Bowie himself, in acknowledgement of his debt to black music – brought his first No 1 single in the US, 'Fame', co-written with John Lennon.

Coincidentally, *Young Americans* also included Bowie's take on the Lennon and McCartney-penned track 'Across the Universe'.

'Fame' was based on a riff that Bowie guitarist Carlos Alomar had developed while covering the Flares' 1961 doo-wop classic 'Foot Stompin', which Bowie's band

had taken to playing live during the Philly Dogs period.

One of the album's backing vocalists was a young Luther Vandross who also co-wrote some of *Young Americans*.

Bowie's 'new sound' jolted and in some cases actually alienated a large portion of his original audience, particularly his UK devotees, but it cemented his stardom in the US, with *Young Americans* staying on the charts twice as long as *Diamond Dogs*

Ironically, at the same time, the UK re-issue of his old single 'Space Oddity' hit No 1 while 'Fame' achieved similar fortune in the US.

LEFT, TOP

Young Americans, poster, 1975. © RCA/Main Man Ltd

RIGHT, TOP

Back catalogue press ad with *Young Americans*, 1991

LEFT

Young Americans, promo mobile, 1975

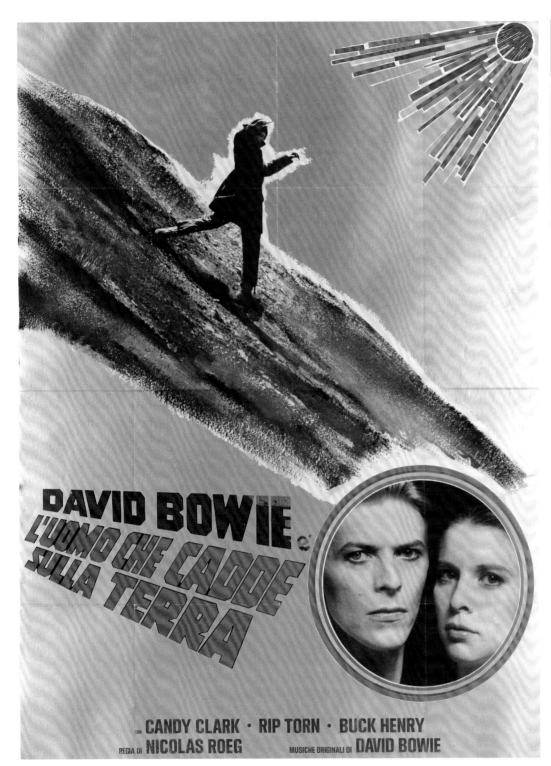

David Bowie starred in the Nicolas Roeg-directed film *The Man Who Fell to Earth* (1976) based on the 1963 novel of the same name by Walter Tevis.

The bittersweet plot involves an extraterrestrial who crash-lands on Earth while seeking a way to transport water back to his home planet, which is locked in a terrible drought.

Thomas Jerome Newton, portrayed by Bowie, is a humanoid alien who uses the advanced technology of his home planet, Anthea, to patent many inventions on Earth. He accumulates great wealth which he secretly directs towards the building of a space vehicle that can fetch water back across the universe and also create an escape route for his people.

Bowie's love interest is played by Candy Clark, who starred in the George Lucas film *American Graffiti* (1973).

Newton's secret life is unveiled and the Bowie-played character is subjected to inhumane tests of will under intense observation, ultimately leaving him broken, lonely and embittered, unable or no longer interested in trying to save his people.

There is no official soundtrack to this movie as legal entanglements caused Bowie to forego creating one.

Station to Station (1976) was David Bowie's tenth studio album. It was notable as the basis for another of Bowie's most memorable 'characters', in this instance the Thin White Duke – one of the last that he was overtly to present.

The album's cover art featured a still from the movie *The Man Who Fell to Earth* (1976), directed by Nicolas Roeg, for which Bowie had just completed his most highly acclaimed cinematic performance.

Famously, during the recording sessions, Bowie became heavily dependent on cocaine, lost considerable weight, and is said to recall almost nothing of the album's production.

Station to Station was a transitional album, bridging the soulful funk of *Young Americans* with a synthesized, brittle sound that German electronica bands such as Kraftwerk and Neu! had introduced. This would lead to Bowie's collaboration with Brian Eno in 1977 – 79 on the 'Berlin trilogy' of albums.

The unusual blend of American funk with Krautrock created some confusion for Bowie's followers. Critics called it either 'accessible' or 'impenetrable'. Yet its single, 'Golden Years' cracked the Top 5 on both sides of the Atlantic and the experimental, often emotionally-detached album itself was to be ranked No 323 on *Rolling Stone*'s list of the 500 greatest albums of all time.

While shooting the film, Bowie began writing a pseudo-autobiography called *The Return of the Thin White Duke*, and had taken on the film's character as his own real-life persona, an amoral, angry and aloof Thin White Duke *aryan*, 'a hollow man of ice masquerading as fire', according to one critic. Thus the Thin White Duke became the symbolic figure for *Station to Station*, particularly as there was no possibility for Bowie to create a soundtrack for what he'd just starred in.

Bowie's *Isolar* 1976 tour supported *Station to Station* and 64 shows were performed across North America and Europe. The tour also is variously referred to as the Thin White Duke Tour, the *Station to Station Tour*, and the *White Light Tour*.

Concert audiences were stunned when each performance commenced with a projected sequence of powerful surrealist images that included a razor blade cutting into an eyeball (culled from the 1928 film *Un Chien Andalou* by Luis Bunuel and Salvador Dali).

Banks of fluorescent white lights set against a stark black backdrop created an overwhelmingly bleak spectacle presaging where Bowie was going next – to Germany to begin the 'Berlin Trilogy.'

BELOW
Promo poster,
1976

RIGHT, TOP
Station to Station,
promo mobile, 1976

RIGHT, MIDDLE
'Golden Years',
press ad, 1976

RIGHT, BOTTOM
Station to Station,
promo poster, 1976

OPPOSITE
German tour
poster, 1976

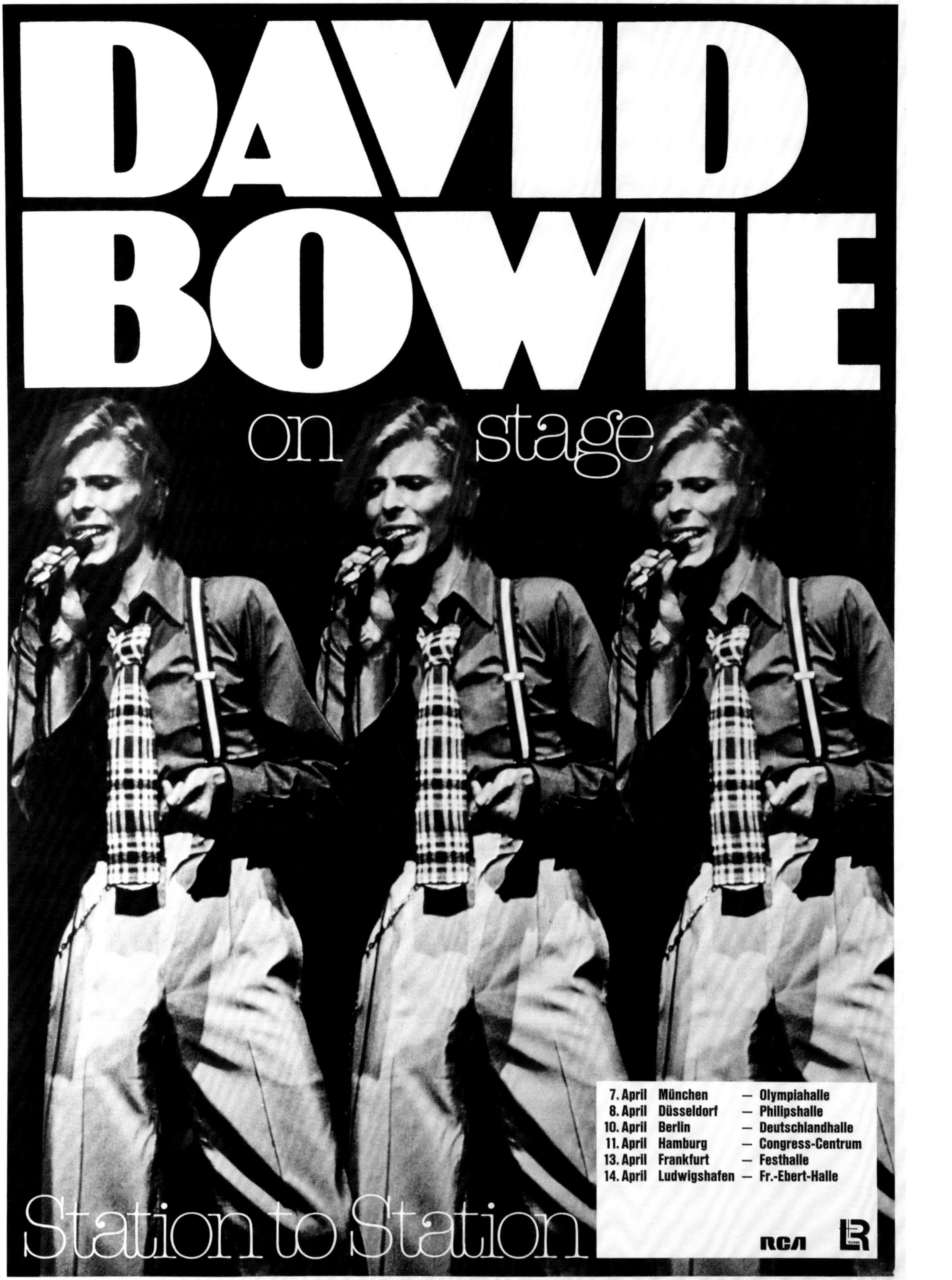

DAVID BOWIE

on stage

Station to Station

7. April	München	— Olympiahalle
8. April	Düsseldorf	— Philipshalle
10. April	Berlin	— Deutschlandhalle
11. April	Hamburg	— Congress-Centrum
13. April	Frankfurt	— Festhalle
14. April	Ludwigshafen	— Fr.-Ebert-Halle

RCA

CPL1-2030

RCA Records

The avant-garde album *Low* (1977) was preceded by Bowie's previous album, *Station to Station* (1976) and also by an unfulfilled project – the music he intended for the soundtrack to Nicholas Roeg's *The Man Who Fell to Earth* (1976). Elements from both were incorporated into *Low*.

A still from the movie – as with *Station to Station* – was selected for the album's cover. It is thought that the juxtaposition of Bowie's image in profile with the album's name was deliberately intended to convey a play on the term 'low profile'.

Low is regarded as an influential release, the first in the 'Berlin Trilogy' (or triptych, as Bowie termed it) of collaborations with Brian Eno (although this first album was actually recorded mainly in France and only mixed in West Germany).

After the cocaine-fuelled *Station to Station*, Bowie would not rely nearly so heavily on drugs for inspiration (or escape). Yet many of the songs concerned depression, estrangement, or self-destructive behaviour, so in effect Bowie's mood was 'low' throughout. *Low* is still seen as being ahead of its time, and Bowie himself was famously to say, 'Cut me, and I bleed *Low*'.

Low had a great effect on post-punk and New Wave musicians including Trent Reznor of Nine Inch Nails. Q magazine was to rank it at No 14 on its list of 100 Greatest British abums ever and the album was to peak at No 2 on the UK charts.

"Heroes" (also 1977) was recorded entirely in Berlin as an even more fleshed-out combination of experimental rock, art rock, Krautrock, electronica and ambient music.

'Heroes,' the title track, is one of Bowie's most beloved songs, the story of two lovers who meet in despair at the Berlin Wall, and it effectively conveys the Cold War zeitgeist of the then-divided city. Co-producer Tony Visconti considered *"Heroes"* (a title using deliberate quote marks) as 'one of the last great adventures in making albums. The studio was about 500 yards from the wall. Red Guards would look into our control-room window with powerful binoculars'.

The cover graphics were inspired by German expressionist Erich Heckel's *Roquairol* painting (as was that of *The Idiot*, a Bowie collaboration with Iggy Pop, also released in 1977).

"Heroes" was marketed by RCA with the astute slogan: 'There's Old Wave. There's New Wave. And There's David Bowie . . .'

A number of the album's tracks were adapted for Bowie's accompanying tour, which was eventually captured on record as *Stage* (1978).

"HEROES" DAVID BOWIE

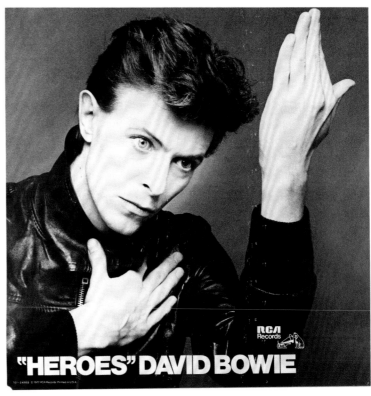

"HEROES" DAVID BOWIE

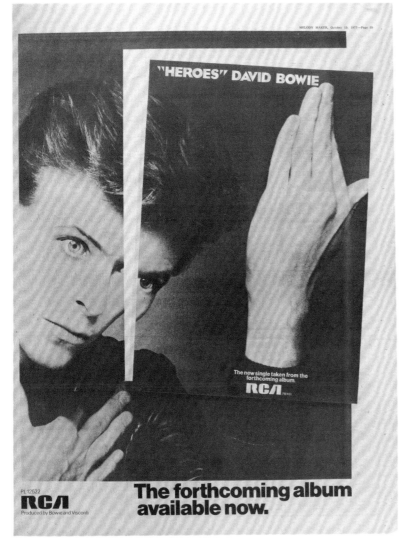

"HEROES" DAVID BOWIE

The new single taken from the forthcoming album.

RCA

PL 12522
RCA
Produced by Bowie and Visconti

The forthcoming album available now.

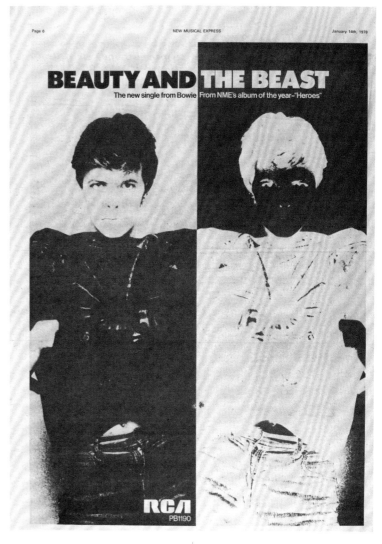

BEAUTY AND THE BEAST

The new single from Bowie. From NME's album of the year–"Heroes"

RCA
PB1190

LEFT
'Heroes' press
kit, 1978

RIGHT, TOP
Stage, UK press
ad, 1978

RIGHT, BOTTOM
Australian tour
programme, 1978

Bowie's second live album was *Stage* (1978). The selections were drawn from US concerts in Philadelphia, Providence and Boston that primarily featured material from Bowie's then most recent studio albums *Station to Station, Low,* and *"Heroes".* To the elation of every fan, it also included a five-song selection from *Ziggy Stardust.*

Critics and fans alike generally feel that *Stage* is a more effective presentation than *David Live* (1974). It captured the electronica from *Low* and *"Heroes"* with great fidelity although this was done by minimizing the crowd reactions that usually give the great live albums their appeal.

Bowie's *Isolar II – 1978 World Tour* (more commonly remembered as the *Low/ Heroes* world tour or the *Stage* tour) performed before 77 audiences in March to December 1978 throughout North America, Europe, Australia, New Zealand and Japan.

In an effort to best the previous 1976 tour, the creepy fluorescent-tube lighting stylings were made even bolder by the creation of a large cage of tube lighting that actually enclosed the entire stage. During the softer instrumental passages, the cage pulsed slowly and somberly and then flashed in great bursts during the hard rock sections. The North American tour leg concluded with three bravura, shows at Madison Square Garden in New York which sold out, as did the final shows of the European leg at Earl's Court in London.

The Australian leg of the tour was Bowie's first concert performances in Australia and New Zealand and his first large-scale outdoor concerts.

DAVID BOWIE · STAGE

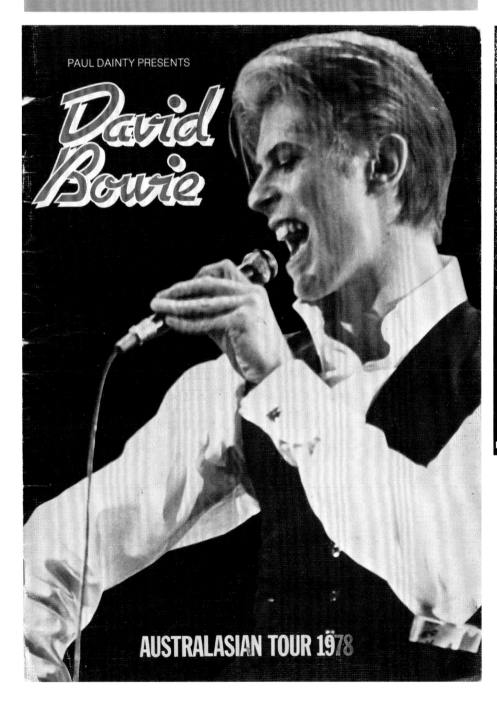

DAVID BOWIE'S NEW LIVE ALBUM STAGE IS NOW AVAILABLE

TOP, RIGHT
Stage, stand-up
display, 1978

TOP, LEFT
UK tour, press
ad, 1978

BOTTOM, LEFT
Australasian tour
programme, 1978

BOTTOM, RIGHT
Stage, promo
poster, 1978

The last of the 'Berlin trilogy' set of albums Bowie recorded in collaboration with Brian Eno was *Lodger* (1979).

Although it was not a major commercial success, fans and critics in retrospect see it as more accessible than *Low* or *"Heroes"* as Bowie determined to leave out any fully impenetrable instrumental tracks. Overall, it was a return to a more cheerful, upbeat spirit with even a few pop flavourings.

Recorded between the legs of Bowie's 1978 *Isolar* world tour, *Lodger* incorporated two major themes: the effects of travel, and

a critique of Western civilization. There was cross-referencing of world cultures throughout, effectively presenting the concept of world music for the first time.

Bowie worked with British pop artist Derek Boshier on the cover design. The original outward gatefold album sleeve featured a full-length shot of Bowie as an accident victim, made up with a seemingly broken nose. For effect, the image was low-res, as though taken with a Polaroid instant camera.

Boshier says: 'The cover for *Lodger* was

a collaboration between photographer Brian Duffy, David and myself. I loved the resolution to the problem of David being photographed falling. We shot him from above, on a specially-made table built to match his falling form.'

The inside of the Boshier-assisted gatefold included pictures of Latin American revolutionary Che Guevara's corpse, Italian Renaissance artist Andrea Mantegna's *Lamentation over the Dead Christ* painting (cir. 1480), and also Bowie being readied for the cover photo.

LEFT, TOP
'DJ', press ad,
1979

RIGHT, TOP
Lodger, promo
mobile, 1979

LEFT, BOTTOM
Lodger, press
ad, 1979

RIGHT, BOTTOM
Lodger, promo poster,
1979. © RCA

OPPOSITE
Lodger, promo
poster, 1979

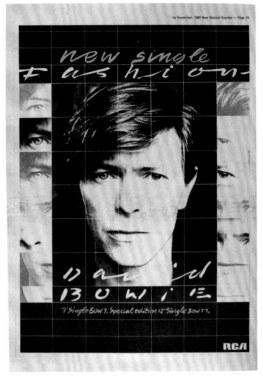

TOP, LEFT
'Ashes to Ashes',
promo poster, 1980

TOP, RIGHT
Scary Monsters,
UK press ad, 1980

MIDDLE, LEFT
Scary Monsters, promo
poster, 1980

MIDDLE, RIGHT
'Fashion', UK
press ad, 1980

BOTTOM
Scary Monsters, limited edition
(150) signed lithograph, 1980

RIGHT
Scary Monsters,
promo mobile, 1980

Scary Monsters (and Super Creeps) (1980) was Bowie's final studio album for the RCA label and his first following the 'Berlin Trilogy' of *Low*, *'Heroes'*, and *Lodger*.

While the trilogy was an artistic watershed, the albums basically were disappointments in the marketplace. So Bowie's return to commercial accessability was welcomed by his fans (and RCA) and *Scary Monsters* debuted at No 1 in the UK.

Bowie would achieve megastardom and his greatest commercial success with *Let's Dance* (1983) and the subsequent *Serious Moonlight* tour, but many critics feel *Scary Monsters* would stand as the true artistic benchmark for every new release to follow. Bowie biographer David Buckley suggested that 'Bowie should pre-emptively sticker up his next album "The Best Since *Scary Monsters*" and have done with it'.

The public's first glimpse of *Scary Monsters* was 'Ashes to Ashes', released as a single that shot to No 1.

The song revisited the character of Major Tom from Bowie's much earlier 'Space Oddity' and was the basis for a highly innovative video directed by Bowie and David Mallet. Bowie would later say that '"Ashes to Ashes" wrapped up the 1970s really well for me … a good epitaph'. It's also been described as 'containing more messages per second than almost any other single!'

A combination of Brian Duffy's photos and a painting by Edward Bell led to the creation of the cover for *Scary Monsters*. Bowie was portrayed in the Pierrot costume that he wore in the 'Ashes to Ashes' video. The overall intent of the packaging was believed to symbolise "the discarding of Bowie's former personae'.

RCA released *Scary Monsters* with the promo line 'Often Copied, Never Equalled', thereby tellingly referencing the many New Wave and cutting-edge acts that Bowie had inspired over the years.

BELOW
Scary Monsters,
UK press ad, 1980

BELOW
Scary Monsters,
US press ad, 1980

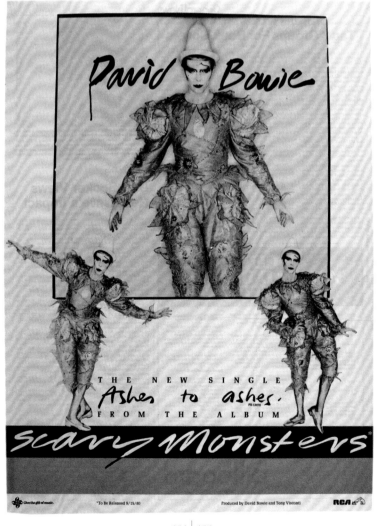

Let's Dance (1983) was a worldwide sensation simply because it was so danceable. Chic's Nile Rodgers co-produced the album with Bowie and it yielded three hits that became standards – the title track, 'Modern Love' and 'China Girl'.

The album itself hit No 1 in the UK and peaked at No 4 in the US. 'China Girl' was a remake of a song which Bowie co-wrote several years earlier with Iggy Pop, who had recorded it for *The Idiot* (1977).

The album was a major milestone in the career of the late Texan blues guitarslinger

Stevie Ray Vaughan, who played lead guitar on all tracks (but did not join the *Serious Moonlight* tour that followed).

One memorable aspect of the *Let's Dance* promotion was the limited edition picture disc. One side showcased the album's front cover graphics and track listing; the other side proclaimed the *Serious Moonlight* tour '83. This was evidence of the album and tour's intertwined intent, a record company, concert promoter, and merchandisers' dream effort. The EMI re-release in 1999 was a cross-promotion with www.david

bowie.com. This was one of the very earliest decisions by a mainstream artist to combine Internet-driven promotions with traditional distribution methods.

The cover graphics for *Let's Dance* included the projection of a Derek Boshier painting across Bowie's figure in boxing gloves. The inner sleeve had line drawings by Boshier, including his characteristic heads and walking figures. Elements of the overall graphic presentation made their way into every aspect of the album and tour promotion, one of the most complete realizations of such an objective to date.

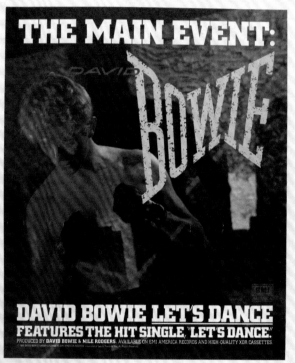

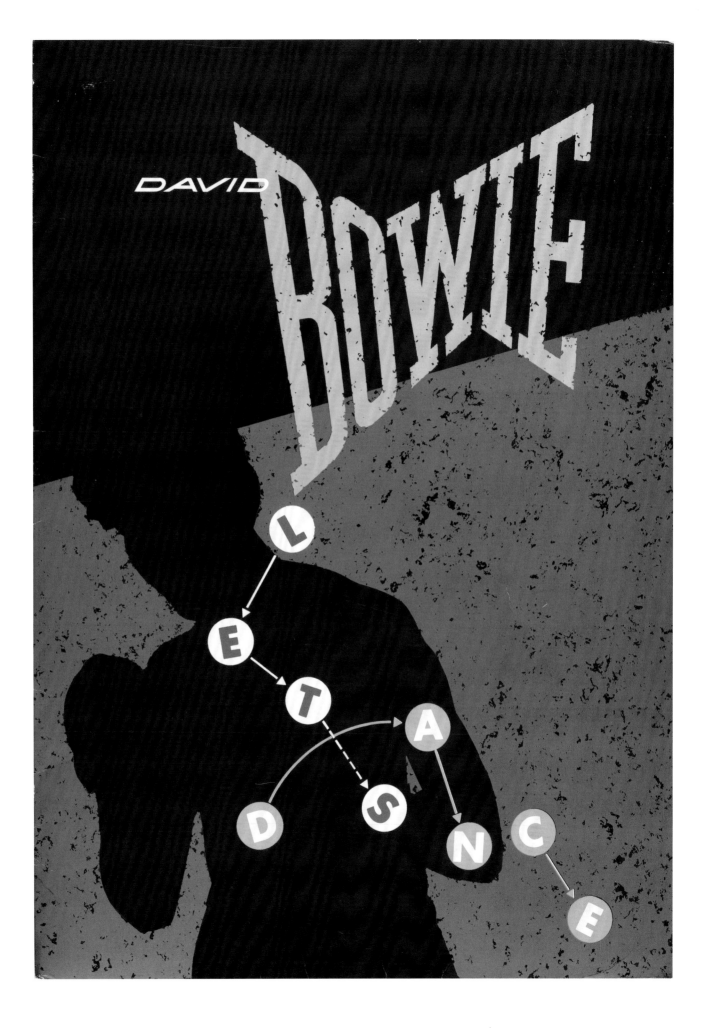

Bowie's Serious *Moonlight Tour* of 1983 was the longest, largest, and most successful concert tour of his career to date, and his first in five years.

It was an exceptional achievement in concert staging, the equal of the best produced by the Rolling Stones, U2, or any other superstar group of the 1980s . . . and beyond. The core team of over 100 hauled 32 tons of equipment across four continents, flying 3,787,000 miles. All the tickets for the tour, combined, alone weighed 5,224 pounds.

Mark Ravitz designed the impressive stage set; he'd previously worked with Bowie on the *Diamond Dogs Tour*. Bowie's close musical associate Carlos Alomar was the lead guitarist and musical director. The tour logo artwork was a collaboration between Bowie and Mick Haggerty (known for his work with Supertramp, the B52s, and especially the sharks-in-the-lawn cover for Ronnie Montrose's *Gamma*).

Serious Moonlight visited 16 countries in Europe, North America, Japan, Australia, New Zealand and Southeast Asia for a total of eight legs and 96 shows over eight months. More than 2,600,000 tickets were sold, and 2,208 songs played.

The Montreal Forum performance on 13 July was broadcast to many more millions worldwide. *Serious Moonlight*, the concert video from the tour, was released in 1984 and on DVD in 2006.

A lavish coffee-table book, *David Bowie's Serious Moonlight: The World Tour* was published in 1984. In his introduction, Bowie said his memories of the tour were vast, from 'American ecstasy and depressions, European familiarity and isolation, and Eastern promise and suspicion'.

TOP, LEFT
Let's Dance,
promo poster, 1983

BOTTOM, LEFT
Serious Moonlight tour,
laminate pass, 1983

MIDDLE, LEFT
HBO show, poster, 1983.
© David Bowie under licence

TOP, RIGHT
Serious Moonlight tour, promo
poster, 1983. © Stenton S.A.

In 1987, Bowie embarked on the *Glass Spider Tour* in support of an album he subsequently would nearly disavow, *Never Let Me Down* (1987), that was emotionally uncommitted hard rock with an industrial/techno dance edge.

Bowie, understandably, was somewhat overexposed as a superstar by this point. Yet the tour itself was the most ambitious of Bowie's career, actually surpassing the previous *Serious Moonlight Tour* of 1983 in terms of audience figures and number of performances.

Preceded by nine promotional press shows, it's been estimated a total of three million people attended 86 concerts over six months in Europe, North America, Australia, and New Zealand. Eight performances alone were given in Sydney, Australia followed by another four in Melbourne.

Peter Frampton, a former superstar in his own right, joined musical director Carlos Alomar as co-lead guitarist in the studio and on the tour. Five dancers appeared on stage for almost the entire duration of each highly elaborate concert.

A video album from the tour, later reissued as a DVD in 2007, was *Glass Spider* (1988,) which documented the performances at the Sydney Entertainment Centre.

*Tonight (*1984) capitalised on the *Let's Dance* album and tour success, but was something of a rushed, even a bit insincere project. Nevertheless it included the Top 10 single 'Blue Jean' which became a stirring video cementing Bowie's long-held interest to interweave music and drama. That video, a 22-minute short film titled *Jazzin' for Blue Jean* and directed by Julien Temple, would win Bowie his only Grammy to date as the 'Best Short Form Music Video'.

The title tune was a collaboration with Tina Turner, and 'Dancing with the Big Boys' once again matched up Bowie with Iggy Pop. It also had a pair of dance version revisions of 'Neighborhood Threat' and 'Tonight', older songs which Bowie wrote with Iggy for his 1977 album *Lust for Life*.

The following year, 1985, Bowie performed several of his greatest hits at Wembley Stadium for Live Aid.

RIGHT, TOP
Glass Spider tour,
laminate pass, 1987

BOTTOM, LEFT
Glass Spider tour,
laminate pass, 1987

BOTTOM, RIGHT
Glass Spider tour,
laminate pass, 1987

Contemporaneous with Bowie forming a hard-rocking (but never fully fan-embraced) new band, Tin Machine, that spawned its own albums and short tours, *Sound + Vision* (1989) was Bowie's long-awaited box set compilation released on Rykodisc, originally in an LP-size box containing LPs, audiocassettes, or CDs.

It's something of an anomaly among box sets because it contains few of Bowie's greatest hits in their original form, instead (in many cases) opting for demos and live versions. Originally it had been intended as a special 'teaser' that would accompany the Rykodisc reissue campaign covering Bowie's entire output from 1969 to 1980.

The set won the 1990 Grammy for Best Album Package, with photography by Roger Gorman.

The tour that followed, Bowie's *Sound + Vision Tour* (1990) actually surpassed the previous *Serious Moonlight* and *Glass Spider* tour statistics by visiting 27 countries throughout Europe, North America, Japan, and South America, lasting seven months, with 108 performances.

For the ten performances in the United Kingdom alone, it was estimated that more than 250,000 fans attended. Several shows were broadcast on television and radio in their respective countries.

Prior to the tour it was announced that the set list for any given performance on the tour would be largely determined by the most popular titles logged by Bowie fans in a telephone poll, with a further declaration that thereafter Bowie would never perform his greatest hits again. But these radical ideas were never fully carried forward, in part because the process for creating 'independent choice' was hacked.

LEFT
Sound + Vision tour
laminate pass, 1990

RIGHT
Sound + Vision tour
programme, 1990

Black Tie White Noise (1993) was Bowie's first solo release in the 1990s, which followed his experiment with Tin Machine. It marked the beginning of a post-modern era for Bowie, who was newly inspired having just married supermodel Iman (notably, the album's first track was 'The Wedding' and its last 'The Wedding Song').

The title track was inspired by the 1992 Rodney King riots in Los Angeles by way of including hip-hop elements and a duet with singer Al B. Sure!

The album was extraordinarily rare until its re-release on CD later in the 1990s (and again on its tenth anniversary in 2003) because the LP's record label, Savage, suddenly went bankrupt upon its introduction.

Bowie's name on the album may actually have been an affront to some purist fans who were distrustful of his pop-style musical allegiances stemming from his success with *Let's Dance*. To test that theory, anonymous club remixes of the album track 'Pallas Athena' were released to American dance clubs and became hugely popular 'most requested' tracks.

An odd sidelight: on the Indonesian release, Bowie sang 'Don't Let Me Down & Down' in Indonesian.

RIGHT
Black Tie White Noise,
US press ad, 1993

BELOW
Outside tour,
laminate pass, 1995

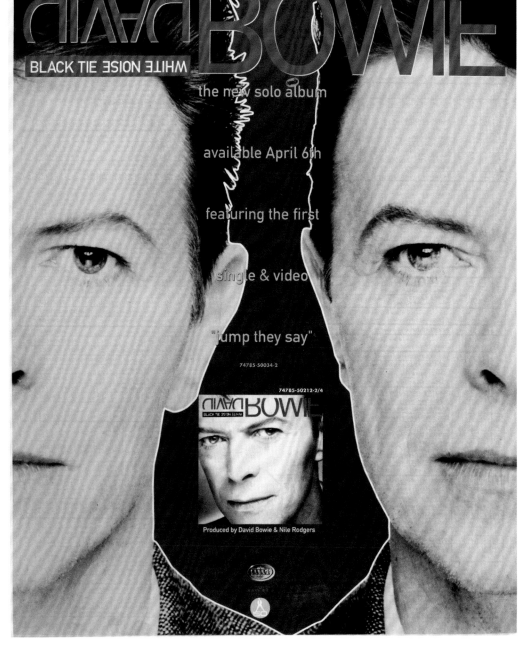

Outside (1995) is a David Bowie quasi-industrial-sounding album portraying a non-linear cyberpunk version of the year 1999 during which an un-named North American government creates a new agency to investigate the phenomenon of Art Crime.

In this supposed future, mutilation of bodies and murder itself has become an art craze. Detective Nathan Adler, the principal protagonist, has the task of deciding what constitutes a legally acceptable artistic acts and what is simply (art) crime. No more odd than any previous concept album, *Outside* was well received by Bowie's mainstream fan base. Brian Eno co-produced and performed as synthesist.

The album's graphics were conceived by Bowie and designer Denovo. The front cover painting was 'Head of DB', an acrylic on canvas (1995) by Bowie himself.

In September, 1995 Bowie began the *Outside* tour. Sixty-eight shows were performed in North America and Europe, which concluded in early 1996.

In a controversial move, Bowie chose Trent Reznor's Nine Inch Nails (NIN) as his co-headlining US tour partner. NIN appeared on stage first, always playing an equal amount of stage time as Bowie.

As the crew changed sets behind a large backdrop, NIN would play several Bowie compositions ('Subterraneans', 'Hallo Spaceboy' and 'Scary Monsters') followed by two NIN songs with Bowie ('Reptile' and 'Hurt').

A subsequent UK/European tour leg with Morrissey as the opening act received an equally mixed reception from the fans, with Morrissey dropping out after refusing to segue his set into Bowie's in the way that NIN had done.

A Bowie-solo summer 1996 festival tour that followed (including shows in Russia and Israel) was better received due to the lack of a split ticket between two equally fervent but diametrically opposed fan bases. The Kremlin Palace Concert Hall performance was broadcast nationwide on Russian state television.

When asked if *Outside* was influenced by Nine Inch Nails' well-acknowledged admiration of his career's work, the ever-forward, ever-inscrutable Bowie answered, 'No, [this time] I was influenced by a [new] Swiss band called the Young Gods.' The Young Gods also toured with Bowie through Europe during the promotion for *Outside*.

On 17 January, 1996 David Bowie was officially inducted into the Rock and Roll Hall of Fame at the institution's eleventh annual induction ceremony.

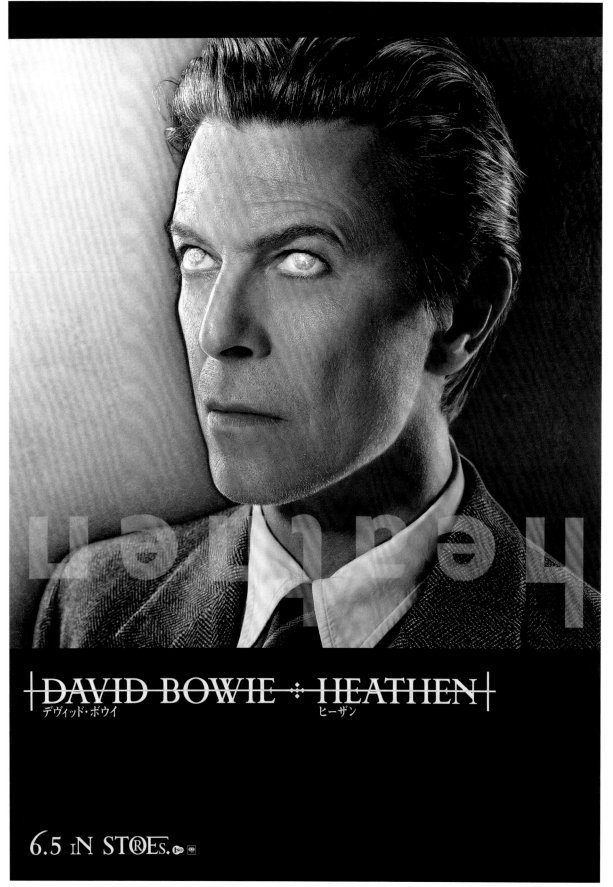

In many circles *Heathen* (2002) is regarded as Bowie's return to mainstream success in the US market, as it was his highest charting album (No 14) since *Tonight* (1984) and earned some of his strongest reviews since *Scary Monsters* (1980). It marked the return of record producer Tony Visconti who had co-produced several of Bowie's all-time classic albums.

Originally Bowie had, in 2000 – 01, recorded what was to be an unreleased album, *Toy*. Some of its tracks appear on *Heathen*. The album features guest appearances from Who guitarist Pete Townshend.

Heathen was supported by the 2002 *Heathen* tour of Europe and North America, a total of 36 shows. This tour was notable for its performance of all the songs from *Low* (1977) and an unusual hopscotch geographical path.

The final seven shows in North America included the first five in each of New York's five boroughs, dubbed by Bowie the *New York Marathon Tour*. The stops included the Music Hall at Snug Harbor (Staten Island); St. Anne's Warehouse (Brooklyn); the Golden Center at Queens College (Queens); Jimmy's Bronx Café (the Bronx), and the Beacon Theater (Manhattan).

As 2003 dawned, a report in the UK's *Sunday Express* named Bowie as the second-richest entertainer in the UK (behind Sir Paul McCartney).

LEFT

Heathen, Japanese
promo poster, 2002

RIGHT

Laminate passes,
2000

ABOVE
Reality tour, laminate
pass, 2004

BELOW
Heathen tour, laminate
pass, 2002

Reality (2003) is David Bowie's latest album to date. It was critically acclaimed upon release, many comparing it to *Scary Monsters* (1980).

Some of *Reality's* lyrics deal with Bowie's prescient view of himself as being a more 'mature', older person, as in the songs 'The Loneliest Guy', 'Days' and 'Never Get Old'. Unusually for Bowie, the recording sessions were held in New York City, with Tony Visconti again co-producing.

The album was supported by a five-leg tour across Europe, North America, New Zealand, Australia and Asia (a total of 113 shows at the point where it was cancelled due to Bowie being felled by a heart attack, diagnosed as an acutely blocked artery likely brought on by years of smoking cigarettes).

Bowie sought to perform with less focus on elaborate staging and more focus on the band members. The musicians were unusually free to move about the stage with wireless amplification.

The set list included tracks spanning Bowie's 30-plus years, from *The Man Who Sold the World* (1970) through to *Reality*. There was some focus on tracks from the albums released since the *Earthling* world tour (1997), which included *Heathen* (2002) and *Reality*. There were no selections from *'hours . . .'* (1999), *Space Oddity* (1969), *Pin Ups* (1973), or *Never Let Me Down* (1987), the albums produced with Tin Machine at the close of the 1980s or *Black Tie White Noise* (1993).

'Ziggy Stardust' (1972) was nearly always the finale of each concert. Bowie also took care to include the most popular tracks from *Let's Dance* (1983) and *Tonight* (1984). 'Rebel Rebel' (from *Diamond Dogs* – 1974) opened most of the shows. In 2004, Bowie released a live DVD entitled *A Reality Tour* of his performances in Dublin the previous November, again notable for the career breadth it showcased.

The cover art to *Reality* was handled by Rex Ray, a designer associated with the San Francisco production company Bill Graham Presents, who had designed over 100 concert posters for bands including the Rolling Stones, Patti Smith, REM, Björk, U2, and Radiohead. Ray had handled several BGP Bowie posters and the first project Bowie himself invited Ray to work on was the 30th anniversary, limited-edition print of *Ziggy Stardust*. Then, he helped

Bowie's staff launch the musician's official website, Bowienet (www.davidbowie.com), which in turn led to his work on *'hours . . .'* (1999)

Rex Ray (interviewed by *RockPopGallery News* in 2008) said, 'I'd worked with many musician "divas" over the years and was braced for a difficult process. Part of being a designer is navigating the collaborative process through each individual's personality while maintaining some measure of self in the process. Sometimes those personalities can be a handful. Some projects go quite smoothly while some projects are a constant negotiation, if not a downright battle. The *'hours...'* project, however, went very smoothly. Working with Bowie's people and the art departments at Virgin Records, we put out the designs for the album package and the singles, as well as all of the promotional POP (point of purchase) materials.

'I'm my own worst critic. Ten years on and I still think the *'hours...'* package is a bit overwrought. The first and only songs I heard while working on the project were rockers, upbeat, and the previous album, *Earthling* (1997) was very upbeat, so that was the visual direction I took. The finished music on the album was more subdued and I would have used a lighter hand had I known the introspective and reflective nature of the whole album. This isn't to say I'm not proud of the finished piece. I think it holds up quite well.

'In 2000, I designed a bonus CD that was included in the collected BBC sessions release *Bowie at the Beeb* (2002), and the first 'collage' Bowienet poster was resurrected for use on the *Best of Bowie* (2002) greatest hits CD and DVD packages.

'Then, also in 2002, Bowie sent me some images as directional material for his next album, *Reality*. Initially, David asked if I knew any illustrators who worked in an anime style who could produce a Bowie character for use on the cover. I asked if I could take a shot at it and developed the character that eventually appeared on the final package.

'While keeping the anime style in mind, I also used the paintings of Margaret Keane as a reference and worked endlessly developing a face and hairstyle for the figure. I can't begin to describe the enormous responsibility of coming up with

a hairstyle for David Bowie. The *Reality* package was a collaborative project between Bowie, renowned British designer Jonathan Barnbook, and myself [Editor's note – Barnbrook had designed the spooky-eyed cover for the *Heathen* record]. I developed the illustrations and imagery and Barnbrook created the amazing typography that appeared on the final package.

'When *Reality* was released, the fans hated the cover. While visiting assorted websites, I was able to grasp people's reaction to the cover and, generally, it wasn't favourable. Bowie has a long history of using a photo of himself on his covers and this marked the first time that no photo had appeared. From my standpoint, I love the cover and think it's among my best. I was challenged to work in a specific style I hadn't worked in before and I'm quite proud of the results. There's no better surprise than surprising oneself.

'Looking back, I remember staring at those amazing covers of Bowie's *Aladdin Sane* and *Diamond Dogs* albums and thinking "I'd like to design covers like this some day" and, some 30 years later, that wish had come true. It was as though I'd reached my goal and I couldn't think of anything else I wanted to do in the field of graphic design. I could also see the writing on the wall – the same writing the music industry can't quite seem to understand.

'Album covers – at least the way I appreciate them – are becoming things of the past. The demands of marketing departments and the disappearance of the actual physical object of an album or CD led me to the conclusion that it was time to move on.

'I still do graphic design work for a few long-time clients and old friends, but I'd rather be painting. After that great run with Bowie, I began phasing out the graphic design work I'd been doing for so many years, not taking on any new clients or large projects and began focusing on the finer, more personal artwork that sustains me today.

'However, if by some chance the phone rang tomorrow and it was Mr Bowie asking for my design services, I'd happily hop on that old horse again.'

On 8 February, 2006, David Bowie was awarded the Grammy Lifetime Achievement Award.

6 ALICE COOPER

ALICE COOPER

The remarkable Alice Cooper has such an instantly recognisable image that he has rightly become one of rock's greatest icons. Cooper was actually born Vincent Furnier, changing his name to Alice Cooper at the time of *Welcome to My Nightmare* (1975). Prior to that, Alice Cooper was the name of the band, and it was as a band that the Cooper style first erupted.

While *Love It to Death* (1971) yielded 'I'm Eighteen' and was notorious for its finger-from-the-pants cover, it was the snake on *Killer* (1971) that became the first graphic to draw millions of kids to the unique Cooper brand of shock-and-awe. Over the next six years of LPs, with those albums backed by defiantly brazen stage shows, the band would throw open the doors to the new school of 'shock rock' and dare parents and politicians to object – which they frequently did. The graphics chosen to support each wave of new outrageousness would drive home the message very effectively.

Cooper himself art-directed *Killer*. The boa constrictor on the cover was Kachina, drummer Neal Smith's pet. Bassist Dennis Dunaway did the lettering using his left hand (he's right-handed) because it gave the words an eerie look. The tour that followed was the first to feature the infamous gallows (built by the Warner Bros. movie-set prop department). It was also when Cooper replaced his earlier 'spider' eye make-up with the notorious 'clown' look, giving him a much darker, more evil character.

Craig Braun (also famous for his package concept for the Rolling Stones' *Sticky Fingers*) art-directed the cleverly-opening desk art for *School's Out* (1972). The album title came from a line in *Angels in Disguise* – an old Bowery Boys movie – where the term 'School's out' was meant to convey 'Hey, wise up!' The song of course was more literal in its message and became Cooper's great break-out hit – bolstered, no doubt, by the salaciousness

of the girls panties stretched right over the album's inner sleeve.

Billion Dollar Babies (1973) portrayed the band at its commercial apex during their 1970s heyday. Here they perfected their concept of an entire unified act – songs, album graphics, and a stage show replete with costumes and props. The album packaging was handled by Pacific Eye & Ear, the first of four-in-a-row for that studio (they would do two more later on, as well). David Bailey took many of the photos, with the album also featuring shots by well-known rock photographer Lynn Goldsmith. The baby on the cover was a girl by the name of Lola Pfeiffer, the daughter of Carolyn Pfeiffer, who handled Alice Cooper's PR in the UK.

The *Billion Dollar Babies* show featured a lavish stage set weighing eight tons with a centre component 25 feet high. Cooper's performance included a variety of mock depraved and sadistic acts before one of several costume changes saw him appear in a black leather outfit, caressing his trademark snake for 'Sick Things'. 'I Love the Dead' commenced as a cloth-covered guillotine was wheeled out, with the magician The Amazing Randi playing the hooded executioner. Alice placed his neck on the block and Randi yanked the rope, leaving Alice's body twitching on the platform. The band came down from their platforms and Randi pulled out the severed head and held it aloft. Show over! Alice was punished for his crimes.

Of course they were all back a few minutes later for

'School's Out', with Alice in his now-traditional top hat, tails, and cane as hundreds of balloons burst and fake money showered the audience.

Drew Struzan, then with Pacific Eye and Ear, painted the cover for *Welcome to My Nightmare* (1975). It was named one of the Top 100 best album covers of all time by *Rolling Stone*. Struzan learned early on in his distinguished career that flexibility was key to his work, as publicity departments and musicians often changed their opinions, viewpoints, and needs throughout recording and post-production.

Struzan commented: 'There is one thing that sets album art and poster work apart from other illustration projects. The demand to change it, change it, and change it again tends not only to screw with the art and the artist, but it can become technically impossible for the artwork itself.

'Most mediums do not lend themselves to making huge alterations on the art – especially when change must be done hurriedly and repeatedly. My technique was developed – well before computer-assisted design – to accommodate this necessary process that is particular to the music and movie industries.'

Once becoming a solo artist in 1975, Alice Cooper experimented with many different musical styles, the album and promotional graphics following suit, with latter-day highlights including the Neil Zlozower photo used for the cover of *Dragontown* (2001). Zlozower's photo will always remind fans that Cooper was doing the devil's work long before Leatherface, Chucky or Freddy Krueger.

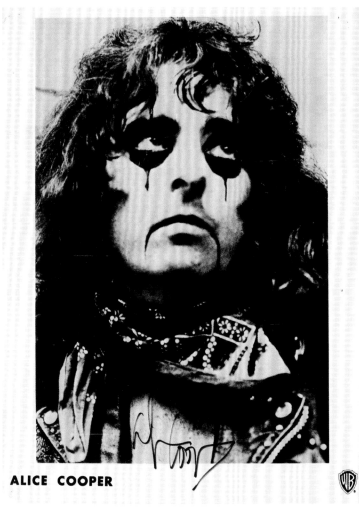

ALICE COOPER

commit yourself!

Find asylum with Alice Cooper on Warner Bros. Records & Tapes

Alice Cooper

TOP, LEFT
'School's Out', signed
promo photo, 1972

BOTTOM, MIDDLE
'How You Gonna See Me Now',
ad (w. Bernie Taupin), 1978

TOP, RIGHT
From The Inside,
promo poster, 1978

BOTTOM, RIGHT
US promo,
poster 1972

BOTTOM, LEFT
'Hello Hurray',
UK press ad, 1973

North Phoenix, Arizona – specifically Cortez High School – was the fertile breeding ground for Alice Cooper, the original band. Cooper himself (then still known as Vincent Furnier), lead guitarist Glen Buxton, rhythm guitarist Michael Bruce, and bassist Dennis Dunaway were pals on the Cortez cross-country team in 1963, and also kicked around in the same art classes. Rocking out was their passion.

'Alice Cooper' was not the first name they chose. Theyhad been called the Spiders and The Nazz until they graduated from high school and learned that multi-instrumentalist Todd Rundgren had also chosen 'The Nazz' as his band's name.

So, the search began again for a name that would be distinctive. Furnier was also convinced that they needed a "gimmick" to succeed. To his everlasting credit, he recognized that other rock bands of the late '60s were not exploiting what he called 'shock-rock'.

Enter the concept of 'Alice Cooper'.

Cooper, nee Furnier, rather swiftly co-opted the quirky name for himself, later admitting that the name change was the most brilliant career move he would ever make.

Alice Cooper: 'We'd found out that another band was called the Nazz. And I said, "We don't have anything to lose, let's do something that no one's going to relate to at all." I could have said "Jennifer Smith" or "Mary Truesdale", but it just happened that "Alice Cooper" came out. It was the very first name that came out. There was something axe-murderish about "Alice Cooper". It reminded me of Lizzie Borden. Alice Cooper – Lizzie Borden. That's got a *What Ever Happened to Baby Jane?* feeling to it. It was feminine, but it wasn't feminine. It had some sort of ring to it, something disturbing.'

Several early gigs in 1968 at the small Cheetah club in Venice, at the western outskirts of Los Angeles, are said to have appalled patrons because of the band's pre-metal 'atrocities' but, despite this, they

did manage to attract the attention of Shep Gordon, who would become their long-time manager. Frank Zappa was also intrigued, and signed them to his new label, Straight Records, and Alice Cooper opened for Zappa on several occasions – including one where famed psychedelic artist Rick Griffin provided a characteristically brilliant cartooned advertising poster.

The band's first album, *Pretties for You* (1969) had a bit of a psychedelic flavour but went nowhere. Likewise, the second album, *Easy Action* (1970), created little action but the third album, *Love It to Death* (1971), locked them in with a great producer, Bob Ezrin, who would become their long-term ally, and earned them some much needed controversy thanks to the album cover and its promotional poster.

Early printings show Cooper's thumb sticking out of his pants, giving the illusion that it was his penis and leading Warner Brothers to censor it (four different versions of the front cover exist on LP).

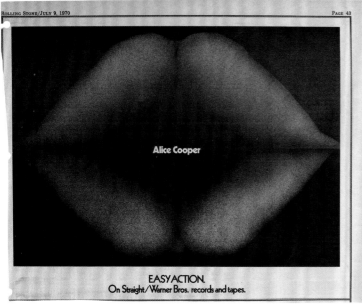

Is *Killer* (1971) the greatest rock album of all time? Johnny Rotten of the Sex Pistols said it was. It always will be the Cooper band's first ear and eye-opener that rock fans of a certain age would call 'classic.'

Killer's music became blood-dripping accompaniment to the group's darkly conceived stage show which by then featured a boa constrictor-hugging lead singer surrounded by cohorts urging on murderous axe-chopping of 'dead babies'.

A gruesome depiction of execution by hanging also rocked the house.

Hanging was on all the Alice Cooper fans' minds because the 'hanging calendar' came free with *Killer*. It was immediately controversial: parents hated it and schools banned it. It was on the walls of the hippest kids' rooms for a full 12 months. Was it intended to provoke controversy? 'Of course!' said Alice, years afterwards. 'Who else was doing anything like that back then? No one!'

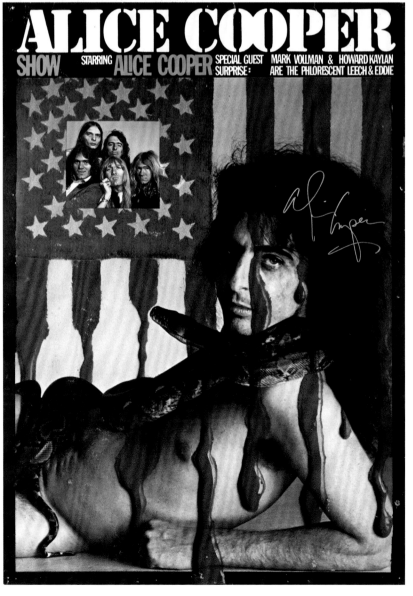

TOP
Killer, promo
poster, 1971

MIDDLE, LEFT
UK press ad,
London, 1972

BOTTOM, LEFT
Killer tour
programme, 1971

BOTTOM, RIGHT
UK tour
poster, 1972

LEFT, TOP
'Under My Wheels',
US press ad, 1971

LEFT, BOTTOM
Killer, US press
ad, 1971

RIGHT
Killer, signed promo
poster, 1971

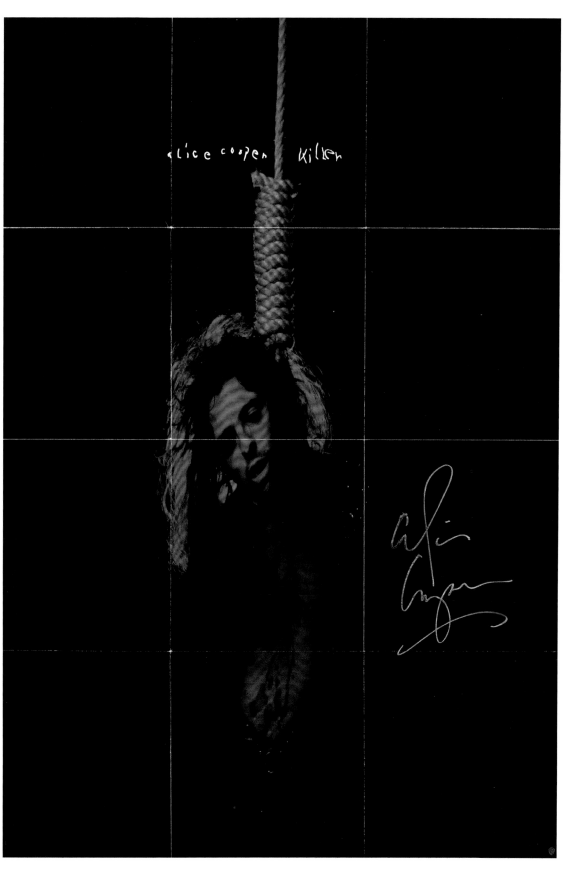

ALICE IN SCOTLAND

John Smith proudly presents
The Alice Cooper Show
Green's Playhouse Glasgow
10th November at 7.30

Tickets £1.50 £1.00 ...
postal applications only plea... m box office
House ... ydsdale Ltd
160 ... Street Glasgow C2

SOLD OUT

'Elected' his smash single

School's Out
Killer
Love it to Death

Released in the hot, sweaty summer of 1972, *School's Out* was Alice Cooper's breakthrough album, peaking at No 2 in the US and selling over a million copies. The title track became a Top 10 hit in the US and a No 1 single in Britain. It remains an evergreen staple on classic rock radio to this day.

Craig Braun designed the original LP cover (he also handled the packaging for the Rolling Stones' *Sticky Fingers*). Uniquely in terms of album design, the *School's Out* LP opened just short of the edge on the front to help make it look like the top of an old school desk. The original knife-carved wooden top hangs in the Orlando Hard Rock Café. The vinyl record inside had a pair of girl's panties stretched over it, although the full original package was recalled because the panties were not flame-retardant.

By the beginning of 1972, Cooper himself was now flaunting his machismo, and the band's travelling circus featured many excellent stagings of filth-mongering and provocation-with-terror, winning over legions of new fans while horrifying equal numbers of parents and pissing off the establishment big-time. British Members of Parliament succeeded in having the BBC ban the video for 'School's Out', but that merely added to Alice Cooper's notoriety.

OPPOSITE

Gig poster,
Phoenix, 1972

ABOVE

Scottish tour,
press ad, 1972

RIGHT

School's Out, promo
inflatable pencil, 1972

In March 1973 *Billion Dollar Babies* appeared, swiftly becoming Alice Cooper's most commercially successful album. It reached No 1 on both sides of the Atlantic and received excellent critical reviews. Four singles were released from the album including 'No More Mr Nice Guy', which reached No 25 in the US charts.

The band ran into some problems by including an oversize 'Billion-dollar bill' with the LP's first release. US law requires FBI approval of reproduction photos of US currency, and the band had to scramble fast. A top-notch graphics crew worked on the package, including Pacific Eye & Ear (graphic concept); Greg Allen (art direction); Hugh Brown (art direction); and three world-renowned rock photographers, David Bailey (cover photo), Neal Preston and Lynn Goldsmith. For the first promo photoshoot, the band had an armoured car deliver one million dollars in actual cash.

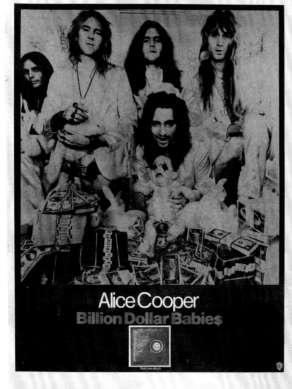

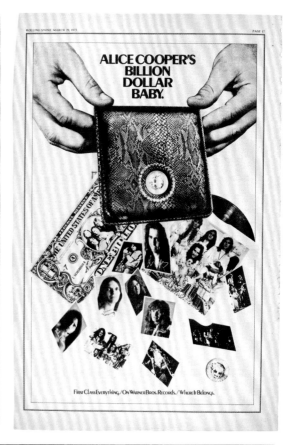

TOP, LEFT
Billion Dollar Babies,
US press ad, 1973

TOP, RIGHT
Billion Dollar Babies,
UK press ad, 1973

MIDDLE, LEFT
Billion Dollar Babies,
press kit, 1973

MIDDLE, CENTRE
Pillowcase from Alice's
Starship jet, 1973

BOTTOM, LEFT
Laminate pass,
1973

BOTTOM, CENTRE
Billion Dollar Babies,
promo mobile, 1973

BOTTOM, RIGHT
Billion Dollar Babies,
tour poster, 1973

OPPOSITE
Billion Dollar Babies
US tour programme, 1973

ALICE COOPER

Muscle of Love (1973) appeared later in the same year as *Billion Dollar Babies* but surprisingly did not have nearly the same impact. It was released just before Alice elected to break up the band's classic line-up, and so Alice Cooper the frontman and 'Alice Cooper' the original group parted company forever.

The LP was boxed in a corrugated cardboard carton, marked in red with a vaguely pornographic message. Clever overprinting also conveyed faux staining at the bottom of the package, as if water or (human?) fluids in the carton had soaked through the box en route to the store.

OPPOSITE
US promo
poster, 1971

LEFT
Muscle of Love,
promo mobile, 1973

RIGHT, TOP
Muscle of Love,
stand-up display, 1973

RIGHT, BOTTOM
Muscle of Love,
US press ad, 1973

alice
cooper
muscle of love

the album in the
plain brown, slightly
greasy wrapper

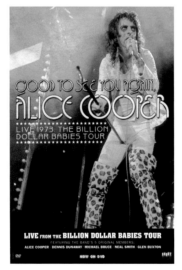

TOP, LEFT
Good To See You Again,
movie poster, 1974

TOP, RIGHT
Good To See You Again,
movie poster, 1974

BOTTOM, LEFT
Good To See You Again,
movie poster, 1974

BOTTOM, MIDDLE
Good To See You Again
DVD, promo poster, 2005

BOTTOM, RIGHT
Good To See You Again,
Mexican movie poster, 1974

While Alice Cooper – the frontman and personality – began appearing regularly on kitschy daytime TV shows such as *Hollywood Squares*, Warner Bros. released *Alice Cooper's Greatest Hits* (1974), which actually performed better in the stores than *Muscle of Love*.

They also put out the band's first feature film, *Good to See You Again, Alice Cooper* (1974), which received a short-lived theatrical run, mostly at drive-in theatres.

The movie mainly consisted of concert footage from the band's *Billion Dollar Babies Tour*, shot in Dallas, Texas on 28 April, 1973. A convoluted storyline and haphazardly introduced comedic sketches made it at times a frivolous experience.

While not a box office smash, the film did show how the Alice Cooper show was developing into almost an 'X-rated' experience, utilizing as it did mannequin stage props dressed out lasciviously with public hair; skewered, blood-drenched baby dolls; and, of course, the Richard Nixon impersonator being beaten up by the band.

If nothing else, it stands as historical proof that Alice Cooper was the first to invent balls-out rock & roll shock and awe.

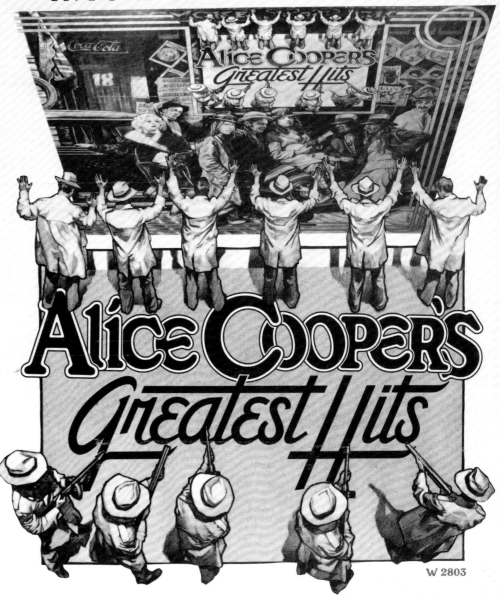

Alice Cooper's first *Greatest Hits* (1974) album was released while the band was on hiatus after its long run of hits and tours. If a fairly standard compilation, it certainly showcased very well their successful amalgam of hard rock, heavy metal, glam rock, garage rock, and shock rock. Plus the cover art was extremely clever, given that no one yet (apparently) had thought of giving a band's greatest hits a Chicago Mob graphics connection.

Welcome to My Nightmare (1975) was Alice Cooper's first solo album under his name alone, the band having been released by then. This was also Alice's first fully-fledged concept album, the songs, when heard in progression, providing an eery glimpse into a child's nightmares – a child (and alter-ego) whom Alice named 'Steven.'

The album also inspired the *Alice Cooper: The Nightmare* (1975) TV special and a worldwide concert tour in 1975 as well as the *Welcome to My Nightmare* (released 1976) concert film shot at London's Wembley Arena later that year.

One of the album's noteworthy songs was 'Only Women Bleed', a ballad about a woman in an abusive marriage, which became one of Cooper's biggest hits

(reaching No 12 on the US *Billboard Hot 100* singles chart in 1975). Etta James, Tina Turner, Lita Ford and Tori Amos all give it their own readings in time. Guns N' Roses used to play it as an intro to their version of Bob Dylan's 'Knockin' on Heaven's Door' in concert.

Drew Struzan illustrated the album cover art. *Rolling Stone Magazine* would later cite it as one of the 'Top 100 Album Covers of All Time.' Horror actor Vincent Price joined Alice's studio musicians (actually Lou Reed's band) to contribute narration and vocal effects. Greg Allen provided the album's overall art direction and design.

The immense success of this project convinced Alice Cooper to continue alone as a solo act.

LEFT
Welcome To My Nightmare,
US promo poster, 1975

TOP RIGHT
Welcome To My Nightmare,
UK press ad, 1975

BOTTOM RIGHT
Sahara Tahoe gig,
US press ad, 1975

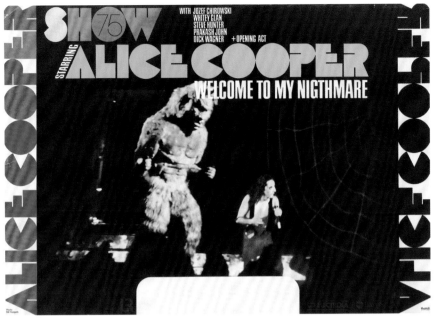

LEFT, TOP
Welcome To My Nightmare
European tour poster, 1975

LEFT, BOTTOM
Welcome To My Nightmare
press ad, 1975

RIGHT, BOTTOM
Gig poster,
Antwerp, 1975

ABOVE
Alice Cooper Goes To Hell,
promo mobile, 1976

BELOW
Gig poster,
Detroit, 1976

RIGHT
'I Never Cry' and tour dates
US press ad, 1976

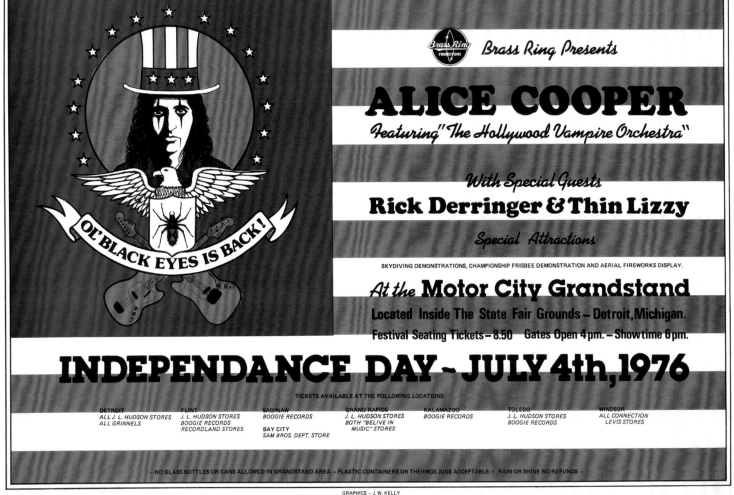

March 1977 began with a tour of Australia and the release of *Lace and Whiskey* that yielded Alice's 'You and Me', a hit that Frank Sinatra added to his own repertoire. Oddly, the previous summer, Cooper had called his tour 'Ol' Black Eyes Is Back', in homage to Sinatra.

Sadly, Cooper's 1977 *King of the Silver Screen* 35-date North American tour was marred to a degree by his alcoholism, a problem that he faced throughout his career but eventually overcame.

TOP
Lace and Whiskey, promo mobile, 1977

MIDDLE, LEFT
US tour programme, 1977

MIDDLE, CENTRE
Lace and Whiskey and tour, US press ad, 1977

MIDDLE, RIGHT
Lace and Whiskey, press kit, 1977

BOTTOM
Lace and Whiskey, promo poster, 1977

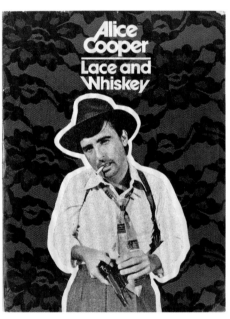

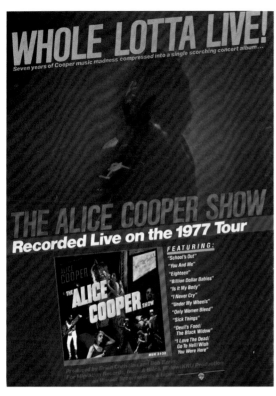

LEFT, TOP
The Alice Cooper Show,
press ad, 1977

LEFT, BOTTOM
The Alice Cooper Show,
UK press ad, 1977

RIGHT
The Alice Cooper Show,
US promo poster, 1977

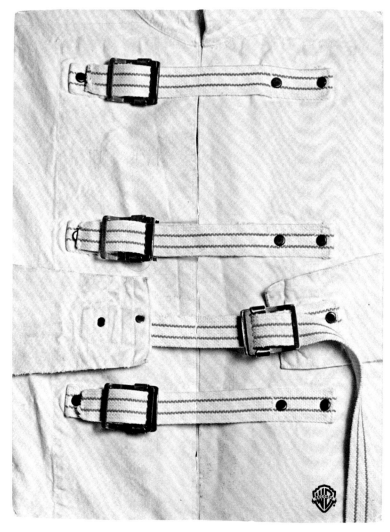

Following Alice Cooper's 1977 concert tour, Cooper had himself hospitalised in a New York sanitorium for treatment of severe alcoholism, during which time the live album *The Alice Cooper Show* was released.

His experience in the sanitarium was the inspiration for his semi-autobiographical album *From the Inside* (1978), which Cooper co-wrote with Bernie Taupin (the career-long songwriting collaborator with Elton John).

Several of the people whom Cooper met in the sanitorium would be incorporated as odd characters in the album's songs.

The subsequent tour's stage show was based inside an asylum and was filmed for Cooper's first home video release, *The Strange Case of Alice Cooper* (1979).

Around this time, Cooper performed 'Welcome to My Nightmare', 'You and Me' and 'School's Out' watched by Kermit and co on *The Muppet Show* for The Children's Television Network.

Cooper concluded the 1970s with the *School's Out for Summer* tour and *Lace and Whiskey 'Part Two' Tour* (both in North America 1978) and the *Mad House Rock* North America tour of 1979.

TOP, LEFT
From The Inside,
UK press ad, 1978

TOP, MIDDLE
From The Inside,
press ad, 1978

TOP, RIGHT
Madhouse Rock US
tour programme, 1978

BOTTOM, LEFT
From The Inside,
press kit, 1978

BOTTOM, MIDDLE
From The Inside, counter
display (open), 1978

BOTTOM, RIGHT
From The Inside, counter
display (closed), 1978

During the early 1980s Alice Cooper continued to release albums and tour but his popularity was on the wane. His first attempt in the new decade was to cop a feel of New Wave, and he released *Flush the Fashion* (1980), considered a hidden gem in his overall catalogue, followed by *Special Forces* (1981).

Zipper Catches Skin (1982) and *DaDa* (1983) were not well received by Alice Cooper fans, and even Cooper himself professes to have no memory of having recorded them, due to his continued alcohol abuse.

Flush the Fashion and *Special Forces* were supported in their years by North American tours. In 1982 Alice Cooper took the *Special Forces* tour to Europe and the UK, but did not tour at all in 1983, 1984 or 1985, when he concentrated on other things, enjoying a period of seclusion.

Alice Cooper's great comeback album was *Constrictor* (1986). It was fueled with some righteous anger, after watching bands try to emulate – not always proficiently – what he had created so splendidly in the 1970s. With new-found inspiration he reached for fresh material designed to turn on a whole new generation of emergent rock fans to the daring music that had long been the hallmark of his career.

These new developments led to one of the most successful tours of the late 1980s – *The Nightmare Returns* outing.

The Nightmare Returns (1987) was a live concert video filmed in Detroit, Michigan on Halloween 1986 towards the start of Alice Cooper's *The Nightmare Returns* world tour, in support of his comeback album, *Constrictor*.

The first stop on the tour, at the Arlington Theater in Santa Barbara, California in October 1986 was the first Alice Cooper show since 1982. The tour brought Cooper back to the UK, where he played three back-to-back nights at the Apollo Theatre in Manchester and three at the Odeon in Birmingham, along with other bravura nights in London and Edinburgh. *The Nightmare Returns* tour continued into 1987, and in the autumn the *Live in the Flesh/Raise Your Fist and Yell Tour* began.

Raise Your Fist and Yell (1987) will be remembered for the songs 'Freedom' and 'Prince of Darkness', the latter actually having played a role in the John Carpenter film of the same name. Cooper had a

cameo appearance as a murderous vagrant. The song can be heard on the Walkman of one of his victims. The album's cover art was inspired by Santa Cruz, California, poster artist Jim Phillips' legendary 'Screaming Hand' graphic long associated with the underground skateboard scene.

Trash (1989) was the follow-up album (produced by well-regarded hitmaker Desmond Child) in the new highly-theatrical mode, this time including guest performances by Jon Bon Jovi, Richie Sambora and Steven Tyler and most of Aerosmith. It became a Top 10 hit in the UK and 'Poison' became Cooper's first Top 10 single since 1977.

The raucous year-long *Alice Cooper Trashes the World Tour* in support of the album began Halloween night 1989 in Los Angeles and ended the next year, again on Halloween night in Los Angeles. It was documented by the video release *Alice Cooper Trashes the World*.

BOTTOM, LEFT

Alice Cooper Trashes The World tour programme, 1989

TOP, RIGHT

Twentieth anniversary press ad, 1987. 'Shep' is manager Shep Gordon

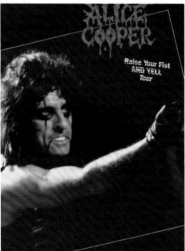

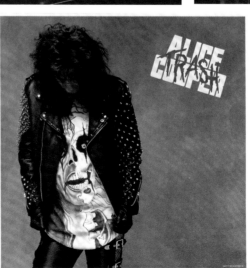

MIDDLE, LEFT

Raise Your Fist and Yell tour programme, 1987

MIDDLE, RIGHT

The Nightmare Returns tour programme, 1987

BOTTOM, RIGHT

Trash, promo poster, 1989

Alice Cooper's *Trash* was a tough act to follow and *Hey Stoopid* (1991) did its best with guest appearances by Slash (of Guns N' Roses and Velvet Revolver), Ozzy Osbourne, Joe Satriani, Steve Vai and Nikki Sixx and Mick Mars (both of Mötley Crüe).

Cooper's alter ego, the character 'Steven' made its appearance once again (after 15 years) on the final track of the album, 'Wind-Up Toy'. Steven had first appeared in *Welcome to My Nightmare.*

Graphically linked references to the songs on the new album were made on the collaged cover art, including a Cobra ('Snakebite'), broken glass ('Dangerous Tonight'), spider webs ('Hurricane Years') and the temptress ('Dirty Dreams').

Other 1990s activity for Cooper included *The Last Temptation* (1994), a concept album revisiting the 'Steven' character. It featured art by British designer Dave McKean, who drew all the *Sandmen* graphic novel covers, and gave rise to a three-part comic book published by Marvel and later reprinted by Dark Horse Comics.

A Fistful of Alice (1997) was Cooper's live album recorded in 1996 at Sammy Hagar's Cabo Wabo club in Cabo San Lucas, Mexico. Slash played guitar on part of the album, returning the favour after Cooper guested on the 1991 Guns 'N' Roses album *Use Your Illusion I.*

Alice Cooper did a brief *Operation Rock N Roll* North American tour in 1991 supporting *Hey Stoopid*, then a quick *Nightmare on Your Street* tour, followed by the official *Hey Stoopid* European Tour that autumn. Just as he had done after the 1982 Special Forces shows, Cooper then took a long break from touring until 1995's four shows in Brazil, Chile and Argentina.

The decade concluded with the release of *The Life and Crimes of Alice Cooper*, a four-CD box set which contained an authorised biography of Cooper: *Alcohol and Razor Blades, Poison and Needles: The Glorious Wretched Excess of Alice Cooper, All-American.* The book was written by long-time *Creem* magazine Canadian editor Jeffrey Morgan.

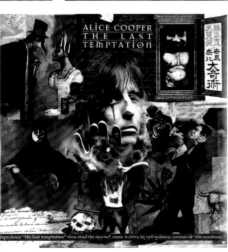
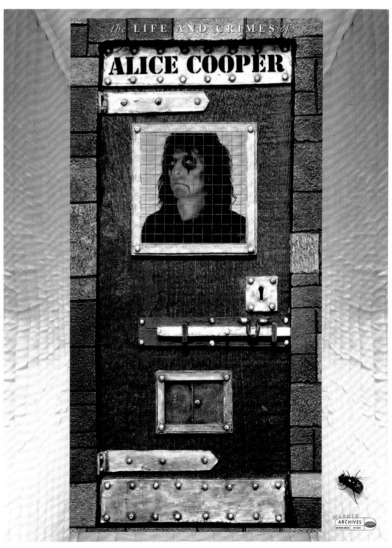

TOP, LEFT
The Life and Crimes of Alice Cooper, press ad, 1999

TOP, MIDDLE
A Fistful of Alice, UK promo poster, 1997

TOP, RIGHT
The Life and Crimes of Alice Cooper, promo poster, 1999

BOTTOM, LEFT
The Last Temptation, poster, 1994. Art: Dave McKean

Brutal Planet (2000) was the 21st studio album by Alice Cooper, beginning the decade in which he turned 60. It was characterized by its ponderous, industrial-metal tone and in-a-dark-mood songwriting wrestling with many difficult, real-life themes appearing on the daily news channels, as Cooper reflected on the brutality of the modern world.

It was followed by an acclaimed sequel, *Dragontown* (2001), described by Cooper as 'the worst town on the Brutal Planet'. Several songs on *Dragontown* were about Hell and who goes there, as opposed to the generally more apocalyptic world of *Brutal Planet*.

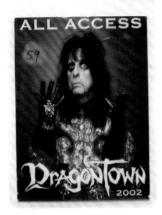

MAIN IMAGE	**LEFT, TOP**
Dragontown tour programme, 2001 – 02	*Dragontown* tour laminate, 2001 – 02
LEFT, MIDDLE	**LEFT, BOTTOM**
Dragontown tour laminate, 2001 – 02	*Brutal Planet* tour laminate, 2000

With *The Eyes of Alice Cooper* (2003), Cooper returned to a more fundamental and fan-familiar garage-rock sound and, with younger studio and road musicians involved, left behind the gloomy 'metal factory' sound with which he had experimented on his previous two albums. That year, he also received a quite worthy (but perhaps unexpected?) music artist's star on the Hollywood Walk of Fame.

Dirty Diamonds (2005) was Cooper's 24th and *Along Came a Spider* (2008) his 25th studio albums respectively. The latter charted at No 53 in America and No 31 in Britain, his best performances since *Hey Stoopid* (1991) and *Trash* (1989).

Cooper's fans loyally continue to support him in large numbers, hence his continued tours of North America, Europe, Australia, and South America with each successive album release.

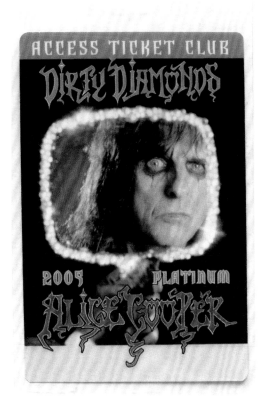

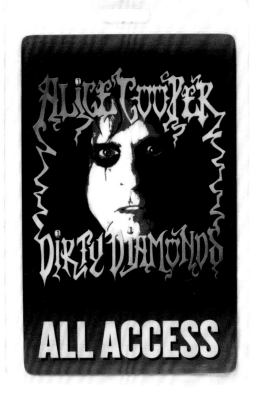

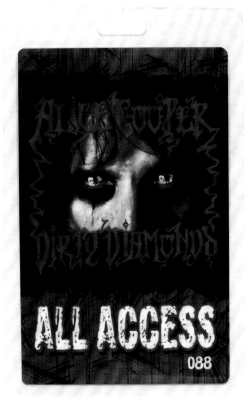

TOP ROW

The Eyes of Alice Cooper tour, laminates, 2003-4

BOTTOM ROW

Dirty Diamonds tour, laminates 2005

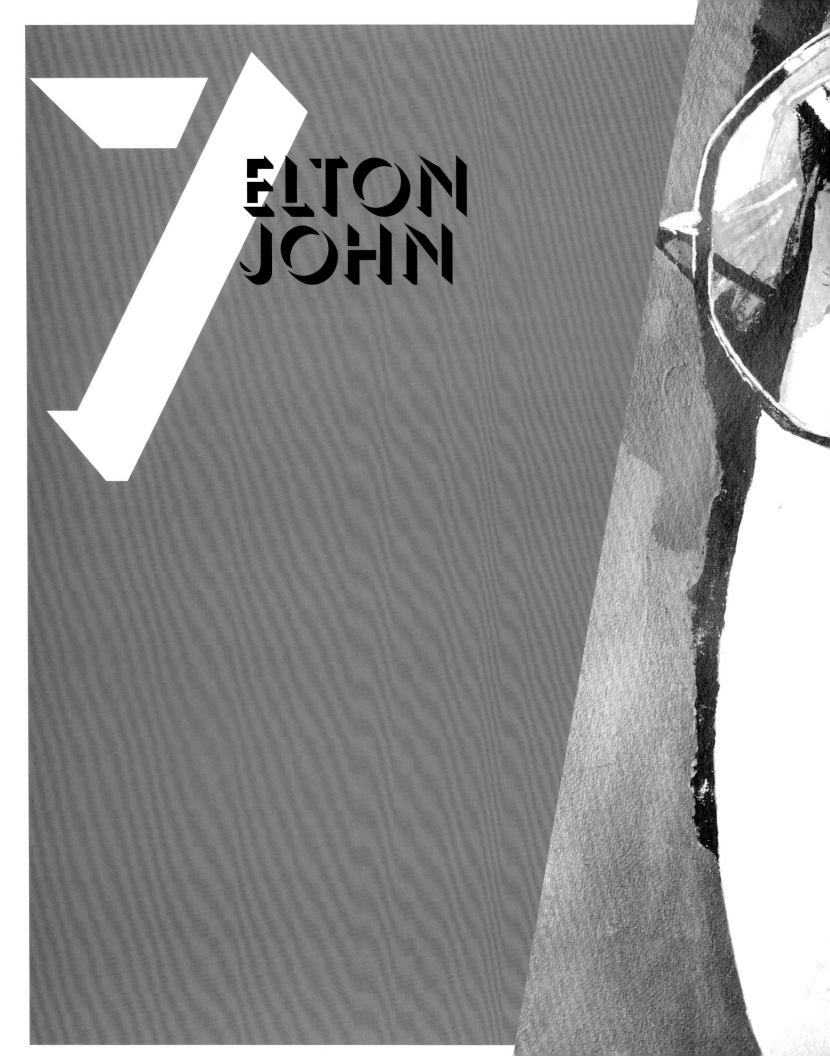

ELTON
JOHN

ELTON JOHN

Sir Elton John and lyricist-collaborator Bernie Taupin's prolific hit-making machine has been virtually unstoppable since 1972. Overall, Elton John has sold nearly 250 million albums and 100 million singles, making him one of the most successful recording artists of all time.

The need for continuous art direction associated with John's stylistic evolution in nearly 30 official albums and decades of concert advertising and merchandised product meant he would become, quite necessarily, one of the most photographed people on the planet.

The consistently strong packaging that has accompanied his career reflects the happy obsession photographers have had with him – not to mention his own delight in being photographed, once he overcame early timidity and stage fright.

The graphic packages accompanying John's work were often striking one-offs: *Don't Shoot Me I'm Only the Piano Player*, *Goodbye Yellow Brick Road* and *Captain Fantastic and the Brown Dirt Cowboy* are probably the highlights. Art director David Larkham (whose designs assuredly played a major role in the marketability of John's hit-streak of albums) headed John's team almost from the very beginning (later joined by Michael Ross and David Costa of Wherefore Art?).

The *Captain Fantastic* artwork was illustrated by the notable Alan Aldridge, who previously edited both of the *Beatles' Illustrated Lyrics* books as well as *Bernie Taupin: The One Who Writes the Words for Elton John* (1976).

John also has been photographed in exemplary fashion for his own album covers and promotional materials by some of the best in the music business, including Ed Caraeff, Chuck Close, and Terry O'Neill (who snapped many informal portraits as well). Photographer/director David LaChapelle collaborated with John on the extraordinary *Red Piano* show that premiered in 2004 at Las Vegas' Caesar's Palace

Considering photography was always necessary to sustain his career, it's not surprising that his eventual enjoyment in being photographed was one reason that led to John and his partner David Furnish together building one of the leading private photography collections in the world.

A 2001 exhibition, *Chorus of Light*, presented key holdings from John's collection at the High Museum of Art in Atlanta (near one of John's homes).

Sir Elton began collecting photography in 1991 and since then has acquired nearly 2,000 superior-quality photographic prints. The collection primarily comprises vintage 20th-century black-and-white photography along with celebrity/musician portraits that include Richard Avedon's head-on portraits of the Beatles and Irving Penn's series of close-ups of Miles Davis' hands.

More recently, photographer Terry O'Neill produced the book *Eltonography*, created as a tribute to the man he calls 'the world's greatest entertainer' and charting the transformation of the former Reginald Kenneth Dwight into stadium rock pianist Elton John.

O'Neill is renowned as the premier portrait photographer of the Swinging Sixties and his early photographs of Elton in 1972 prior to the release of the singer's first Number 1 album *Honky Chateau*, show a quiet young man, but with a hint at the showman within. O'Neill said, 'He was such a great person to photograph – though the amazing thing was he *hated* it at first. Then when he got into [each role] he dropped his inhibitions and just went flat out.'

John said in response to O'Neill's book, 'Turning the pages was like gazing through a window at the most extraordinary and exciting moments of my life. Terry was "court photographer" and I'm so glad he was with us throughout the madness.'

O'Neill countered, 'You can't help but love Elton. He's a genius, an enigma and a star, possibly one of the greatest of all time.'

For you
from Elton John,
Bernie Taupin,
and David Nutter
an exciting new paperback book
with more than 200 photos!
Elton: It's a Little Bit Funny
available at better bookstores.

Penguin
Books

Printed in U.S.A.

TOP, LEFT
Back catalogue,
promo poster, 1975

TOP, RIGHT
It's A Little Bit Funny book,
promo poster, 1977

BOTTOM, LEFT
Rock of the Westies tour,
promo poster, 1975

BOTTOM, RIGHT
Caribou, promo
poster, 1974

Elton John (born Reginald Kenneth Dwight) embarked upon his musical career in the early 1960s. He began playing piano at the age of four, and won a scholarship to the Royal Academy of Music aged 11. After six years, he left with the intention of breaking into the music business.

He first went to work for Dick James Music (a top London music publishing house) where his first responsibilities were as messenger and tea boy. To supplement his income, John also played the piano in bars and clubs and eventually joined up with a band called Bluesology.

Bluesology backed up soul artists such as Doris Troy and Patti LaBelle until around the mid-1960s. During this period John picked up his stage name, a combination of the middle name of Bluesology's singer, Long John Baldry, and the first name of the saxophone player, Elton Dean.

In 1968, an advertisement placed by Liberty Records in the British music magazine *New Musical Express* seeking writers and performers brought John together with Bernie Taupin, the man who would become his prolific – and nearly career-long – songwriting partner. At DJM Music, working on material for singers like Lulu, the pair collaborated as staff song-writers at a hectic pace, with Taupin submitting batches of lyrics every week or so, after having written, sometimes, more than a song an hour. Never together with Taupin in the same room, John would then write the music without changing Taupin's words, often completing a particular song in under half an hour.

In 1969, John released his debut album *Empty Sky*. It received decent reviews but few sales. That same year, he played piano on the classic Hollies single, 'He Ain't

Heavy, He's My Brother'.

John and Taupin brought in fledgling producer Gus Dudgeon and esteemed arranger Paul Buckmaster to achieve a measure of gravitas with the second album, *Elton John* (July 1970). It spawned his first hit single, 'Your Song', which climbed into both the US and UK Top 10.

In August 1970, John gave his first American concert at the Troubadour in Los Angeles. Introduced by Neil Diamond, he received effusive praise from seasoned producers Quincy Jones and Leon Russell. John managed to kick over his piano bench Jerry Lee Lewis-style and performed handstands on the keyboards.

In 1971 *Elton John* was nominated for the Album of the Year Grammy Award. In the same year, he released the album that was to prove his watershed, *Tumbleweed Connection*.

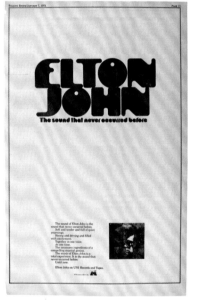

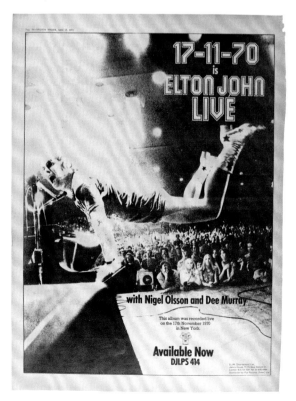

TOP, MIDDLE
Elton John, US
press ad, 1970

ABOVE
Elton John, promo
poster, 1970

TOP, RIGHT
Promotional material for
*Captain Fantastic and the
brown Dirt Cowboy*, 1975

BOTTOM, RIGHT
17-11-70, UK
press ad, 1970

MIDDLE, RIGHT
Rocket Record Company
drinks coaster

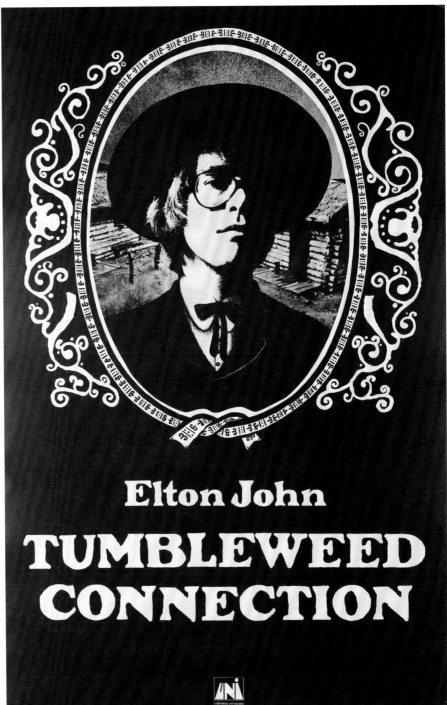

Elton John

TUMBLEWEED CONNECTION

SOUVENIR PROGRAM $1.50

TOP, LEFT

Japanese tour
poster, 1971

TOP, RIGHT

Tumbleweed Connection,
US promo poster, 1970

BOTTOM, LEFT

Tour programme,
1971

BOTTOM, RIGHT

UK tour
programme, 1971

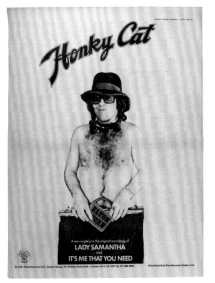

LEFT, TOP

Madman Across The Water,
promo poster, 1971

RIGHT, TOP

'Honky Cat', UK
press ad, 1972

RIGHT, MIDDLE

Madman Across The Water,
US press ad, 1971

RIGHT, BOTTOM

Honky Chateau tour, US
press ad, 1972

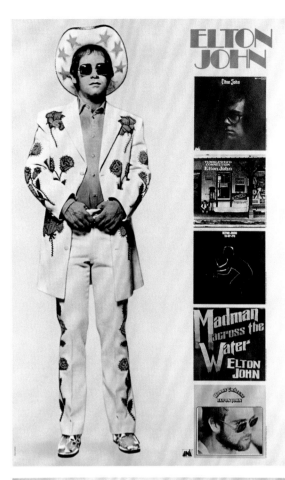

Without the release of even one single, the 'western Americana'-styled *Tumbleweed Connection* (October, 1970) achieved gold status in the US, although songs like 'Burn Down the Mission' would prove to be concert evergreens. It was the second album with Gus Dudgeon at the production helm and the second with David Larkham handling the album-package art direction. Both would become closely associated in those roles, helping to secure John's recording success for many years.

The curiously titled *11-17-70* (*17-11-70* in the UK) (May 1971) was a 40-minute album created from elements of a live radio broadcast on 17 November, 1970.

Ironically, at the time a bootlegger also issued the entire hour-long show and nearly sabotaged the official release. It remains a rare example of an official live recording issued very early in the career of still-to-be-fully-emergent musician.

Madman Across the Water (November, 1971) was John's fourth studio album, but was not the commercial success his label was banking on.

It would take the high-stepping, irresistible, New Orleans-funky *Honky Chateau* (May 1972) and the hits 'Honky Cat' and 'Rocket Man' to earn critical approval by fans and critics alike to set concert stages ablaze around the world.

LEFT, TOP
Back catalogue,
promo poster, 1972

LEFT, BOTTOM
Honky Chateau,
UK press ad, 1972

RIGHT
Honky Chateau, stand-up
display, 1972

If Elton John lit a commercially viable bonfire with 1972's *Honky Chateau* he burned down the house and most of the village with *Don't Shoot Me I'm Only the Piano Player* (January 1973). It was his most direct, pop-oriented album to date.

An impeccably well-woven-together amalgam of classic and contemporary pop styles, the album demonstrated the diversity of the John/Taupin hitmaking team. The singles, 'Daniel' and 'Crocodile Rock' among them, kept the album at the top of the charts for months.

But there was a new development. In effect, in the several years after the release of *Goodbye Yellow Brick Road* (October 1973) Elton John's stage personality began to gather even more attention than his music. He was headed for the cover of *Time Magazine* (indeed, there is where he landed, on 7 July, 1975 as 'Rock's Captain Fantastic').

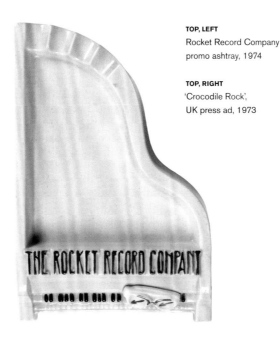

TOP, LEFT
Rocket Record Company promo ashtray, 1974

TOP, RIGHT
'Crocodile Rock', UK press ad, 1973

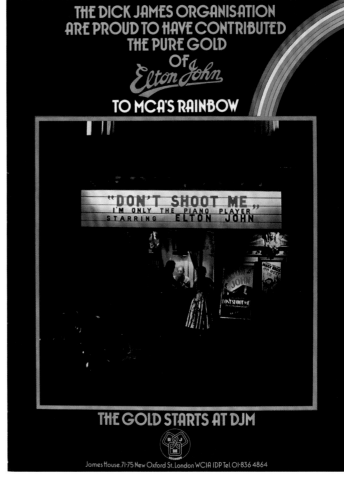

MIDDLE, LEFT
Don't Shoot Me...
UK promo poster, 1973

MIDDLE, RIGHT
Don't Shoot Me...
US press ad, 1973

BOTTOM, RIGHT
Don't Shoot Me... tour, cloth stage pass, 1973

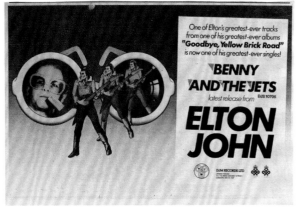

MAMA CONCERTS PRESENT **ELTON JOHN**
9. DIENSTAG
APRIL
20⁰⁰ UHR DEUTSCHLANDHALLE BERLIN

Vorverkauf:
An den Kassen
der Deutschlandhalle
und den bekannten
Vorverkaufsstellen

TOP
Gig poster,
Berlin, 1974

BOTTOM, LEFT
Greatest Hits, US No 1 at
Christmas, press ad 1974

BOTTOM, RIGHT
UK tour programme,
1974

TOP, RIGHT
Fan club
poster, 1974

TOP, LEFT
US 'Thank you'
press ad, 1974

BOTTOM, LEFT
US tour
programme, 1974

Throughout the mid-1970s Elton John's concerts were enormously popular, on a level with with his mega-selling singles and albums.

Midway through 1974, he played and sang on John Lennon's comeback single, 'Whatever Gets You Through the Night', and Lennon kept his promise to John that if the single hit No 1 – as it did – he would join him on stage at Madison Square Garden on Thanksgiving Day. This would prove to be Lennon's last live performance before his tragic murder.

Caribou (June 1974) was John's fourth album to hit No 1 on both sides of the Atlantic. Recorded in Colorado, the album took its name from the Caribou Ranch recording studio in Nederland where John had completed it in a scant two weeks. The apparently rushed schedule had been to accommodate the recording between live bookings. Two singles, 'The Bitch is Back' and 'Don't Let The Sun Go Down on Me' ensured the album's success.

Later that same year, in November, *Elton John's Greatest Hits* was released. The album spanned the years 1970 to 1974 and topped the album chart in both the US and the UK, staying at No 1 for ten consecutive weeks in the US and 11 weeks in the UK.

It continues to be his best-selling album to date, being the first to have received an *RIAA Diamond* certification for US sales of more than 10 million copies.

For seven intoxicating weeks, *Captain Fantastic and the Brown Dirt Cowboy* (May 1975), John's ninth album, stayed at No 1 on the US Pop Albums chart – having shot straight to the top spot on its release.

Captain Fantastic was a concept album that provided a surprisingly intimate peek into the struggles John (the Captain) and lyricist Bernie Taupin (the Cowboy) had in the early years of their musical careers.

The lyrics and the accompanying photos included specific references to times and places in both their lives, unusual as John and Taupin were not normally so intimate with their audience. 'Someone Saved My Life Tonight' was the only single to be released from the album.

Captain Fantastic's successor, *Rock of the Westies* (October 1975) also made its debut at No 1 on the US Billboard album chart, the only two back-to-back albums to achieve such chart success during those years. *Westies* was only slightly less successful in the UK, where it reached No 5 (*Captain Fantastic* hit No 2). Some fans and critics regard *Westies* as John's last 'great' album from his middle period.

To celebrate five years of unparalleled success since he first appeared in America at the venue, John played a two-night, four-show stand at the Troubadour. With seating limited to under 500 per show, the chance to purchase tickets was determined by a postcard lottery. Everyone who attended received a gilt-embossed hardbound 'Yearbook' of the band's history, entitled *Elton John: Five Years of Fun*, art directed by David Larkham.

TOP, LEFT
'I Feel Like A Bullet in the Gun of Tom Ford', US ad, 1975

TOP, RIGHT
Playboy magazine, promo poster, 1975

MIDDLE, RIGHT
Captain Fantastic... UK press ad, 1975

BOTTOM, LEFT
Rock of the Westies, promo poster, 1975

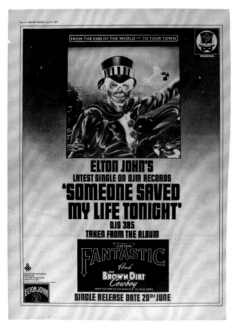

BOTTOM, MIDDLE
'Someone Saved My Life Tonight', UK press ad, 1975

BOTTOM, RIGHT
Rock of the Westies tour, luggage tag, 1975

From April to June, Elton John embarked upon the *Louder Than Concorde (But Not Quite as Pretty)* UK tour, while releasing his second official live album, *Here and There*, in May 1976. This was culled from two concerts: 'Here' from the Royal Festival Hall in London, and 'There' from Madison Square Garden in New York City (with guest John Lennon).

Blue Moves (October 1976), John's eleventh studio album (his second double album and the first of his own under his own record label, Rocket Records) was one of his personal favourites, once more produced by Gus Dugeon. David Costa now took over the art direction duties, with long-time graphics associate David Larkham coordinating.

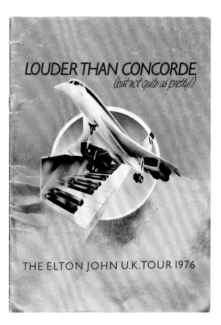

Containing a booklet with lyrics to all its songs, even to the covers of The Beatles' 'Lucy in the Sky with Diamonds' and The Who's 'Pinball Wizard' – plus an illustration for each of those songs as well, *Elton John's Greatest Hits Volume II* debuted in September, 1977.

The first post-*Blue Moves* album that John created without his long-time collaborator Bernie Taupin involved was *A Single Man* (October 1978). He did not write the entire album himself, though many fans misinterpreted the title. The image used on the album's front cover was a photograph taken in Windsor Great Park at the Long Walk that leads to Windsor Castle. It was the first album cover photo of Elton John without his glasses.

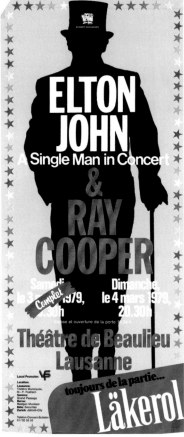

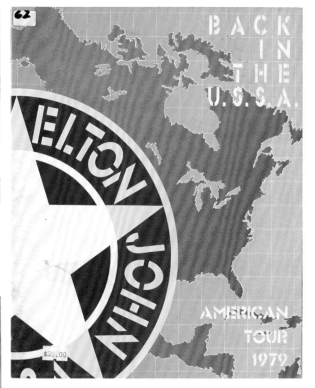

TOP, LEFT
Gig poster,
Lausanne, 1979

TOP, RIGHT
A Single Man, European
tour poster, 1978

MIDDLE, LEFT
A Single Man,
tour poster, 1978

MIDDLE, RIGHT
Back in the U.S.S.A.
US tour programme, 1979

BOTTOM, LEFT
A Single Man,
press ad, 1978

Elton John
The Fox

One of Elton John's more forgettable albums was his thirteenth, *Victim of Love* (October, 1979), about which one critic opined, 'a less than thrilling disco album released at the peak of disco fever'. John only handled the vocals but strangely did not play either piano or any keyboards.

Curious title, that fourteenth album. *21 at 33* (May 1980) refers to it being John's twenty-first album in total (live albums and compilations included); it was released two months after he'd celebrated his 33rd birthday. *The Fox* (May 1981), *Jump Up!* (April 1982) and *Too Low for Zero* (May 1983) followed in due course.

All the lyrics on *Too Low for Zero* were written by Bernie Taupin, the first time since *Blue Moves* (1976) that he had worked with John. It was at the insistence of Taupin that John 'went back to basics' and, in addition to returning to working with Taupin full time, he also reunited with the core of his early-1970s band: Dee Murray, Nigel Olsson, and Davey Johnstone.

The album yielded a strong streak of singles that included 'I'm Still Standing' and the Top 10 hit 'I Guess That's Why They Call It the Blues'.

Generally, Elton John albums were straightforward graphic presentations. The *Too Low for Zero* LP, however, was something of a departure from the norm, featuring a die-cut cover and special inner sleeve. The clever inner inking created a striking effect showing through the die-cut shapes on the cover as splashes of colour.

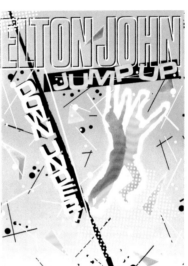

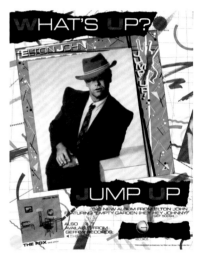

TOP, LEFT
The Fox, promo
poster, 1981

TOP, MIDDLE
Jump Up Australian
tour programme, 1982

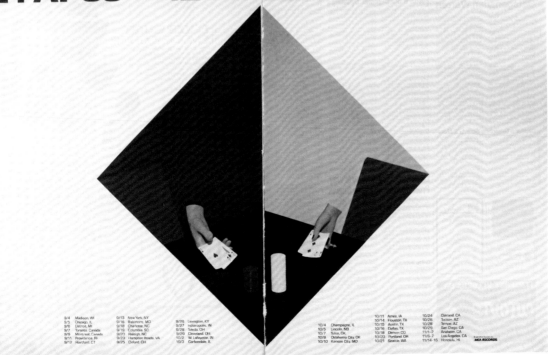

TOP, RIGHT
Jump Up,
press ad,1982

BOTTOM, LEFT
21 at 33 tour,
US press ad, 1980

BOTTOM, RIGHT
Tour luggage tag and laminate
pass, 1980

ELTON JOHN
ICE ON FIRE

NEW ALBUM
ON RECORD, CASSETTE & COMPACT DISC

INCLUDES THESE SONGS

CRY TO HEAVEN	WRAP HER UP
SOUL GLOVE	TELL ME WHAT THE PAPERS SAY
NIKITA	SATELLITE
THIS TOWN	CANDY BY THE POUND
TOO YOUNG	SHOOT DOWN THE MOON

Produced by Gus Dudgeon
Lyrics by Bernie Taupin
CASSETTE & COMPACT DISC CONTAINS EXTRA TRACK 'ACT OF WAR'

LP-HISPD 26 M/C REWND 26 CD 826 2-3-2

WRAP HER UP
NEW SINGLE OUT NOW

ELTON
JOHN

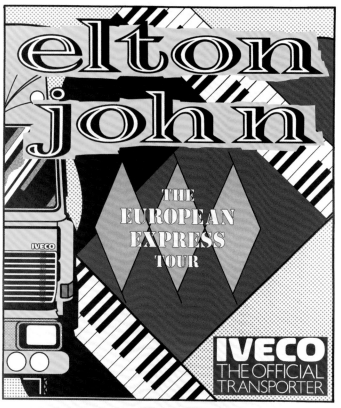

elton john

THE EUROPEAN EXPRESS TOUR

IVECO
THE OFFICIAL TRANSPORTER

Sonntag 20 Uhr
20. Mai '84
Bad Segeberg
Freilichttheater

20. Mai '84

aus dem Hause
phonogram

ELTON JOHN breaking hearts
THE BRAND NEW ALBUM
AND CHROME TAPE
RELEASED SOON ON COMPACT DISC
Includes "SAD SONGS"

ELTON JOHN
EUROPEAN EXPRESS

ACCESS ALL AREAS

ELTON & GEORGE
JOHN MICHAEL

NEW SINGLE
WRAP HER UP

NOW AVAILABLE AS A
LIMITED EDITION PICTURE DISC

EJSP 10

SASSON PRESENTS
ELTON JOHN breaking hearts tour

ACCESS ALL AREAS

TOP, LEFT	**TOP, MIDDLE**	**TOP, RIGHT**
The Night Time Concert video, promo poster, 1984	*Ice on Fire*, UK promo poster, 1985	'Wrap Her Up', promo poster, 1985
MIDDLE, LEFT	**MIDDLE, CENTRE**	**MIDDLE, RIGHT**
US tour programme, 1984	*European Express* tour, promo poster, 1984	*Breaking Hearts*, promo poster, 1984
BOTTOM, LEFT	**BOTTOM, MIDDLE**	**BOTTOM, RIGHT**
'Wrap Her Up' promo poster, 1985	*Breaking Hearts* tour, laminate pass, 1984	*European Express* tour, laminate pass, 1984

Twenty albums in, Elton John was ready for a 'comeback.' His twenty-first studio album, *Reg Strikes Back* (June 1988) also had a purpose – to rail against the critics who had been assailing him for lack of effort. John did not play a grand piano on *Reg*; he replaced it with a Roland RD-1000 digital piano, the anchor of a revamped sound that would last until 1994.

Also in 1988, John performed five more sold-out shows at New York's Madison Square Garden, giving him (at that point) 26 for his career – breaking the Grateful Dead's formidable house record.

In later interviews, John deemed 1989 to be the worst period of his life, comparing his mental and physical deterioration to Elvis Presley's last years. John then auctioned off – netting over $20 million – all of his theatrical costumes and thousands of pieces of memorabilia, a symbolic turning-of-the-page as he was battling drug addiction. But by 1991 he was sober, and in 1992 he established the Elton John AIDS Foundation.

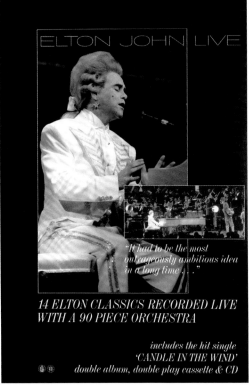

For tax purposes, Elton John recorded *Sleeping with the Past* (August 1989) in Denmark. It featured John's first solo British No 1 single, 'Sacrifice', and the album itself also hit the top in the UK. The title and substance of the album reflected John and Taupin's intention to revisit the style of 1960s R&B icons such as Marvin Gaye, Otis Redding, Sam Cooke, and others whom they admired.

The Very Best of Elton John (October 1990) was his fourth official greatest hits album, this time accompanied by a companion music video compilation.

To Be Continued (November 1990) was John's four-CD/four-cassette box set presenting his career from Bluesology through to mid-1990. The cover art went through some revision when John determined the first version was too

frivolous a presentation considering the changes he was making in his personal life.

The Lion King: Original Motion Picture Soundtrack (July 1994) featured songs from the film written by Elton John and lyricist Tim Rice, including 'Circle of Life' and 'Hakuna Matata'. It would eventually go 10x platinum by 1995.

'Can You Feel the Love Tonight' won the Academy Award for Best Original Song as well as the Grammy for Best Male Pop Vocal Performance.

The 1991 film documentary *Two Rooms* described the unusual writing style that John and Bernie Taupin had used nearly from the beginning of their distinguished collaboration, which involved Taupin writing the lyrics on his own, and John then putting them to music, with the two never in the same room during the process.

TOP, LEFT
Assorted laminate
passes, 1992 – 06

BOTTOM, LEFT
Love Songs, promo
poster, 1996

BOTTOM, RIGHT
To Be Continued,
promo poster, 1990

TOP, RIGHT
Sleeping With The Past,
promo poster, 1989

BOTTOM, MIDDLE
Duets, promo
poster, 1993

elton *john.*
sleeping with the past.

featuring the future classics
"healing hands"
"whispers"
"club at the end of the street"
"sacrifice"

Elton John
Love Songs

17 classic
love songs
on 1 album

SACRIFICE
CANDLE IN THE WIND
YOUR SONG
CAN YOU FEEL THE LOVE TONIGHT
DANIEL
PLEASE
DON'T LET THE SUN GO DOWN ON ME
(WITH GEORGE MICHAEL)

AND MANY MORE

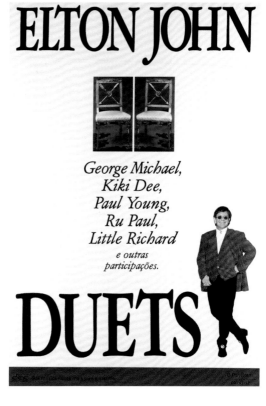

ELTON JOHN

George Michael,
Kiki Dee,
Paul Young,
Ru Paul,
Little Richard
e outras
participações.

DUETS

elton john to be continued...

The Definitive Elton John Collection.
A 67-Song, 5-Hour Musical Journey.

MADE IN ENGLAND MADE IN

ELTON JOHN MADE IN ENGLAND

rocket

ISLAND

314 528 185POS2

ELTON JOHN

THE BIG PICTURE TOUR

Today, 'Candle in the Wind' is most closely associated with Elton John having performed the song as an anguished, heartfelt tribute, live at Princess Diana's funeral service at Westminster Abbey on 6 September, 1997.

In fact it was originally written in 1973 (music by Elton John, lyrics by Bernie Taupin) in honour of Marilyn Monroe, who had died 11 years earlier. It appeared on *Goodbye Yellow Brick Road*, and in 1974 reached only a surprising No 11 on the UK singles charts. Looking back, it is surprising that it was not released as a single in America at the time, considering its iconic aspects. 'Bennie and the Jets' was the track chosen instead.

Blues/rock singer Janis Joplin (whose career ran from 1965 – 71) actually inspired the song's title. Taupin heard a

friend speak of Joplin and utter the phrase 'She was like a candle in the wind.'

Elton John's album *Live in Australia with the Melbourne Symphony Orchestra* (1987) included the song, originally recorded in Sydney on 14 December, 1986 and his record label broke it as a new single. In 1988 this latest version reached No 5 in Britain and No 6 in America, and for many years it was the most popular version played on radio.

On 7 April, 1990, at *Farm Aid 4*, John dedicated his singing of the song to Ryan White, his young friend who was suffering from AIDS. Tragically, White died from AIDS complications the next day.

'Candle in the Wind 1997' or 'Goodbye England's Rose' as many call it, was the third re-make, the lyrics altered by Taupin for the state occasion. It immediately

soared to No 1, becoming John's fourth No 1 career single in his homeland.

There remains some controversy as to whether 'Candle in the Wind 1997' became the biggest selling single of all time, or whether Bing Crosby's 'White Christmas' has sold more (archival records from much earlier decades being imprecise).

However, John's song was the fastest-selling hit of all time in both Britain and America, and spent 14 weeks at No 1 between the two countries. In 1997 alone, it sold 30 million copies, netting $47 million, all donated to the charitable trust established in Diana's name.

Following his heroic public response to Diana's tragic death, and subsequently reflecting upon the grief that he personally experienced, Elton John said he would never sing the song live again.

TOP, LEFT

The Big Picture tour,
laminate passes, 1997

BOTTOM, LEFT

The Big Picture,
promo poster, 1997

BOTTOM, RIGHT

'Candle in the Wind 1997',
promo poster, 1997

ELTON JOHN THE BIG PICTURE

ELTON JOHN

Something About The Way You Look Tonight

Candle In The Wind 1997

In loving memory of Diana, Princess of Wales

All artist and composer royalties and record company profits
from sales of this single will be donated to the
DIANA, PRINCESS OF WALES MEMORIAL FUND

TOP, LEFT
*An Evening with Elton John
Solo,* laminate pass, 1999

MIDDLE, LEFT
*An Evening with Elton John
Solo,* tour programme, 1999

BOTTOM, LEFT
The Road to El Dorado,
promo poster, 1999

TOP, MIDDLE
One Night Only,
laminate pass, 2000

TOP, RIGHT
One Night Only,
promo poster, 2000

BOTTOM, RIGHT
One Night Only,
promo poster, 2000

OPPOSITE
Gig poster,
Prague, 1999

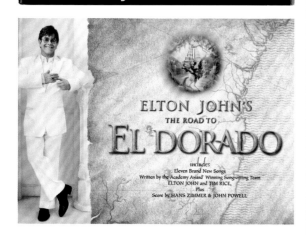

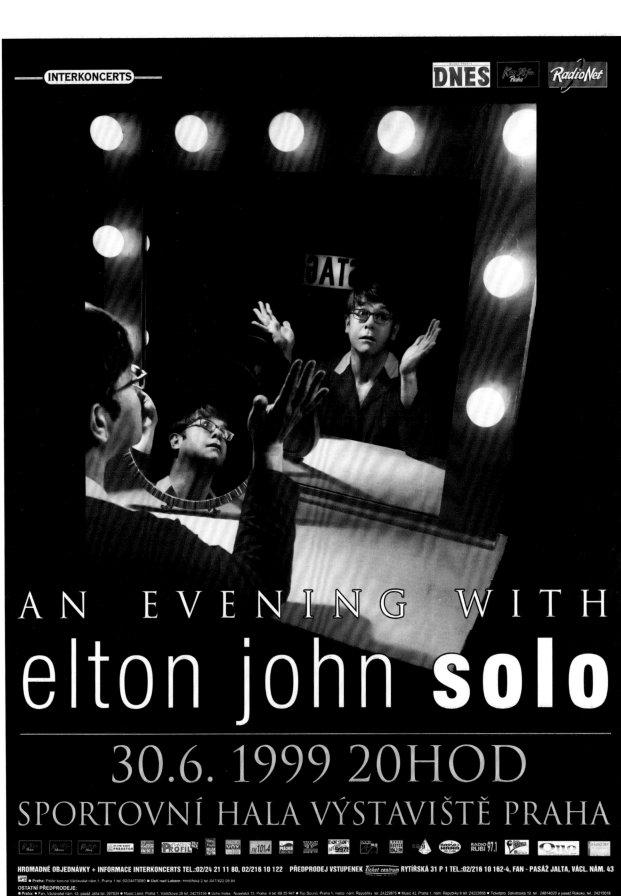

AN EVENING WITH
elton john solo

30.6. 1999 20HOD
SPORTOVNÍ HALA VÝSTAVIŠTĚ PRAHA

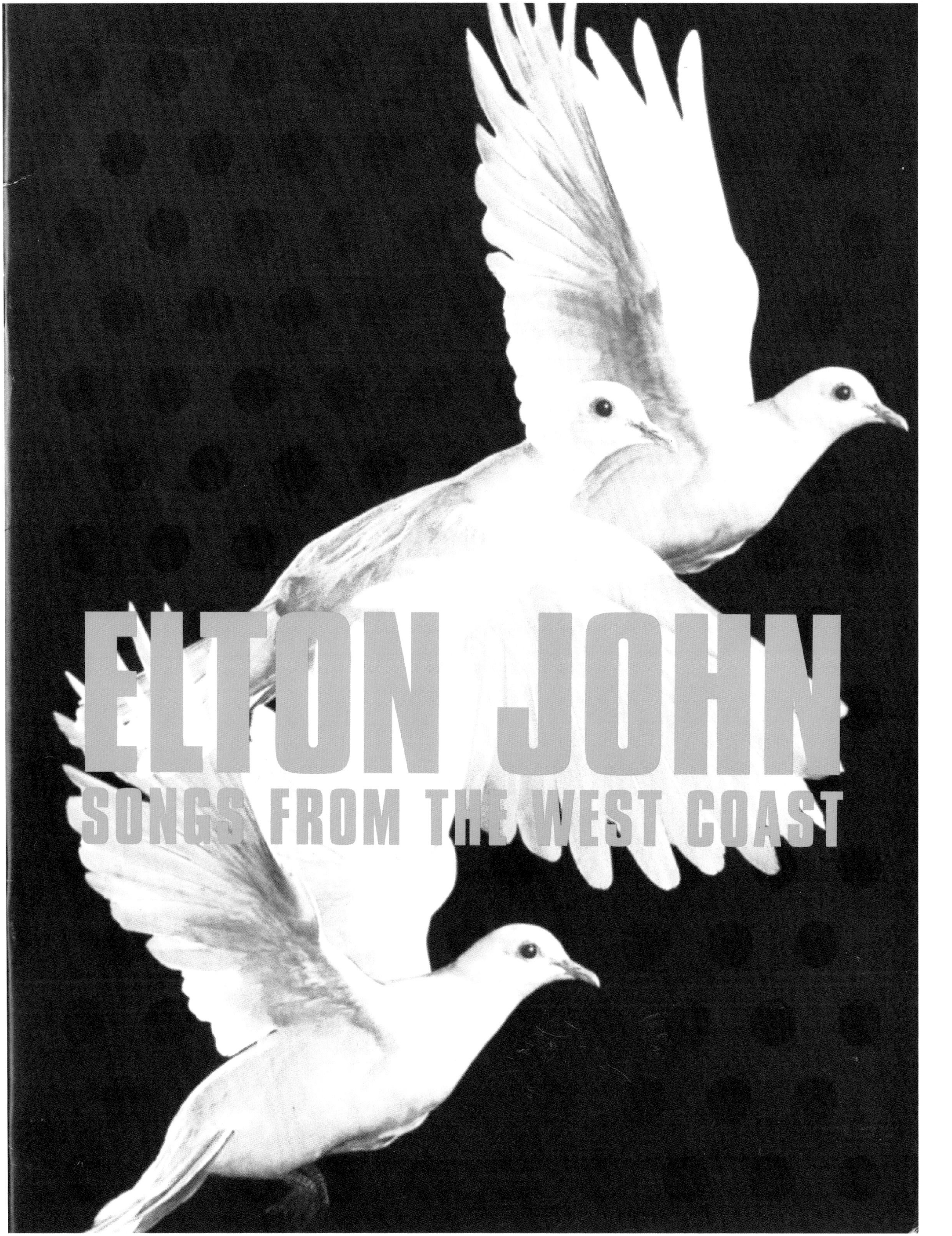
ELTON JOHN
SONGS FROM THE WEST COAST

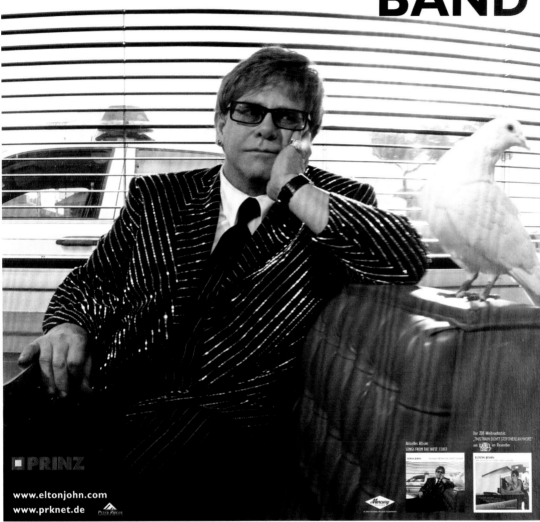

OPPOSITE
Songs From The West Coast
US tour programme, 2001

TOP, LEFT
Gig poster,
Frankfurt, 2002

TOP, RIGHT
Songs From The West Coast
tour, Australian poster, 2001

BOTTOM, RIGHT
Laminate passes,
2002 – 03

Following a successful personal drug rehab in late 1991, John sallied forth once again, releasing over the next ten years The One (June, 1992), Duets (November 1993), The Lion King Soundtrack (July 1994), Made in England (March 1995), The Big Picture (September 1977), Elton John and Tim Rice's Aida (March 1999), The Muse Soundtrack (August 1999), The Road to El Dorado Soundtrack (March 2000), and ultimately his twenty-seventh studio album (another strong collaboration with Bernie Taupin) Songs From the West Coast (October 2001). Drummer Nigel Olsson then also returned to John's band.

The restaurant shown on the album's cover is Rae's Restaurant, frequently used as a location for many Los Angeles-based film shoots.

In October 2003, Elton John announced that he had signed an exclusive agreement to perform 75 shows over three years at Caesars Palace on the Las Vegas Strip. The show, entitled *The Red Piano*, was a multimedia extravaganza on a massive stage featuring extraordinary props and eye-opening video montages created by artist/photographer David LaChapelle. Effectively, Celine Dion shared performances at Caesar's Palace with John throughout the year – while one performed, one rested.

The first of these shows took place on 13 February, 2004. On 21 June, 2008, he performed his 200th show in Caesar's Palace. A DVD/CD package of *The Red Piano* was released in November 2008.

RIGHT, TOP
The Red Piano, laminate passes, 2004 – 07

RIGHT, MIDDLE
Gig programme, NY Radio City Music Hall, 2004

BOTTOM
Gig poster, Gibraltar, 2004

OPPOSITE
The Red Piano, Vegas, press ad. Art: David Lachapelle

London-based photographer Sam Taylor-Wood shot the introspective cover of *Peachtree Road* (November 2004). It was taken at a Southern railroad crossing near the western suburb of Douglassville, outside Atlanta.

Peachtree Road is the northern extension of Peachtree Street, the avenue that in effect 'defines' Atlanta, where Elton John had established one of his four worldwide homes.

On assignment for the album, Taylor-Wood had shot literally thousands of photos throughout Georgia. While she also visited the posh Buckhead district near John's home, she and John subsequently felt Buckhead to be too chaotic and excessively contemporary – not sufficiently 'bluesy' for the album's introspective, contemplative nature.

The album was dedicated to the memory of John's studio producer Gus Dudgeon and his wife Sheila, who sadly had died together in a car crash earlier that year.

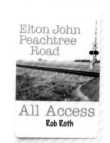

TOP
Laminate passes,
2004 – 05

RIGHT
Peachtree Road, Swedish
promo poster, 2004

BOTTOM
Summer Orchestral Shows
tour programme, 2005

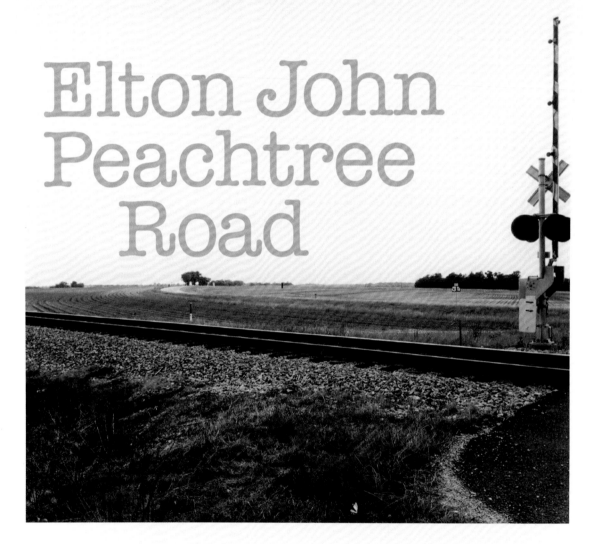

TOP, LEFT
The Captain & the Kid tour,
laminate pass, 2006

TOP, MIDDLE
Australia/New Zealand tour
laminate pass, 2006

TOP, RIGHT
The Captain & the Kid tour,
laminate pass, 2006

BOTTOM
The Captain & the Kid tour
programme, 2006

With his twenty-ninth studio album, *The Captain & The Kid* (September 2006), Elton John once again adopted an autobiographical approach, picking up where 1975's *Captain Fantastic and the Brown Dirt Cowboy* left off. The new album, in similar fashion, portrayed the events in the lives of Elton John and lyricist Bernie Taupin from where they'd started working together nearly 40 years before, reflecting upon their phenomenal success, creativity, optimism, and even the sadness inherent in what has been a nearly career-long partnership.

This is the first Elton John album that has Taupin pictured on the album cover along with John.

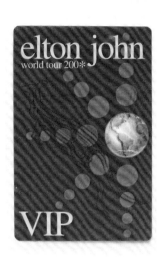

Early in 1997, vestiges of the flamboyant Elton John resurfaced as he threw a 50th birthday party – he was himself costumed as Louis XIV – for 500 friends (the costume itself cost more than $80,000).

March 2007 saw John celebrating his 60th birthday in more ways than one.

He engaged in a joint party with Sam Taylor-Wood (who photographed the cover art for *Peachtree Road*) in London's East End, and then flew to New York to perform at Madison Square Garden for the 60th time (which is a record) to mark his 60th birthday.

John's Madison Square Garden show was a three-hour long and 33-song concert streamed live, called *Empty Garden*. It also inspired a television special called *Happy Birthday Elton!* (the concert began with the audience singing 'Happy Birthday'). He opened with a classic song from his second album, 'Sixty Years On', doubly paying homage to his 60th birthday. The show also featured behind-the-scenes footage from the superstar's private party. In October 2007, the DVD *Elton 60 – Live at Madison Square Garden* and a box set with the live CD was released.

To celebrate his record-setting achievement at Madison Square Garden, a banner marking 'Most Performances by a Single Artist' at the Garden was raised to the rafters and placed within Madison Square Garden's Music Hall of Fame.

TOP
60th birthday show, NY,
VIP pass, 2007

BOTTOM, LEFT
60th birthday show, NY,
All Access pass, 2007

BOTTOM, MIDDLE
60th birthday show, NY,
choir pass, 2007

BOTTOM, RIGHT
60th birthday show, NY,
TV backstage pass, 2007

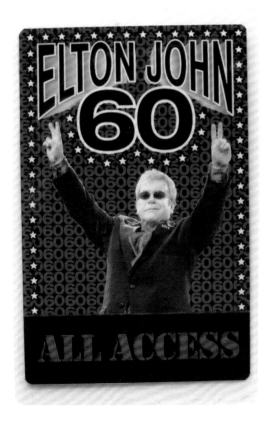

On 1 July, 2007, Sir Elton John performed at the Concert For Diana. He started the concert with 'Your Song' and finished the show with three songs; 'Saturday Night's Alright For Fighting', 'Tiny Dancer' and 'Are You Ready For Love'. He then commenced a European Tour and played at the Live at the Marquee festival in Cork to a rapturous reception.

John then played in September 2007 in Vevey, a small village situated on Lake Geneva, Switzerland. Of this he said: 'The market square in Vevey is one of the most beautiful and magical places in Europe. Since visiting the area by chance in Summer 2003, I have always wanted to sing there. My friend Shania Twain who lives there, convinced me to set up the gig.'

Other memorable concert projects in the decade have so far included the extension of the *Face-to-Face* tours with fellow pianist Billy Joel that have been commercially very successful throughout the world since the mid-1990s.

In deference to Elton John's well-acknowledged support of emerging performing artists, concert promoters sometimes issue commemorative advertising posters that are the work of talented young graphic artists.

The Alaska poster shown here is a case in point. It was designed by Dan Knapp, whose screenprint studio is now based in Philadelphia. It commemorates John's first-ever shows in Alaska.

The promoter asked Knapp for a 1930s WPA-style poster with a bear and a salmon, and Knapp focused their attention around a classic grand piano.

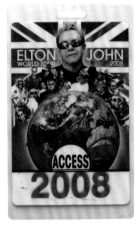

5.28 SULLIVAN ARENA • ANCHORAGE
5.29 CARLSON CENTER • FAIRBANKS
5.30 SULLIVAN ARENA • ANCHORAGE

SOLD OUT

SMG POSTER BY DAN KNAPP

QUEEN

'I thought up the name Queen,' Freddie Mercury was quoted saying, several years before his untimely death. 'It's just a name, but it's very regal obviously, and it sounds splendid. It's a strong name, very universal and immediate. It had a lot of visual potential and was open to all sorts of interpretations.'

Mercury, born Farrokh Bulsara, earned Graphic Arts and Design diploma from Ealing Art College in London in 1969 and was to design the Queen logo, also known as the 'Queen Crest'. The band's first bass player, Tim Staffel (eventually replaced by John Deacon in February 1971), was also a student at Ealing. Guitarist Brian May, then a student at London's Imperial College, first formed the band with Staffel, and placed an advert on his college's bulletin board seeking a drummer. Roger Taylor answered the call.

Mercury built the Queen Crest around the Zodiac signs of all four band members:
• two lions for Leo (John Deacon, born 19 August, and Roger Taylor, born 26 July)
• a crab for Cancer (Brian May, lead guitarist, born 19 July)
• two fairies for Virgo (Freddie Mercury, born 5 September)

The lions support a stylised letter 'Q', with a royal crown inside the 'Q', and the crab is resting atop the 'Q' with flames showing directly above it. Each of the fairies is nestled below a lion, and a great winged phoenix rises from the flames on top of the entire logo.

The original logo was created as a simple line drawing and was first used on the reverse of the first album cover. More intricate and fully-realized colour versions (with further variations by Mercury) were used on later album covers, notably their fourth and fifth LPs, *A Night at the Opera* (1975), and *A Day at the Races* (1976).

Like the Rolling Stones' tongue-and-lips and the

Grateful Dead's skeleton-and-roses, the Queen logo would carry the band's album and tour promotions throughout their career, and was a major unifying presence in their merchandising.

It was when the band created *Queen II* (1974) that they really began to develop a distinctive visual image, due in large part to their meeting photographer Mick Rock, who'd been working with David Bowie. Rock, a 24-year-old Cambridge graduate, was at that point a bigger player in the music business than Queen. The four band members were impressed that Rock had shot covers for Lou Reed's *Transformer* (1972) and the Stooges' *Raw Power* (1973).

The styling decisions made on *Queen II* and on *Sheer Heart Attack* (1974) – for which Rock also handled the cover photo assignment – were genuinely democratic, all decisions depending upon majority approval. But, said Rock subsequently, 'While, collectively, they had a sense of their own destiny, I also realized after a while that when it came to the visual end of things, Freddie's opinion was the strongest. So he was the one I had to zero in on.'

Queen's most distinctively 'arty' album cover was created for *News of the World* (1977). Drummer Roger Taylor, scouring his personal collection of sci-fi comics and magazines, found *Astounding Science Fiction* from October 1953, with cover art by New York-born artist/illustrator Frank Kelly Freas (1922 – 2005) who had, for over 50 years, produced a wealth of excellent work in

advertising as well as book and magazine publishing. He was also known for his many covers for *Mad* featuring 'twisted' renditions of the iconic character Alfred E. Neuman. Queen's Mercury, May and Deacon immediately agreed on Freas' potential, and the artist was soon located.

Freas called his original illustration 'Please . . . Fix It, Daddy'. It portrayed a giant robot holding the body of a man that the robot had just accidentally squished – with the robot looking to his 'daddy' for help. Queen commissioned Freas to re-work the original painting for use on the new record's packaging and the promotional materials that would ensue. Freas replaced the single figure in the robot's hand with the band's four members, all apparently having been killed. Deacon and Taylor were depicted falling away from the robot. Queen loved the final version, and it 'merchandised' terrifically as well.

While Queen worked collaboratively to reach joint decisions on the artworks that supported their music, with imagery largely art-directed by Richard Gray, Mercury would later admit: 'We have the most outrageous rows sometimes. There are so many things that we don't see eye-to-eye about in the group, even as to the titles of our albums. We row about everything, even about the air we breathe. I think that's good because then we get the cream of the crop [from our work]. Artistically, none of us think anything should ever be compromised – rather, everything should be done to perfection.'

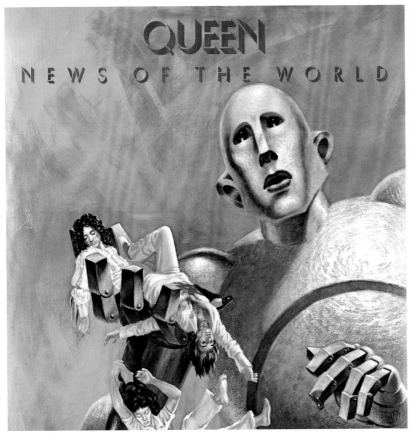

TOP
Queen I, UK press ad with
the 'Queen crest', 1973

BOTTOM, LEFT
News of the World,
promo poster, 1977

BOTTOM, RIGHT
Queen II, UK
press ad, 1974

MELODY MAKER, March 30, 1974—Page 25

Queen AT THE Rainbow

promoted by
MEL BUSH

MARCH 31
SOLD OUT

other dates

new album
QUEEN II EMA 767
OUT NOW
ALSO ON CASSETTE AND CARTRIDGE

including their
HIT single
'Seven Seas of Rhye'

WITH 10cc

ABOVE

Rainbow Theatre, London
gig, press ad, 1974

Queen owes its genesis to two very well regarded recording studios. The band had been playing the London club and college circuit for roughly two years when, in 1971, they had the opportunity to test out the new De Lane Lea Studios where the Beatles, the Stones, The Who, Pink Floyd, and Deep Purple would subsequently record. Despite creating an exceptionally polished demo tape, however, Queen received only a low bid from one label.

Then, in 1972, brothers Barry and Norman Sheffield gave them a major break as they were setting up Trident Studios, where the Beatles would put to wax 'Hey Jude'; George Harrison would record much of the *All Things Must Pass* LP; and where David Bowie would produce Lou Reed's

Transformer. Trident would go on to be booked by Elton John, Marc Bolan and T-Rex, Carly Simon, Frank Zappa, the Yoko Ono/John Lennon Plastic Ono Band, Jeff Beck, Rod Stewart, and the Mahavishnu Orchestra, among others.

For six months Queen was given the opportunity to record using the studio's high-tech equipment (including the UK's first Dolby noise reduction unit, and the first eight-track, reel-to-reel recording deck) but only during the studio's downtime, after the paying artists had left, usually between 3 o'clock and 7 o'clock in the morning.

Queen I (1973) was produced by Roy Thomas Baker. Trident spent nearly a half year attempting to interest a major label with it. When it finally came out in July (but

only under Trident's own self-named independent label), it was barely noticed by the public. Nevertheless, Queen was furiously writing new and stronger material for a second album. They were frustrated by the first album's delayed release, understandably feeling that they had developed well beyond this point, even if their fans were just beginning to discover there was an initial record to purchase.

Brian May was to explain: 'So [by the beginning of 1973] we had matured as a group and had an audience, even before the press caught on to us. I think that actually gave us a better start because we were better prepared for what came next."

August 1973 found Queen back at Trident. This time, they were allowed to book 'normal' studio hours. Generally regarded as a complex and challenging album with multi-tracked vocals, harmonies, and instruments all benefiting from Trident's advanced equipment, *Queen II* (1974) took only one month to record.

Mick Rock was contracted to handle the album cover photography. One noted aspect of the LP was the band's decision to label the two sides 'Side White' and 'Side Black.' One of Rock's most dramatic photos ever taken of Queen was on 'Side Black' (that side's music was composed entirely by Mercury). The band later used it again to dramatic effect in the legendary 'Bohemian Rhapsody' (1975) promo video.

Their new label, EMI/Parlophone (Elektra in the US) was forced to delay *Queen II's* release because *Queen I* had only just appeared in Britain and had still not been seen in the US. *Queen II* finally hit UK stores in March 1974.

Queen II, with its breakout single 'Seven Seas of Rhye' (reaching No 10) was the band's first UK Top 5 album; strangely, it was a poor seller in the US and remains the only 1970s-era Queen album not to be certified gold or platinum in America.

During 1973 – 74, Queen made the rounds of the UK and the US as support to Mott the Hoople. It was then they began to earn richly deserved applause for what fans were beginning to see on stage night after night: intellectually heady and physically balls-out performances uniquely 'Queen.'

Brian May was to explain, 'Led Zeppelin and The Who were among our favourite groups at the time, but what we were trying to do differently from either of them was a sort of layered sound.

'Our music was more based on an overdriven guitar sound, with texture behind the main melody lines. *Queen II* was the sort of emotional music we'd always wanted to be able to play, although for a while we couldn't play much of it on stage because it was too complicated.

'We were trying to push studio techniques to a new limit for rock groups. It went through our minds to call the album *Over the Top.*'

And as for the look, Freddie Mercury added, 'The wardrobe that we used at the time described it perfectly well.'

RIGHT
Queen II,
promo poster, 1974

Their New Album on Elektra Records

LEFT
Sheer Heart Attack,
promo poster, 1974

ABOVE
Japanese tour
programme, 1975

OPPOSITE
Back catalogue
promo poster, 1974

Sheer Heart Attack (1974), recorded July through September and released in November, gave Queen their first real taste of commercial success.

The album reached No 2 in the UK, sold exceptionally well throughout Europe, and went gold in America. It showcased a variety of musical genres, including British music hall, heavy metal, ballads, ragtime and Caribbean rhythms.

Queen were starting to put a little bit of distance to the studio-embellished tendencies of their first two albums and were moving into a more radio-friendly style. *Sheer Heart Attack* introduced highly

listenable melodic patterns that they would take to even greater heights on their next album, *A Night at the Opera*.

'Killer Queen', written by Freddie Mercury, became their first US hit, reaching No 12 on *Billboard's* Top 40 singles. It was a winning combination of camp, vaudeville and hardcore rock, replete with Brian May's virtuosity.

Another single, 'Stone Cold Crazy' anticipated the metal sub-genres of speed and thrash metal through May's guitar fireworks, while 'In the Lap of the Gods . . . Revisited' had a powerful chorus and stadium-ready bigness that would presage

their later terrace anthem, 'We Are The Champions'.

Wearing Zandra Rhodes-created costumes and basking in banks of newly acquired lights and effects, Queen headlined for the first time, touring Europe, North America, and Japan in 77 shows behind *Sheer Heart Attack*. Live, their effect upon Japanese fans produced sheer hysteria.

From the *New Musical Express*' album review: 'This is a *feast*. No duffers, and at least four songs that will just run and run.'

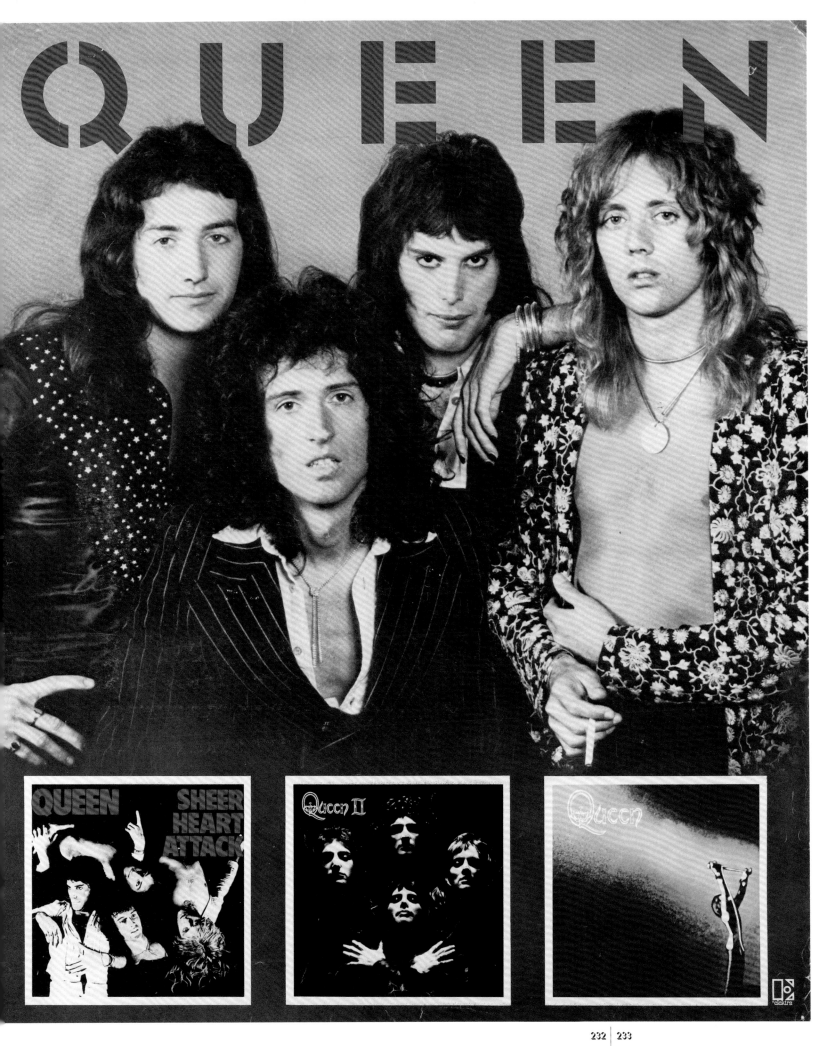

Was *A Night at the Opera* (1975) the most expensive rock album ever made up to that time? Many reports say that it was. It was named after the band watched the Marx Brothers movie of the same name 'one night at the recording studio complex.'

A Night at the Opera sat proudly atop the British album charts for nine weeks; in America it was certified triple platinum (three million copies sold). Like its predecessor, *Sheer Heart Attack*, the new album featured diverse musical styles and experimentation with stereo effects. But it also broke entirely new ground for rock on the strength of just one song.

The album's centrepiece was 'Bohemian Rhapsody', written by Freddie Mercury. The song flew to the top of the UK charts and like the LP stayed there for nine weeks. But it also drew attention to Queen from all over the world. It since has been voted – on both sides of the Atlantic and many times over – as the 'most revered song of all time' in part because of its contribution to an inspired driving-in-the-car segment in the movie *Wayne's World* (1992).

'Bohemian Rhapsody' effectively ushered in the MTV age, establishing a new form of visual communication for rock bands. Though some artists, including Queen themselves, had made video clips to accompany songs, it wasn't until after the success of 'Bohemian Rhapsody' that it became regular practice for record companies to produce creative short-form videos to maximize mainstream TV attention on the promotion of artists' singles.

'Bohemian Rhapsody' consists of six sections: introduction, ballad, guitar solo, opera, rock, and outro. Performed live, Queen split it into three sections in order to compensate for the complex studio effects. Their *Night at the Opera* tour (78 shows) visited Europe, North America, Japan and Australia between late 1975 and 1976.

Songwriter Freddie Mercury reflected, '"Bohemian Rhapsody" is one of those songs that has such a fantasy feel about it. You know, it didn't just come out of thin air. I did a bit of research. Yes, it was tongue-in-cheek and mock opera. But why not?'

Queen's studio producer, Roy Thomas Baker, related how one day Mercury played for him the opening ballad section on a piano. 'Freddie stopped and said: "This is where the opera section comes in." Then we went out to eat dinner.'

Interestingly, the piano used by Mercury in the video had also been used by Paul McCartney to record 'Hey Jude'.

LEFT
A Night At The Opera, US poster (withdrawn), 1975

RIGHT, TOP
A Night At The Opera, US poster, 1976

RIGHT, BOTTOM
Gig poster, Saginaw, 1976

A NEW TRACK RECORD

QUEEN
A DAY AT THE RACES

6E-101

THEIR NEW ALBUM ON ELEKTRA RECORDS & TAPES ⓔ

SOMEBODY TO LOVE
B/w White Man
EMI 2565 Released November 12th

EMI

Harvey Goldsmith in association with John Reid present the

QUEEN
Summer Tour

Queen's follow-up album to *A Night at the Opera* was *A Day at the Races* (1976). It seemed appropriate for the band again to borrow the name of another Marx Brothers movie (originally released in 1935 and 1937). It was the band's first fully self-produced album. It reached No 1 on the British album charts, led by the single 'Somebody to Love' for which Freddie Mercury, Brian May, and Roger Taylor multi-tracked their voices to achieve the effect of a full-on gospel choir.

May's 'Tie Your Mother Down' became a featured staple in their stage show. He had written it in Tenerife while researching his Ph D in Astronomy in 1975.

On Elektra Records and Tapes ⓔ

News of the World (1977) was without doubt a milestone of achievement for Queen in the development of arena-friendly album rock, in large measure because of two singles forevermore used to crown sports champions the world over. The album quickly went platinum in the UK and four times platinum in the US.

News contained the arena staples 'We Will Rock You' and 'We Are the Champions'. While Mercury was thinking football (soccer) when he wrote it in 1975, fans of American football and basketball also would find it ringing in their heads when their team won.

TOP, RIGHT
News of the World, mirror, 1977

MIDDLE, LEFT
News of the World, press kit, 1977

MIDDLE, 2ND LEFT
News of the World, press ad, 1977

MIDDLE, 3RD LEFT
News of the World, promo mobile, 1977

TOP, LEFT

News of the World,
promo poster, 1977

TOP, RIGHT

News of the World,
promo poster, 1977

OPPOSITE, MIDDLE, RIGHT

News of the World,
stand-up display, 1977

BOTTOM, RIGHT

News of the World,
staff pin, 1977

OPPOSITE, BOTTOM, LEFT

'Spread Your Wings'
single sleeve, 1977

OPPOSITE, BOTTOM, RIGHT

News of the World,
mirror/clock, 1977

Queen played 59 shows from January to June in 1977, touring North America, Europe and Britain while supporting *A Day at the Races*. The final two shows on the tour, at Earls Court in London, employed a technically advanced lighting rig called 'the crown' for the first time; these shows were filmed for video but the bootleg versions were avidly traded among fans before the official videos became the first of many live video merchandise staples for Queen.

In October, the band re-entered the studio to record *News of the World*. In November they re-commenced touring, now behind the new album. From then to the end of May 1978 they played another 46 shows in North America, Europe and Japan.

TOP
US tour 1977, laminate pass

RIGHT, TOP
News of the World, spring tour programme, 1977

LEFT
News of the World, US tour programme, 1977 – 78

RIGHT, BOTTOM
News of the World, tour programme, 1977

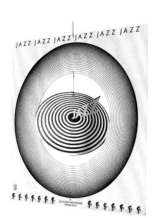

Despite its title, *Jazz* (1978) contained no music of that type *per se*, although it incorporated many other styles including vaudeville, music-hall swing, disco, funk, and hard rock, and there even was a classic American Southern-style stomp. Its many flavours were the subject of much critical discussion but the album did reach No 6 on the *Billboard* Hot 200. The highlights were the singles 'Fat Bottomed Girls', 'Bicycle Race', and 'Don't Stop Me Now'.

Queen promoted the album and 'Fat Bottomed Girls' with a much in-demand poster imagining an all-female nude bicycle race. Queen's sexed-up humour was now also reflected on their backstage laminate passes.

The album's mesmerizing artwork was suggested by Roger Taylor, who had previously seen a similar design painted on the Berlin Wall.

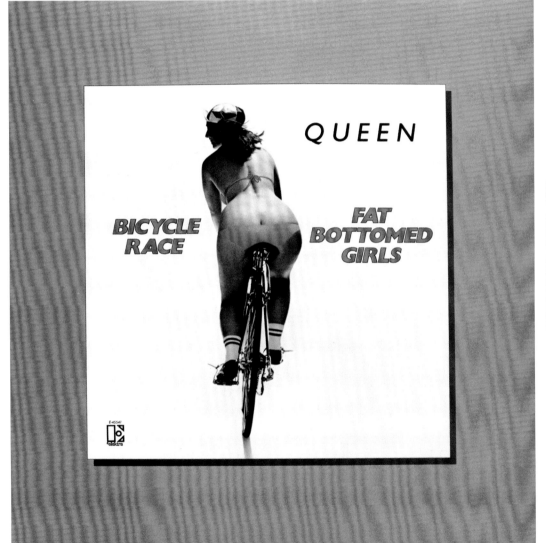

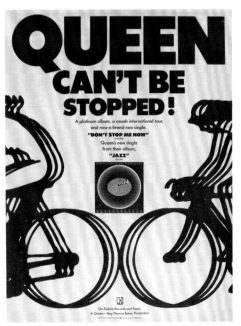

TOP

Gig poster,
Boblingen, 1979

BOTTOM, LEFT

Live Killers European
tour, UK press ad, 1979

BOTTOM, RIGHT

Live Killers, promo
poster, 1979

OPPOSITE

Live Killers Japanese tour
programme, 1979

QUEEN

Question: what was the only Queen album to become simultaneously the No 1 album in both the UK and the US? That would be *The Game* (1980), which would sell four million copies in the US alone – an achievement besting even *News of the World*.

Two songs stood out from the rest: 'Another One Bites the Dust' and the rockabilly-sounding 'Crazy Little Thing Called Love'. Both singles reached No 1 in the US. To back the album, Queen played 83 shows in Europe, North America, Japan, and Latin America. Their concerts on November 24 and 25, 1981 were released in 2007 as the album Queen Rock Montreal (ten years to the date before Freddie Mercury died).

TOP LEFT
The Game US tour,
laminate pass, 1980

TOP RIGHT
The Game, US
press ad, 1980

BELOW
Gig poster,
Bremen, 1980

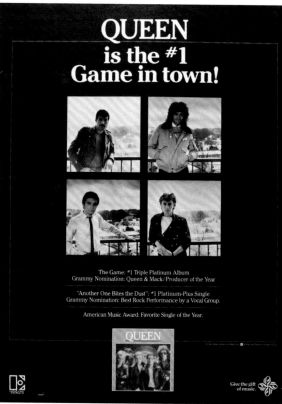

Flash Gordon (1980) was the Queen-composed soundtrack album to the science fiction movie of the same name. Queen's band members were avid science fiction fans; the film was based on the eponymous comic strip character, Flash Gordon.

It was one of the first high-budget feature films to use a score primarily created by a rock band, and although it did poorly at the box office, it is still regarded as a camp classic in the UK.

All but two of the album tracks are instrumentals. The album made extensive use of synthesizers, which Queen introduced into their work for only the second time.

ABOVE
Flash Gordon soundtrack,
US press ad, 1980

ABOVE
Flash Gordon soundtrack,
UK press ad, 1980

In 1981, Queen became the first major rock band to play in Latin American stadiums. The band played to a total audience of 479,000 people on the first leg of their South American tour, including five shows in Argentina and two in Brazil (where they played to more than 130,000 people the first night and more than 120,000 people the following night in two different cities). On the second leg they would perform before more than 150,000 fans (combined) in Monterrey and Puebla in Mexico.

The Game tour's February and March 1981 stops at South American stadiums in Argentina and Brazil were re-named by the band *South America Bites the Dust*. Resuming in September and October, the stops in Venezuela and Mexico were called *Gluttons for Punishment*.

Queen's *Greatest Hits* (1981) is the UK's all-time best-selling album (currently in excess of 5.6 million units). Combined with the later-released *Greatest Hits II* (1991), these would be the definitive Queen compilations of singles.

While Queen released *Greatest Hits* worldwide, there was no universal track listing or even cover art in common for all the countries involved. Each territory's tracks were dependent on what singles were released there and what tracks charted. In some cases, despite Queen's popularity, not enough songs were issued as singles to fill a territory's compilation album and so a few album tracks were used as filler.

As of 2008, all of the *Greatest Hits* album versions together had sold, worldwide, in excess of 43 million copies, with the hits on the albums collectively selling over 110 million units worldwide.

In the UK and the US the standard was raised by only including top 20 hits on the *Greatest Hits* original issue. To date, *Greatest Hits* has sold eight-times-platinum in the US.

TOP
Greatest Hits, promo mobile 1981

MIDDLE, LEFT
South American tour, luggage tag, 1981

MIDDLE, RIGHT
Japanese tour programme, 1981

SOUTH AMERICA BITES THE DUST

VENUE	DATE	ATTENDANCE
BUENOS AIRES	28 FEBRUARY	54,000
BUENOS AIRES	1 MARCH	52,000
MAR DEL PLATA	4 MARCH	30,000
ROSARIO	6 MARCH	34,000
BUENOS AIRES	8 MARCH	58,000
SAO PAULO	20 MARCH	131,000
SAO PAULO	21 MARCH	120,000

THANK YOU QUEEN

The first group ever to tour outdoor stadiums in South America, and to play to 479,000 people.
The first group ever to fill 3 nights in a stadium in the same city—Buenos Aires, playing to 164,000 people.
The first group ever to go live on T.V. coast to coast in Argentina and Brasil—to 35,000,000 people.

And for creating rock & roll history on 20 March, 1981 in Sao Paulo.
The largest ever paying audience for one group anywhere in the world.

Jose Rota
The Twenty-Eighth Company
4211 Kester Avenue
Sherman Oaks, CA 91423

Alfredo Capalbo
Alfredo Capalbo Producious S.A.
Avda. Alvcar 1891
Buenos Aires

Photo: Neal Preston

BOTTOM
South American tour, 'Thank you' press ad, 1981

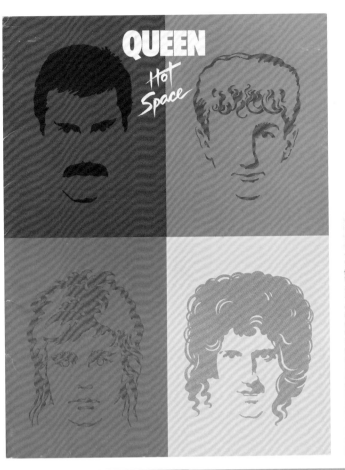

1982 marked a brief change in direction for Queen, exemplified by their album *Hot Space*. Here, the band's focus was on black music, specifically funk and rhythm-and-blues, marrying those forms to disco, pop-rock and electronica. This decision was influenced by the success of their own dance-oriented hit from two years before, 'Another One Bites the Dust' (1980).

In a spontaneous studio collaboration, David Bowie joined voices with Queen on the track 'Under Pressure'. Queen and Bowie fans together ensured it would reach No 1 on the British singles charts.

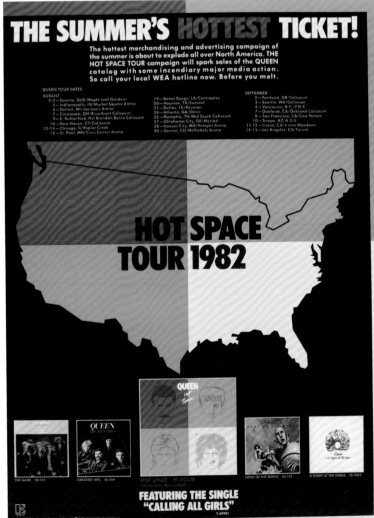

Drummer Roger Taylor could not have put it more precisely: 'It was time to give 'em [the Queen fans] the works!' What Taylor meant was, Queen necessarily abandoned their brief foray into black music and returned to their hard rock roots. The resulting album was *The Works* (1984), their eleventh.

The band members had taken a year's break from recording and touring after *Hot Space*, determining not to perform live at all in 1983. *The Works* tour began in August 1984 and ended in mid-May 1985, covering 48 stops in Europe, South Africa, South America, Australia and Japan.

In a controversial move, Queen performed nine times before integrated audiences in October 1984 at the Sun City Super Bowl in Bophuthatswana, South Africa. This was during the height of apartheid, when nearly every rock band refused to play in that country. Queen also played twice at the 'Rock in Rio' festival in Rio de Janeiro, Brazil in January 1985 (before 325,000 people on each night).

In July 1985 Queen performed at 'Live Aid,' broadcast to an estimated 400 million viewers across 60 countries.

TOP, LEFT
The Works,
press ad, 1984

TOP, RIGHT
Gig poster,
Stockholm, 1984

BOTTOM, LEFT
The Works, UK and European
tour programme, 1984

BOTTOM, RIGHT
The Works, promo
poster, 1984

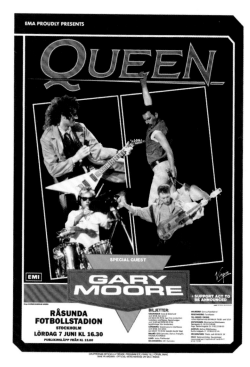

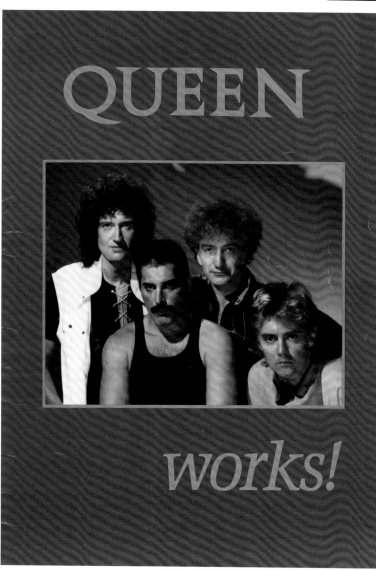

VENUE	ATTENDANCE	VENUE	ATTENDANCE	VENUE	ATTENDANCE
STOCKHOLM, RÅSUNDA FOTBOLL STADION	37,500	MUNICH, OLYMPIAHALLE	11,200	VIENNA, STADTHALLE	12,000
LEIDEN, GROENOOR DHAL	12,800	ZURICH, HALLENSTADION	11,400	VIENNA, STADTHALLE	12,000
LEIDEN, GROENOOR DHAL	12,800	ZURICH, HALLENSTADION	11,400	† BUDAPEST, NEPSTADION	80,000
PARIS, HIPPODROME DE VINCENNES	40,000	DUBLIN, SLANE CASTLE	85,000	FREJUS, THE AMPHITHEATRE	15,000
BRUSSELS, FORÉT NATIONAL	9,200	NEWCASTLE, ST. JAMES PARK	38,000	BARCELONA, MONUMENTAL PLAZA DE TOROS	18,000
LEIDEN, GROENOOR DHAL	12,800	LONDON, WEMBLEY STADIUM	72,000	MADRID, RAYO VALLECANO	45,000
MANNHEIM, MAIMARKTGELÄNDE	85,700	* LONDON, WEMBLEY STADIUM	72,000	MARBELLA, ESTADIO MUNICIPAL	37,000
BERLIN, WALDBUEHNE	22,600	MANCHESTER, MAINE ROAD	35,000	STEVENAGE, KNEBWORTH PARK	120,000
MUNICH, OLYMPIAHALLE	11,200	COLOGNE, MUENGERSDORFER STADION	50,000	TOTAL	969,600

* FILMED FOR WORLDWIDE TELEVISION
† FILMED FOR WORLDWIDE CINEMA

Queen's twelfth studio album, *A Kind of Magic* (1986) was in essence a soundtrack to the film *Highlander* (1986) directed by Russell Mulcahy. Six songs from the album appeared in the film.

The album was largely unsuccessful in the US (charting no higher than No 46) but in the UK it hit No 1, afterwards holding its own on the album charts for 63 weeks and yielding three hit singles. A curious side note to the album: it was Queen's first with a title track. For the first time in their career, the band allowed cameras to film them while they were in the studio. The video for 'One Vision' shows them in various stages of writing and recording the song.

Due to Freddie Mercury's illness, the *Magic Tour* was the final tour by Queen with Mercury as lead singer. It was relatively short (26 shows, from June to August 1986) but the band's biggest ever money-earner, although only involving European stadiums.

In the spring of 1987, Mercury was officially told he'd contracted HIV but previously, seeing him obviously weakened (but not clear exactly why), the band had made the decision to cease touring, making the concert at Knebworth on 8 August, 1986 the last time the four members of Queen would perform on stage together. The show sold out within two hours and over 120,000 fans packed the site.

Over the course of the *Magic Tour*, Queen played to nearly one million people – 400,000 in the UK alone, and from this tour Queen released *Live at Wembley Stadium* (12 July, 1986) in 1992, *Live Magic* (much from Knebworth) in late 1986 and *Live in Budapest* (27 July, 1986), also in 1986.

The Miracle (1989) originally was to be titled 'The Invisible Men.' But three weeks before its release the band spontaneously decided on a name change. It was Queen's thirteenth studio album.

The cover art utilized then-cutting-edge image-manipulation technology to combine photographs of the faces of the four band members into one morphed image. The band would explain that this was in line with their decision to dispense with individual credits and simply present their music as the product of 'Queen itself'.

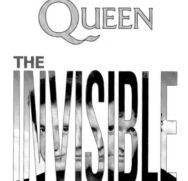

LEFT
The Miracle,
press ad, 1989

RIGHT, TOP
'The Invisible Man',
promo poster, 1989

RIGHT, BOTTOM
The Miracle,
promo poster, 1986

The final studio album composed entirely of new material and the first of two final albums released while Freddie Mercury was still alive was *Innuendo* (1991).

Designer Richard Gray collaborated with Queen on the album's cover art, which was something of a departure for the band. The album's singles' graphic art were the work of (or inspired by) the painter Grandville

The music video for the song 'These Are the Days of Our Lives' was Mercury's last appearance in that promotional role. By the time the video was shot, it had become impossible to disguise that Mercury was seriously ill. Despite his frail appearance, he made a game appearance and gave to it all the energy he had left. It was filmed in black and white in a decision made to help preserve his dignity.

The single was first released in the US on Mercury's birthday, 5 September, 1991. In Britain, it was released in December 1991 following his death.

On 23 November 1991, in a prepared statement made on his deathbed, Mercury finally revealed that he had AIDS. Within 24 hours of releasing that long-expected and confirming word, he died from the disease at the age of 45. The sad news shocked the rock world to its core.

LEFT
'I'm Going Slightly Mad', promo poster, 1991

RIGHT
Innuendo, promo poster, 1991

QUEEN

INNUENDO

THE ALBUM

AVAILABLE NOW

COMPACT DISC • CASSETTE • RECORD
INCLUDES THE HIT SINGLE 'INNUENDO'

PARLOPHONE

The *Freddie Mercury Tribute Concert* was held at Wembley Stadium in London on 20 April, 1992 and televised to one billion viewers worldwide. The concert is listed in the Guinness Book of Records as the largest-ever benefit honouring a rock star.

Performers included Def Leppard, Elton John, David Bowie, Robert Plant, Tony Iommi, Annie Lennox, Guns 'N' Roses, Roger Daltrey, George Michael, Metallica, and actress Elizabeth Taylor, along with the three remaining members of Queen.

Queen's Greatest Hits II (1991), came less than a month before Mercury's passing, the last Queen release of any kind while he was still alive. It was a compilation containing most of Queen's European hits from 1981 to 1991 and became the 12th best-selling album of the 1990s in the UK.

Live at Wembley '86 (1992) is regarded as a tribute album of a unique sort, the band at the top of their game (despite Mercury's frailty), their performance serving as an appropriate salute from one of the world's top rock bands to one of its founding members.

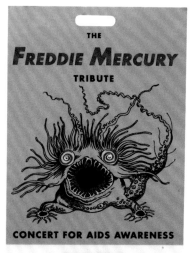

PART 2

ABOVE
Freddie Mercury Tribute,
laminate pass, 1992

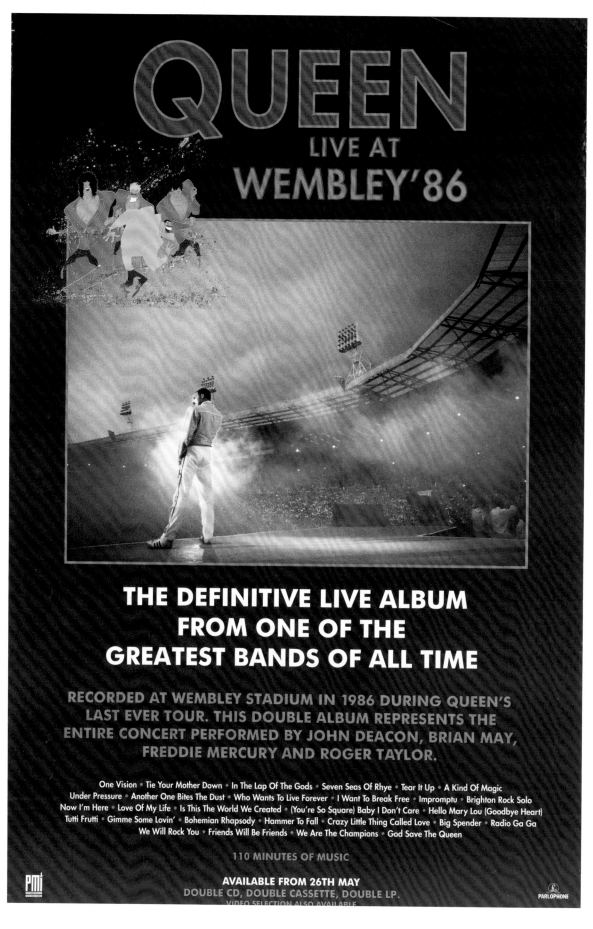

ABOVE
Live at Wembley '86,
promo poster, 1992

OPPOSITE
Freddie Mercury Tribute,
Wembley, programme, 1992

THE

FREDDIE MERCURY

TRIBUTE

CONCERT FOR AIDS AWARENESS

EASTER MONDAY APRIL 20th 1992

WEMBLEY STADIUM

And so, in the end, there were fifteen studio albums recorded by the four members of Queen. The last was *Made in Heaven* (1995). After Mercury's death in 1991, the remaining band members worked on-and-off in the following years with vocals that Mercury had recorded before he died.

In one more honour befitting Mercury, *Heaven* debuted at No 1 in Britain and went six times platinum.

Both stages of recording (before and after Mercury's death) were completed at the band's studio in Montreux, Switzerland. A picture of the studio appears on the album cover, juxtaposed with a typically flamboyant image of Mercury with his arm and fist up in the air.

The next studio album, *The Cosmos Rocks* (2008), would be recorded by Queen with singer Paul Rodgers (formerly of Free, Bad Company, and The Firm).

Other key albums followed Mercury's death. One, *Queen At The Beeb* (1989) was a live album comprising tracks from two sessions recorded in 1973 for BBC Radio 1's *Sounds of the Seventies* show.

Queen Rocks (1997) was a compilation of songs from Queen's heavier side. It included 'No One But You (Only The Good Die Young)', the last original studio recording from the 1990s featuring Brian May, Roger Taylor, and John Deacon (but the first ever Queen recording without Freddie Mercury).

In 2002, a rock musical based on the songs of Queen, titled *We Will Rock You*, opened at the Dominion Theatre in London's West End. Subsequently, it was restaged all over the world, but in London, it became the venerable Dominion's longest running musical ever, overtaking the previous record holder, *Grease*.

BELOW
Queen at the BBC,
promo poster, 1995

BELOW
Made in Heaven,
promo poster, 1995

AFTERWORD

ABOVE
Rob Roth and Elton John
aboard Elton's private jet
as they return to NY from
a concert in Buffalo.

Rob and I met in 1994 backstage at Royal Albert Hall in London. I was wearing a pink vinyl suit. Rob was not. We were about to begin work on the first of our musical theater collaborations. It was clear right away that we would be friends, we shared a love for music, movies, art, and of course, collecting.

I first became aware of Rob's obsessive/compulsive collecting behaviour, which I share and approve of, when he presented me with a rare Honky Chateau stand-up display for my birthday. I hadn't seen one of these since Tower Records in LA in 1972. Rob was excited that he had found it. I told him the truth, "I love that you found this for me, but it means more to you than me. I want you to have it." So I gave him back his present. Secretly, I knew he was happy I did.

I don't usually look to the past, I'm always looking forward, but I did sit down with Rob back at Royal Albert Hall again, 16 years after we first met, to look at this book. I couldn't wait to see the Queen and Zeppelin chapters, I was less excited about seeing my own. I ended up being surprised and delighted by my own promotional artwork, some of which I had never seen before. And so much of it! I loved the other bands' artwork too. Lots of history here.

With the decline of record stores, we are losing this incredible, beautiful, unique form of art. How great that my crazy compulsive friend is collecting and preserving this vast treasure trove of artwork.

INDEX